Of Solitude and Silence

Of Solitude and Silence

Writings on Robert Bly

Edited by
Richard Jones and Kate Daniels

BEACON PRESS   BOSTON

Beacon Press books are published under the auspices
of the Unitarian Universalist Association,
25 Beacon Street, Boston, Massachusetts 02108
Published simultaneously in Canada by
Fitzhenry & Whiteside Limited, Toronto

Printed in the United States of America

(hardcover) 9 8 7 6 5 4 3 2 1
(paperback) 9 8 7 6 5 4 3 2 1

Library of Congress Cataloging in Publication Data

Of solitude and silence.

   Bibliography: p.
   1. Bly, Robert — Criticism and interpretation —
Addresses, essays, lectures. I. Jones, Richard,
1953 –   . II. Daniels, Kate, 1953 –
III. Bly, Robert.
PS3552.L9Z8   811'.54   81 – 68357
ISBN 0-8070-6360-6   AACR2
ISBN 0-8070-6361-4 (pbk.)

Foreword

Robert Bly has contributed much to poetry in the twenty-five years he has been writing, translating, and editing. Besides his own prodigious and provocative outpourings of poetry and prose, his work has generated a barrage of commentary by others. In light of this, it is surprising to note that this is the first collective critical work on Bly. What we have attempted to do is to present a forum of discussion that is not necessarily one of homage, however much we personally admire Bly, but one that is dedicated to a realistic evaluation of what he has aspired to and of what he has accomplished. Robert Bly has said, "The criticism of my own poetry that has been the most use to me has been criticism that, when I first heard it, utterly dismayed me." Let us hope, then, that there is something here that dismays Robert.

Needless to say, one does not undertake such a gargantuan project as this without a strong personal feeling and interest in the subject. What we most appreciate about Robert Bly is his constant attempt to reintegrate poetry with life—daily life, the life of the body, political life, moral life. In an era of increasing specialization in every conceivable area, the expansiveness of Bly's approach to poetry has been for us a way of combatting the ever-increasing solipsism of the modern world and its art. We have often thought that the narrow, elitist concerns of much recent American poetry have fostered an atmosphere in which it has become unfashionable to hold a position on anything outside one's own personal life. As Americans with freedoms that the rest of the world does not always enjoy—that is, to say whatever the hell we want without reprisal—it is often seen as meaningless or pretentious in our society to hold a political or moral position. Robert Bly has shown us that this situation does not necessitate the death of one's political life and conscience. Even in a society such as ours, where people do not suffer or die for their beliefs, the realm of decision-making, of political and personal morality, continues to exist, and to deny this, to retreat from one's responsibilities, has never been Bly's way.

A critical anthology devoted to a poet one enjoys should not only point out the poet's strengths, but his or her weaknesses, as well. Talking to Bly once, he said that to really understand the older poets, the younger writers should study them for their faults; only then can their powers really be appreciated. But Bly, as usual, is beating all of us to the punch! In a recent article in *Field,* he admits what he has yet to excel in—the sound of a poem, its music. He pushes himself further in the essay written for this collection, talking now about form. In an age of conformity, an age in which the writing professors are calling out for more prosody, this perhaps is a dangerous announcement for Bly, of all people, to make. Wasn't it he who turned the 1950s poetry community on its head by his pronouncement that most of the poetry being published in America at that time was "too old-fashioned," too tied to the formal traditions of English poetry? Yet again it seems his thinking is one step ahead of the mob. Although his ideas are not clear just yet, he seems to be struggling with the notion that form is "out there beyond the poem." One of the most interesting aspects of Bly's career as a poet and critic has always been his willingness to think and develop his ideas in public. Just as his ideas on leaping, political, and nature poetry were crystallized in *Leaping Poetry* and *News of the Universe,* we anticipate the final resolution these initial thoughts on form will take in the upcoming issues of *The Eighties,* which Bly is rejuvenating.

The generous outpouring of time and energy that has resulted in this collection was more than we ever expected. Not only did we mercilessly demand rewrites and revisions from our numerous authors, but we pressed deadlines on them in the middle of summer vacations, trips abroad, family illnesses. The good humor and the cooperation of everyone involved has been one of our main pleasures in putting together this collection, and we thank all of you. Simply put, *Of Solitude and Silence* would not exist without the good spirits and heavy labors of our contributors. Especially, of course, we want to thank Robert Bly, for the enthusiasm with which he participated in the project, the wealth of materials and documents he provided, and for the good humor with which he ran the gauntlet. Bly's readings are notable for the amount of time he devotes to the poetry of others. We like to think that his generosity of spirit is reflected and returned by the more than ninety poets, critics, and translators who took the time to write for this issue.

It should be obvious to anyone reading this volume not only that Robert Bly has made enormous contributions to poetry and the age, but that he is still working, talking, thinking, and turning over new ground, while, as is his way, always reminding us of old and unexpected places where we can find spiritual water. We look forward to seeing and hearing Robert Bly in the eighties; it is an exciting prospect, and we hope this collection will move us all forward.

Kate Daniels and Richard Jones
Earlysville, Virginia
August 1981

Contents

Notice: A Bly Prescription

These pages are good for you; they enhance your life. A few of them every day, mixed with ordinary reading, will keep up your appetite, provide incentive, and maintain hope.

One page supplies twenty percent of the minimum daily requirement of wonder and mystery. Along with religion, they will sustain you, even in conditions of extreme stress.

For chronic spiritual anemia, you should consult your family poet.

No government has established the minimum daily requirements of honesty and trust, but no society has ever lasted without at least trace elements of these essentials—richly present in these pages.

New Work by Robert Bly

Ten Poems

Four Translations from Rilke

Form that is Neither In nor Out, *An Essay*

Words Rising

I open my journal, write a few
sounds with green ink, and suddenly
fierceness enters me, stars
begin to revolve, and pick up
caribou dust from under the ocean.
I see the music, and I feel the bushy
tail of the Great Bear
reach down and brush the seafloor.

All those lives we lived in the sunlit
shelves of the Dordogne, the thousand
tunes we sang to the skeletons
of Papua, the many times
we died wounded under
the cloak of an animal's sniffing,
all of these return, and the grassy
nights we ran for hours in the moonlight.

Watery syllables come welling up.
Anger that barked and howled in the cave,
the luminous head of barley
the priest holds up, growls
from under fur, none of the sounds are lost!
The old earth fragrance remains
in the word "and." We experience
"the," in its lonely suffering.

We are bees then; honey is language.
Honey lies stored in caves
beneath us, and the sounds of words
carry what we do not. When weeping

a man or woman feeds a few words
with private grief, the shames
we knew before we could invent the wheel,
then words grow larger. We slip out

into farmyards, where rabbits lie
stretched out on the ground for buyers.
Wicker baskets and hanged men
come to us as tremors and vowels.
We see a million hands with dusty
palms turned up inside each verb,
lifted. There are eternal vows
held inside the word "Jericho."

Blessings then on the man who labors
in his tiny room, writing stanzas on the lamb;
blessings on the woman, who picks the brown
seeds of solitude out of the black seeds of
        loneliness.
And blessings on the dictionary maker, huddled
        among
his bearded words; and on the setter of songs,
who sleeps at night inside his violin case.

Written at Mule Hollow, Utah

After three days of talk, I long for silence and
    come here.
It's called Mule Hollow. I love this granite steep
    shooting
upward. The base seems to remain
in grief—all the children killed when you return
    to the cave.

Haven't you ever longed for all these cheerful
    noises
to end? These hellos and goodbyes? We fall
    asleep speaking.
Perhaps talking we sleep;
our ability to wake stays hidden in rocks that we
    never visit.

This tree I stand beside—a stone wall behind it,
sedimentary, moving in waves—it is neither tree
    nor pine;
it has half-leaves, half-needles,
and a scaly bark, like someone constantly waking
    up in the night.

All the failures of the slate are perfectly clear—
    spoken—
how it gave way to pressures, bent between
    humps,
as when a man lets his hands
climb up over his head, and says, "It's true, it's
    true, why say it isn't?"

How many failures we hide, talking. When I am
    too public,
I am a wind-chime, ringing, to cheer up the black
angel of Moroni, and feed him
as he comes dancing, prancing, leaving turkey
    tracks in the mist.

Talking, we do not say what we are! Sensing what
    others want,
used to hiding from our parents, talking,
not saying what we want, by agreeing,
we sustain the brilliant glass skeleton on which
    we hang.

A Meditation on Philosophy

There is a restless gloom in my mind;
I walk grieving. Leaves are down.
I come at dusk,
where, sheltered by poplars, a low pond lies.
The sun abandons the sky, speaking through cold
    leaves.

A deer comes down the slope toward me,
sees me, turns away, back up the hill
into the lone trees.
It is the doe out in the cold and air alone,
the woman turned away from the philosopher's
    house.

Someone wanted that. After Heraclitus dies,
the males sink down to *a-pathy,*
to not-suffering.
When you shout at them, they don't reply.
They turn their face toward the crib wall, and die.

A Tang painter made ''The Six Philosophers.''
Five Chinamen talk in the openwalled house,
exchanging poems.
Only one is outdoors, looking over
the cliff, being approached from below by rolling
    mists.

It must be that five of me are indoors!
Yesterday, when I cleaned my study,
I laid your paints,
watercolor paper, sketches and sable brushes

not on the bookcase, where mine were, but on
the floor.

But there are thunderstorms longing to come
into the world through the minds of women!
A bird of yours came,
it was a large friendly bird with big feet,
stubby wings, arrows lightly stuck in the arms.

Last night I dreamt that my father
was an enormous turtle—the eyes open—
lying on the basement floor.
The weight of his shell kept him from moving.
His jaw hung down—it was large and fleshly.

The New King

It is late morning.
Sultry mood-moths
come to grief
among the ruling masses.
How blue the sky is!
The sooly man says:
Who is king now?
The toft needs
the rule of stakes,
what keeps out
the wolf-filled birches,
long-nosed pigs
swooning on darkness.
A young man answers:
The King is Hoom.
The unruly Celtic
snakes, twining,
dark-hued, make room
for the New King.

Crazy Carlson's Meadow

Crazy Carlson cleared this meadow alone.
Now three blue-
jays live in it.
Crazy Carlson cleared it back to the dark firs.
Volunteer poplars have stepped
out in front,
their leaves trembling.
They hold their leaves in the motionless October
    air,

color midway between pale green and yellow,
as if a yellow
scarf were floating
six inches down in the Pacific. The dark firs
make sober, octopus caves,
inviting the heavy-
lidded eyes
of the women in whose bark huts Gaugin lived.

A blue sky rises over the trees, pure blue,
too pure and blue.
There is no room
for the dark-lidded boys who longed to be
    Hercules.
There is no room even for Christ.
Breaking off
his journey toward the Father,
he leaned back into the mother's fearful tree.

Then he sank through the bark. The energies the
    Jews

refused him
turned into nails,
and the wine of Cana turned back to vinegar.
Blessings on you, my king, broken
on the poplar tree.
Your shoulders quivered
like an aspen leaf before the storm of Empire.

You fell off then and the horse galloped away
into the wind without
you, and disappeared
into the blue sky. Your orbits never reached your
     father's house.
But the suffering is over now, all
consequences finished,
the lake closed
again, as before the leaf fell, all forgiven, the path
     ended.

Now each young man wanders in the sky alone,
ignoring the absent
moon, not knowing
where ground is, longing once more for the
     learning
of the fierce male who hung for nine days only
on the windy tree.
Beneath his feet
there is darkness; inside the folds of darkness
     words hidden.

Fifty Males Sitting Together

After a long walk in the woods clear cut for
    lumber,
lit up by a few young pines,
I turn home,
drawn to water. A coffin-like shadow
softens half the lake,
draws the shadow
down from westward hills.
It is a massive
masculine shadow,
fifty males sitting together
in hall or crowded room
lifting something indistinct
up into the resonating night.

Closer to me, out of shadow, the water lies lit,
some of it pinkish from western clouds.
Near shore, reeds
stand about in groups, unevenly,
as if they might finally
and at once ascend
to the sky all together!
A thin thread
of darkness lives
in each reed, so it is relaxed,
private. When the reed dies,
it dies alone, as an animal does.
Rooted, it waits only for itself.

The woman stays in the kitchen, and does not
    want

to waste fuel by lighting a lamp,
as she waits for the drunk
husband to come home.
Still leaving the kitchen
dark, she
serves him food in silence.
Closest in to shore,
motionless water
lies calm, protected by reeds.
So the son who lives
shielded by the mother lives protected
by reeds in the joy of the half darkness.

He lives thousands of years ago. He does not
     know
what he should give, as herds slowly
pass the cave mouth,
what the world *wants* from him.
Blood rises
from dark neck-holes.
But how far he lives
from working men!
The blood asks:
Whose head has been cut off?
The dark comes down slowly, the way
snow falls...or herds pass the cave.
I look up at the other shore; it is night.

The Whole Moisty Night

The Viking ship sails into the full harbor.
The body meets its wife far out at sea.
Its lamp remains lit the whole moisty night.
Water pours down, faint flute notes in the sound
    of the water.

At Midocean

All day I loved you in a fever, holding on to the
    tail of the horse.
I overflowed whenever I reached out to touch you.
And my hand moved over your body
covered with its dress,
burning, rough, the hand of an animal's foot
    moving over leaves,
the rainstorm retiring, sunlight
sliding over ocean water a thousand miles from
    land.

A Bouquet of Ten Roses

The rose bodies rise from the green strawberry-like leaves, their edges slightly notched, for the rose is also the plum, the apple, the strawberry, and the cherry. Petals are reddish-orange, the color of a robin's breast if it were silk. I look down into the face of one rose: deep down inside there are somber shades, what Tom Thumb experienced so low under chairs, in the carpet-darkness...those unfolding currents of gathering shadows, that eyes up near lamps do not see. It is the calm fierceness in the aborigine's eye, as he holds his spear polished by his own palm. These inviting lamb-like falmers are also the moist curtains of the part of the woman she cannot see; and the cloud that opens, swarming and parting for Adonis.... It is an opening seen by no one (only experienced later as rain). And the rose is also the skin petals around the man's stalk, the soft umber folds that enclose so much longing; and the tip shows violet, blind, longing for company, knowing already of an intimacy the thunder storm keeps as its secret, understood by the folds of purple curtains, whose edges drag the floor.

And in the center of the nine roses, whose doors are opening, there is one darker rose on a taller stem. It is the rose of the tumbling waters, of the strumming at night, the color of the Ethiopian tumblers who put their heads below their feet on the Egyptian waterfront, wheeling all over the shore.... This rose is the man sacrificed yesterday, the silent one wounded under the oak, the man whose dark foot needs to be healed. It is the color of the clumsy feeling that can only weep. It is the girl who has gone down to the world below, disobeying her mother, in order to bring calm to the house, travelling alone...and the rose windows of Chartres, the umber moss on the stag's antler....

Eleven O'Clock at Night

I lie alone in my bed; cooking and stories are over at last, and some peace comes. And what did I do today? I wrote down some thoughts on sacrifice other people had, but couldn't connect them to my own life. I brought my daughter to the bus—on the way to Minneapolis for a hair cut—and I waited twenty minutes with her in the somnolent hotel lobby. I wanted the mail to bring some praise for my ego to eat, and was disappointed. I added up my bank balance, and found only $65, where I need over a thousand to pay the bills for this month alone. So this is how my life is passing before the grave?

The walnut of my brain grows. I feel it irradiate the skull. I am aware of the consciousness I have, and I mourn the consciousness I do not have.

Stubborn things lie and stand around me—the walls, a bookcase with its few books, the footboard of my bed, my shoes that sit up on the blanket nervously, as if they were animals sitting at table, my stomach with its curved demand. I see the bedside lamp, and the thumb of my right hand, the pen my fingers hold so trustingly. There is no way to escape from these. Many times in poems I have escaped from myself: I sit for hours and at last see a pinhole in the top of the pumpkin, and I slip out the pinhole, gone! The genie expands and is gone; no one can get him back in the bottle again; he is hovering over a car cemetery somewhere.

Now more and more I long for what I cannot escape from. The sun shines on the side of the house across the street. Eternity is near, but it is not *here*. My shoes, my thumbs, my stomach remain inside the room, and for that there is no solution. Consciousness comes so slowly, half our life passes, we eat and talk asleep—and for that there is no solution. Since Pythagoras died, the world has gone down a certain path, and I cannot change that. Someone not in my family invented the microscope, and Western eyes grew the intense will to pierce down through its darkening tunnel. Air itself is willing without pay to lift the 707's wing, and for that there is no solution. Pistons and rings have appeared in the world; valves usher gas vapor in and out of its theatre box twenty times a second, and for that there is no solution. Something besides my will loves the woman I love. I love my children, though I did not know them before they came. I change every day. For the winter dark of late December there is no solution.

Mourning

Heart, whom will you cry out to? More and more
    alone,
you make your way through the unknowable
human beings. All the more hopeless perhaps
since it holds to its old course,
the course toward the future,
that's lost.

Happened before. Did you mourn? What was it?
    A fallen
berry of joy, still green.
But now my oak of joy is breaking,
what is breaking in storm is my slowly
grown oak of joy.
The loveliest thing in my invisible
landscape, helping me to be seen
by angels, that are invisible.

Paris, July 1914

Imaginary Biography

First childhood, no limits, no renunciations,
no goals. Such unthinking joy.
Then abruptly terror, schoolrooms, boundaries,
    captivity,
and a plunge into temptation and deep loss.

Defiance. The one crushed will be the crusher
    now,
and he avenges his defeats on others.
Loved, feared, he rescues, wrestles, wins,
and overpowers others, slowly, act by act.

And then all alone in space, in lightness, in cold.
But deep in the shape he has made to stand erect
he takes a breath, as if reaching for the First,
    Primitive...

Then God explodes from his hiding place.

Schöneck, September 1923

Fox Fire

We have an old association
with the lights out on the moors.
I have the feeling they are great-aunts....
More and more I notice between them

and me a kind of family resemblance
that no force can suppress:
a certain jump, a leaping, a turn, a curve—
others can't seem to do it.

I too live where there are no roads,
in the mist that turns most people back,
and I've seen myself often too
go out under my own eyelids.

Muzot, February 1924

Just as the Winged Energy of Delight

Just as the winged energy of delight
carried you over many chasms early on,
now raise the daringly imagined arch
holding up the astounding bridges.

Miracle doesn't lie only in the amazing
living through and defeat of danger;
miracles become miracles in the clear
achievement that is earned.

To work with things is not hubris
when building the association beyond words;
denser and denser the pattern becomes—
being carried along is not enough.

Take your well-disciplined strengths
and stretch them between two
opposing poles. Because inside human beings
is where God learns.

Muzot, February 1924

Translated from the German by Robert Bly

Form that is Neither In nor Out

I have been thinking lately that we have not been very faithful servants of art.

What did Yeats say—

> I know what wages beauty gives,
> How hard a life her servant lives,
> Yet praise the winters gone:
> There is not a fool can call me friend,
> And I may dine at journey's end
> With Landor and with Donne.

By "we" I mean the poets of my generation. We have been lively and fierce servants, but was it of art? Or was it of art but not the single work of art?

The other day a stranger repeated a thought of Goethe's that set me thinking what actually makes up a work of art. Goethe said something like this: "In a work of art the content is easiest to understand, the meaning more difficult, and form still more difficult to understand; and few take it in."

I don't know how Goethe distinguished between content and meaning, so I have had to set up my own fences. I associate content with the griefs we have experienced since birth, that is, the so-called accidents of our genetic inheritance, our relationship to our mother and father, the sorrows of friends and lovers, the knowledge that we are mortal. When a poem has an emphasis on content we may call it a confessional poem.

Meaning I take to be associated with a master. I assume that we meet meaning mainly outside our or our parents' house. Meaning comes down, passed to us through centuries by old men and old women, hand to hand, so to speak, and something secret comes with it. We can speak of a descending line of meaning.

The concept that there is a consciousness in trees or hills came to Rilke from Goethe, to Goethe from the Alchemists, to the Alchemists from Hermes Trismegistus and Heraclitus, to Heraclitus from the Orphic teachers and so on. Yeats carries meaning that came to him through Blake, and to Blake through Swedenborg, and to Swedenborg through Raymond Lull and the Renaissance occult masters. Whitman's meaning, which carries a transcendental reconciliation of opposites, comes partly from Asian masters. We could say that Whitman's poems have moving and marvelous content, and a subtle and wide-ranging meaning.

I imagine content to be close to the chest, perhaps inside the chest; it is dear to us; we have to be careful that we don't say too publicly what is deeply private; and yet through its warmth and closeness to our lungs and heart it gives life to the poem.

Meaning I imagine to be floating several feet out from the chest, between the chest and the human community. Meaning is more intense than content, in the way that Blake is more intense than a poet solely of content such as Oliver Goldsmith. I'm not sure I've made the right choice there, but I think we can imagine such a difference, two such roles, whichever poets we choose to illustrate them. Meaning often carries hints of the hidden traditions, that which the established religions do not include, what is not always acceptable at the time, as Blake's ideas were not acceptable to most English readers at the time. Meaning, in the way I am using the word, is not publicly taught, partly because the established religions reject much of it, and partly because teachers in this tradition know the teaching will be destroyed if it is given to everyone. So secret teaching needs a strong container, created again in each generation, so that the meaning remains fresh.

If content lives somehow inside the chest, and meaning a few feet away, between the body and the human community, then, if we follow Goethe's three steps, I would have to say that form lives still farther out, still farther from the chest, and is still wilder. Perhaps that is why it is more difficult to understand. This view comes as a surprise to me because I have often thought of form as a prison, which would put it inside the chest, or below the chest, a kind of dungeon in which heart material gets imprisoned. Suppose I were wrong on that. If so, we need to find a way to speak of form so that its wild or intense quality becomes clear.

The distinction between form as prison and form as wildness may correspond to a distinction between kinds of forms, in particular, the mechanical and the organic. The one form would be drawn from human economy, the other from the economy of nature. This set of opposites is over simplified, but we'll stick to it for a few minutes. The first — overly regular iambic, for example — depends on certain repetitive patterns that human beings have developed; the second draws from the success nature has had in its plant and animal adaptation. It is the second form which would deserve the word "wild," since the word "wild" itself refers to what humans have not domesticated, what is still receiving nourishment from nature.

What would such form look like? We note that "form" is close to "shape" and the word suggests a container that contains certain energies in the way a "successful" animal (that is, one that endures) — a snail — contains conflicting energies. What did Wallace Stevens say? "I placed a jar in Tennessee." Form also implies order, for example, a beginning, middle and end, something which chaos lacks. A snail shell certainly has a beginning, middle and end. Thirdly, form implies some sort of return. We say the universe has form because Venus returns, and at the time we expect it. The moon returns to full each month; spring and fall return, the salmon returns. In the snail shell, a certain curve, which can easily be plotted, returns again and again.

I think we could say that form, in nature and art, is not an either/or matter, but a matter of degree. A poem can have more or less, as it has more or less meaning. A poem is still a poem, even with a moderate amount of meaning or form. I'll set down a poem of my own here which has a modest amount of form:

> Early in the morning the hermit wakes,
> hearing the roots of the fir tree stir beneath his
> floor.

Someone is there. That strength buried
in earth carries up the summer world.
When a man loves a woman, he nourishes her.
Dancers strew the lawn with the light of their feet.
When a woman loves the earth, she nourishes it.
Earth nourishes what no one can see.

Certain sounds return here as the curves in the snail shell, or as certain notes return in a musical key. The poem has a specified number of syllables, as well. Finally, it has a slow movement associated with calm or ordered breathing.

Attention to breathing is important in adaption. In certain animals and birds, the speed of the heartbeat seems associated with their successful adaptation. Hummingbirds and tigers might be examples. The heartbeat, as well as the interior bone structure, the sinews in legs and neck, the lungs, all of these help it to be a container that contains fierce energies, and to help it move among other fierce energies.

By contrast, if we think of a poem written in mechanical form today, in second-rate iambic for example, the poem would appear rigid, stiff-kneed, with English coloring, and so poorly adapted to the ground and trees around it that the first hawk flying over would see it immediately and eat it.

If we imagine a typical long Whitman poem as an animal, it would be an animal about a mile and a half long with not enough bone structure between head and tail, long in the stomach, and so cumbersome it would be killed by the first lion that entered the forest. The true animal that survives, such as the tiger or horse, has just the right number of bones, just the right number of feet, a good balance of lung and heart, and just the right number of vertebrae. Moreover, it somehow fits the continent it lives on.

So when we speak of form as a wildness, and consider a poem's form as drawn from the careful economy of nature, we then can imagine the poem as a being that moves fast, can leap in the air, escape from tigers or professors, and live for generations, even during lean times.

I maintain then that the more form a poem has—I mean living form—the closer it comes to the wild animal.

The subject is so complicated we can't go into it here, or be fair to it; and the notes on form here are preliminary and inadequate. But we could guess that for a poet today to grasp this second idea of form would require a study of music as well as study of ancient poetry, and memorization of some Anglo Saxon poetry, Provençal poetry, and Homeric poetry, as well as poems in the stanzas that Sappho and Alcaeus invented. I'll set down here, to close this essay, a stanza written in Latin—by Horace—but using the sequence or pattern of drum beats that Alcaeus settled on. It goes:

> O matre pulchra filia pulchrior
> quem criminosis cumque voles modum
>   pones iambus, sive flamma
>   sive mari libet Hadriano.

This time I will add the pauses, and an "o" above the syllables where the drum beat comes down.

The lines say something like this:

> O mother so beautiful   daughter still more,
>   take my satirical poems   and end them
>   anyway you choose   fire is all right,
>   or the waters of the Adriatic Sea!

If one memorizes the lines in Latin sound and gives them in "passionate speech," as Yeats would call it, one notices that because certain drum beats come down harder than others, a third rhythm runs over and above the words, and it curiously resembles the running of a wild animal.

The drummer Michael Meade from Seattle told me that the ancient Celtic women would sometimes lay hard conditions on a man who wanted to sleep with them. Conflicting loyalties and obligations often made going to bed dangerous for both parties. And besides, no woman wants to go to bed with a man who can't solve riddles, or is too straight-laced, or has no playfulness in his soul. So she might say, you can come to me, but neither in the day nor the night, and neither riding nor walking, and you should be neither in the house nor out.

We see the threshold coming in here—on the threshold one is neither in the house nor out, neither in the conscious or unconscious, neither in this world or the other world. That is where living form takes the poem. And thresholds belong to all inbetwixt and between places, to the heron that is neither land bird nor sea bird, or mercury that is neither metal nor liquid. So the wise lover might arrive riding a sheep, or lying across a short pony, with his legs dragging, so he is neither riding nor walking, at dusk, which is neither day nor night, and he wouldn't call to her until the pony's front legs were inside the house and the back legs outside. Then they could do what they wished.

Writing poetry with open form, which I've done a lot of, is a little like walking over the threshold right into the house, and saying, "I'm a Protestant, I don't believe in all of this, let's just go to bed." And writing in mechanical form, rigidly iambic and rhymed, which I've done some of, is a little like riding the horse right up to the threshold, all four hooves outside, putting the head in, and saying, "I'm a Catholic, we can cancel the pagan conditions, come out and marry me."

But writing in an inbetween form, a form for which one has gone to nature, drawing it from her subtle abundance of snail shells and herons, that is like arriving at the inbetwixt time, neither night nor day, neither walking nor riding, and the horse neither inside nor out.

Essays, Memoirs, Poems,
& Documents about Robert Bly

Donald Hall

Poetry Food

These occasions allow the expression of gratitude. I met Robert Bly in February of 1948, when I tried out for *The Harvard Advocate* of which he was already an editor. We have remained closest friends over the decades—through many disagreements and even quarrels, our friendship based on the bewildered but unflagging affection that opposites sometimes feel for each other. We have bickered so much—I have made many essays out of these bickerings!—that he may find it outrageous that I recommend him as a model of behavior.

As vain as anyone, and as avaricious of praise—yet among my acquaintances of poets he is the most nearly disinterested. (I refer to Keats's favorite moral idea, a word which alas loses meaning every day as people use it to mean "uninterested.") A thousand times, I have observed with amazement Bly's cordial response to negative criticism: if there is an *idea* lurking in the denunciation, he lifts the idea up to the light, examines it like a dog a bone, remarks it, wonders at it, sniffs learnedly, and then chews on it—for nourishment and to keep his teeth sharp.

Of course such behavior is only sensible—what use are the complaints against us unless we learn from them?—but most people respond to blame not with curiosity but with plots of murder. Many artists as they grow older become experts at defending themselves against taking criticism seriously. They build castles out of the praise they get from younger writers, from old students, from sycophants, and from editors seeking their names. They build moats of exclusiveness; they surround themselves with dragons and princesses. Bly on the other hand seems to look for blame, as if he were daring himself to improve.

Writers who will grow and improve through their fifties and sixties, even into their seventies and eighties, are writers who

31

In James Wright's apartment, New York City, 1974.

LAYLE SILBERT

best develop dissatisfaction with themselves. Only from disappointment with one's old work can one possibly move ahead. Lately Bly has become aware that much of his work lacks sound, and lacks variety of syntax. Therefore he tries to begin again, to hear vowel and consonant sound as if for the first time.

It takes a doughty temperament. It means of course that one will never be satisfied. (To be a satisfied poet, to believe what the flatterers say. . .this is to be dead.) So one goes to the grave in labor. But the labor's end, if one is serious and persistent, is not the gratification of one's ego but a stewardship. Not long ago, when I felt discouraged, I wrote Bly a long letter; I whined to him as I would to no one else. He answered me with these words: "That the poems are useful to other people, that they are bread, that they can be eaten, and strengthen strangers, that is precisely our goal, our reward, and our vocation. . . ."

Deborah Baker

Making a Farm: A Literary Biography

Introduction

The life of Robert Bly is by no means over and it is not the intention of this biography to settle the dust. That is one obvious point. The other is that any biography will be incomplete; this one, because of length limitations, is even more so. Bly's contributions to American poetry can only really be understood in time and in the poets he inspired and exasperated: they will have to voice their own objections and homilies. This biography tries to follow major currents in Bly's literary criticism and poetry in the last three decades and to suggest their possible sources and implications. (Because Bly has been heavily influenced by Jung it will probably be a sore temptation for some psychobiographer in the future to identify the teeth-mother in Bly's past. I have not tried to do that.) As a subject for a biography Bly can be very elusive—he is the poet shaman, he is the political activist, and he is the critical voice defining the paths and traditions of American poetry. These have been his public voices; his poetic voice can speak the doubts and conflicts underlying this authority.

> I am only half-arisen.
> I see how carefully I have covered
> my tracks as I wrote
> how well I dusted over my past with my tail.

If one is to begin looking for Bly, this is where he should be found.

Early Life

Robert Bly was born on December 23, 1926 in Madison, Minnesota. His mother's name was Alice Aws Bly, his father's Jacob Thomas. Bly was the second son; his brother James was a year and a half older. His mother worked at the courthouse for some years, and the two Bly children were taken care of by a woman named Marie Schmidt. His father always had a hired hand living with the family, and one, Art Nelson, was with the Blys for nine years.

The father, Jacob Thomas, was the oldest son in his family and had quit school at eighteen to go to work. Bly describes him as a man who was both a reader and a strong farmer. The inheritance, however, was divided between the two sons. Robert became a reader of books and his brother James became a farmer. Bly has written very little about his family life, apart from the details of farm work, and about his father only once.

> He had a gift for deep feeling. Other men bobbed like corks around his silence, and his swift decisions; that did not bring him more company, but it did help carry the burdens higher up the mountain. His heart beat very fast, and he felt himself tied to this earth. At church he kept his arms crossed over his chest.[1]

This may suggest more about Bly than about his father. The idealization here suggests both Bly's strong identification with his father and also a certain observational distance.

A story that Bly tells about his father suggests more precisely the particular tone of his father's character, but even this story reveals less about Bly's relationship with his father than the importance of the example he set for Bly as a young boy. When Bly was young, and the Midwest was still recovering from the Depression, men from the southern Midwest would come north to help harvest the grain, living in camps and working as hired hands. One man had been working for Bly's father for a few weeks, when one morning he didn't appear. Instead of hiring someone else, Bly's father sought him out, learning that over the weekend he had been sent to the Stillwater jail for twenty years. Apparently he had made a date with a local waitress and had walked her home, when there occurred a misunderstanding of some sort, and he had slapped her face. Her parents called the sheriff, who tried and sentenced the hired man in a manner that suggested the zeal of the law before the coming election. Bly's father drove to St. Paul for the attorney general; then both men drove to Stillwater and brought the man back to the county jail. Eventually, after a new trial, the man was released.

In retrospect Bly states, ''I learned then that the indignation of the solitary man is the stone pin that connects this world to the next. I learned so much from that one story!...one moral example will do for a lifetime.''[2] This story goes to some of the roots of Bly's later political activism and his inability to withdraw into a poetic worldliness, eschewing these responsibilities and spurning the community that his father had reaffirmed. Yet Bly's father's actions on behalf of the hired man were not explicitly political. In his own activism Bly remains aloof; the largeness of his political and moral visions precluded the kind of affirmation that his father had acted on by saving one man.

The roots of this elevation can perhaps be inferred from the title of Bly's essay, ''Being a Lutheran Boy-god in Minnesota.'' It is in this context that Bly refers to his mother, Alice Aws Bly. Here, Bly's attitudes are less apparent than in his description of his father. Though Bly has written several essays on the importance of the mother image in symbols, literature and myth, his one sentence about his own mother is generous but curiously neutral in tone.

> As I understand the idea, boys towards whom the mother directs a good deal of energy, either warm or cold, tend to become boy-gods. They are boys, and yet they feel somehow eternal, out of the stream of life, they float above it. My mother was and is a good mother, without envy or malice, affectionate, excitable, living with simplicity and

energy—one of the servants of life. This embodied itself in a sense that I was "special" and so in
a general lack of feeling for others. If someone
were suffering, or in a rage, I would feel myself
pull away, into some safe area, where I did not
"descend" to those emotions, and get tangled in
them, but neither did I help the person at all.
What helping I did tended to be from above.[3]

In a recent interview Bly described the psychological
"wound" that drove him to solitude in New York in his early
twenties.

The male is wounded, and the question is, is he
wounded by the father's coldness to him, or is he
wounded by the actual animus, attacks and remarks of his mother. . . the remarks of the mother
cause deeper wounds. My father was a strong
enough power in the house, so that the remarks of
my mother. . . but she wasn't that way anyway, so
it doesn't really come true.[4]

The ambiguity of this remark has the unhappy effect of piquing
curiosity about Bly's family life while preventing speculation.
In any case, there appears to be a relationship between Bly growing up as a "boy-god" and this "wound," whatever its origins
in Bly's early life. The aloofness he affected was nurtured by the
"Sunday-school cheerfulness" of the Norwegian-American culture of the farms where the social tone was "a maddening cheerfulness, with no one ever admitting to being depressed or sui-
cidal."[5] Bly himself, however, would later be bothered by this
superficial cheeriness of his early life and would try to come to
terms with the darker, more melancholy intuitions of his wound.
He exclaimed later, "How high I was all through high school!
What a terrible longing I had to come down."[6] This "coming
down" would begin in his early twenties, after he had left Minnesota for Harvard and New York.

Bly and his brother James went to the District 94 county school at the time when one-room school houses were disappearing. If one taxpayer objected to the closing of the school, it had to remain open and Jacob Bly did object; sometimes the two Bly boys were the only students. They usually walked the mile to school, or rode double on the back of a family mule. Bly kept a diary when he was in the sixth grade. His entries are short and to the point.

> Jan 25
> Neither James nor I went to school today on account of blizzard, I practiced my music lesson in granma's room on Clara's piano. Got my magnifying glass from Post Toasties.[7]

It is doubtful that school played a very important role in the Madison community where the emphasis was on farming. Bly says most farmers regarded teachers "as a curious kind of bird-trainer, whom one humored." The men from the town were even more suspect. Bly's own attitude towards the cashiers and clerks who came out to the farms to watch the bank's grain being collected is, in itself, telling, reflecting on his later decision not to become an academic.

> How we pitied these creatures! Getting out of the car with a white shirt and necktie, stepping over the stubble like a cat so as not to get too much chaff on his black oxfords. . . . What a poor model of a human being! It was clear that the teller was incapable of any boisterous joy, and was nothing but a small zoo animal of some sort that locked doors on itself. . . . How ignoble! How sordid and ignoble! What ignobility![8]

Bly was as certain of the nobility of his father's occupation as he was of the ignobility of the bank clerk's.

Despite his idealization of the farmer's life and the pleasures of shocking grain and threshing, Bly admits that he would often make himself ill in the summer in order to lie in bed and read books.

> My father was very understanding. He would say "You just take a couple of weeks off and lie in bed and read, and you'll be well again." So I became the reader, the poet. My brother is absolutely the opposite of me. He's a farmer. He's never read to the second page of any of my books.[9]

The decision to become a poet, however, was hardly automatic. The idealization of the farming life and his father's importance in the shaping of Bly's early life would persist. These feelings would contribute to Bly's later conflicting conception of the role of the poet in American society, as if being a poet in itself was insufficient or incomplete.

The Navy

Upon graduation from high school, Bly stayed on the farm a few months and then enlisted in the Navy. Recruits were given the Eddy test, which essentially tested mathematical abilities. Though it was late in the war, the United States was still losing ships to German submarines; the Navy needed men who could master the new radar technology. Bly, to his surprise, passed the test, and after boot camp began the mathematics preparation at Wright Junior College in Chicago. In the middle of his session at Wright he caught rheumatic fever and was sent to Palm Beach, Florida for six months to recover. He then continued the tourse in Del Monte, California and Navy Pier, Chicago, but just before he was ready to go to sea the war ended.

In the Navy Bly met two men, Izy Eisenstein and Warren Ramshaw, both of whom were aspiring men of letters.

> I doubt I would have ever become a writer if I hadn't gone into the Navy and met Izy, who wrote poetry, and Warren, who knew about books and lived with books.[10]

Bly met Izy in Chicago, where they were the only recruits just out of high school taking the mathematics course. "We didn't know what the hell was going on and we didn't care, and we both considered ourselves literary even at that time." Bly's first contact with poetry, as he tells it, was hearing Izy describe the Chicago slums as a "running sore" on the city's body. Witnessing this creation made a powerful impression on Bly, and began his own thinking about poetry. Before Bly came down with rheumatic fever, he and Izy developed a plan to flunk out of the mathematics course by answering all multiple choice tests by repeating the firing order of the Model T's four cylinders. Their commanding officer, however, guessed something was up and promised them, if they flunked one more test, a front seat in the next landing barge invading a Pacific island.

> They didn't fool around at that time, boy. That was a *Yes Sir*. No one wrote to their congressman and said, "I got threatened" because it wasn't that kind of a war; you goddam well fought the war.[11]

When Bly was in Florida he met Warren Ramshaw and his family who were Unitarians from Chicago.

> I had never met any people that read books. My father read books but fathers don't count anyway. So I met a man named Warren Ramshaw who actually read books, and he was reading *Razor's Edge* by Somerset Maugham. That book was the farthest out thing that I had ever heard of.[12]

To Bly, reading books appeared a sort of family institution. "Their whole life was organized around books." With them as with Izy, Bly discovered a bookish camaraderie. No one in Bly's early life had ever read the same books he had, or with the same sort of passion.

These literary enthusiasms planted during Bly's time in the Navy probably contributed to his dissatisfaction with St. Olaf

College, which he entered in 1946 after he was released from the Navy. St. Olaf College was established in 1874 in Northfield, Minnesota by a Norwegian missionary and still retains strong ties with the American Lutheran Church. Bly later described St. Olaf as "dead spiritually." Still, the main reason for Bly's transfer to Harvard in 1947 was that he found the literary life not intense enough at St. Olaf. It is likely that the "holy Olies" kept up the atmosphere of "maddening cheerfulness," the Norwegian-American culture of the farms that Bly, at this time, was intent on escaping.

Harvard 1947-1950

From St. Olaf Bly transferred to Harvard and stayed three years, graduating *magna cum laude* in 1950. Here he found the literary community he wanted, on the *Harvard Advocate,* where he became a senior editor. With him at Harvard were the aspiring poets John Ashbery, Frank O'Hara, Kenneth Koch and Donald Hall, all four undergraduates who would later gain varying degrees of fame though they were far from an homogeneous group. Richard Wilbur, older, was also there. Bly later described the feeling of his undergraduate years and the first contact he had with poetry: "There was a wonderful air of seriousness about poetry; many people at Harvard had intended to be poets since they were about twelve or thirteen years old...something one rarely met in the Midwest."[13] Donald Hall has remained a close associate of Bly's throughout his career, both as a friend and as a critical observer of Bly's own work and poetry. He met Hall in the offices of the *Harvard Advocate*—there is a story that Hall arranged a blind date for Bly with Adrienne Rich who was then at Radcliffe.

Bly contributed poetry, short stories and book reviews to the *Advocate*. At Harvard, Bly wrote in the traditional forms of English poetry, maintaining the iambic line and rhythm. His criticism reveals a sensitivity to poets like William Carlos Williams, but also a vague suspicion of them. Their sense of form, Bly felt, was "unsure." A book review in 1949 reveals Bly analyzing the trends in contemporary poetry, already describing the mistakes of the "old Auden group," although Auden wouldn't be dead for another twenty-four years. His essay reviewed Kenneth Rexroth's anthology of new British poets. Bly was skeptical about Rexroth's finding a new movement in poetry in England, the "New Romanticism." Rexroth, through his translations of French, Japanese and Chinese poetry, precedes Bly in the search for alternatives to the British traditions in American poetry, though Bly was not yet at the point of recognizing this affinity. His criticism of Rexroth's editing and viewpoint sounds remarkably similar to later criticism of Bly's own work, particularly his moralistic statements and the political poetry he would begin writing five or six years later.

> ...what Mr. Rexroth means by "moral quality" becomes clear several pages later, when we realize that he is quietly sifting the whole movement down to a single grain of anarchism, in which Rexroth is known to have a rather vigorous interest. Perhaps it is unfortunate that Rexroth should have been let loose on the Romantics; there is, I think, a difference between the desire to express personal emotion by increased direct reference to the world of nature, and the desire to overthrow all external discipline of morals of government.[14]

The distinction Bly makes between the interior Romantic vision of nature and the political or moral involvement of the poet is significant in his career. Moreover, he was later to recognize Rexroth's contribution to the poetry Bly would further in his own magazine. In 1949, however, he concluded

> New Directions is to be commended, I think, for risking the publication of this volume which for all its value as poetry and as stimulation to American poets, must be by its nature [Rexroth's political bias] of small appeal and a smaller history.[15]

Thus, in neither his poetry nor his critical outlook did Bly show a serious interest in the trends that he would later defend and support in his own magazine.

New York 1951-1954

After graduating from Harvard in 1950, Robert Bly made the decision to live by himself for a time. At first he stayed in a cabin in the North Woods of Minnesota, and then he moved to New York where he spent about three years. The reasons for Bly's self-imposed exile are difficult to understand; at the time Bly was not clear himself. He describes the move as an "instinct" to be alone. Having graduated from Harvard with high honors in English Bly was in a position to go to graduate school, to become a professor. Instead he chose a more difficult path.

Bly had chosen not to be a farmer before he chose not to become an academic. Perhaps his scorn of those who worked at desks, such as the small "zoo-animal" bank clerks, contributed to the discomfort now of being a "literary man." Bly would later say half-seriously that he often felt like "apologizing for being a poet" and that perhaps he should have been a truck driver. Bly probably felt his separation from the land and from the harmonious ideal he had seen in his father. In this sense, Bly's instinct for seeking solitude, separated both from the Harvard and New York literary communities and from his father's farm, can be understood. It is only recently that Bly has identified the "wound" that sent him into exile in New York, stemming not from his father's approbation, but rather from his own conflicting expectations.

> I was wounded by something which I interpreted in the attitude or remarks of my father. . . . I am saying that a young man cannot join the community until he has dealt with that wound. And what I did, the intelligent thing that I did, was to go alone with my wound for three years in New York. And it is exactly like an animal that goes into a cave and licks its wounds.[16]

Bly's earlier explanations of his need for solitude are much more diffuse, related more to projected ideals of a poet's role in society rather than explicit personal reasons. In earlier interviews, given in the sixties and seventies, Bly's representation of the period in New York suggests conflicts; there is a tension between his vision of a poet and the difficulties this period posed in the development of his own creativity. It is perhaps for this reason that Bly for a long time did not care to talk about the period in New York. When he did, he described his poverty, depression and loneliness, while maintaining that the time alone was necessary for his development as a poet.

> In the early fifties I spent a couple of years alone, about three years, some in a room in New York. Part of that I did from an instinct to be alone... and part of it because I was too poor. Once I got alone I was too poor to get out of it. So I was forced to remain alone, in a way longer than I intended to. But it was in those years that I learned everything that I tried to bring into my poetry.[17]

At the time, however, Bly's efforts at writing were for the most part unsuccessful. He was foundering; he had yet to discover his own voice and even understand the benefits of solitude. He later said that he could not write about his wound, possibly because he had not yet articulated the personal basis of his instinct to be alone.

Though Bly has remained convinced throughout his career of the importance of solitude for the poet, he speaks of it as important for the poet's relationship to society as well as for personal understandings. In another interview Bly claims that the role of the poet is similar to that of the shaman in ancient society. Yet this representation of the poet as moral leader by virtue of isolation from society can become Bly's own mask.

> Yeats stood for values completely different from those I had understood before [my graduation

from college]. And one of those was that poetry was written in solitude. I spent about three years in solitude as a result of that. After I did that I had to make a choice between going back to school or remaining in solitude, and I decided to do the second. I didn't do it by going to a Trappist monastery I just did it myself. I got the taste for it. . . . I didn't go back to the university.[18]

The fact remains, however, that in 1955, the year Bly married and a year after his departure from New York, Bly finally did go to graduate school at the University of Iowa enrolling in the Writer's Workshop for an M.A. in creative writing. The time in New York, Bly claimed, had helped him learn what to bring to his poetry. At the time, however, the creative block, the poverty and isolation were sufficiently disheartening to make him waver in his effort to fulfill his Yeatsian ideals and pursue his instinct for recovery from his wound.

Later, Bly would maintain that the wound which sent him to New York had still not healed by the time he left.

> I know males and I know that the wound is there and to try to hide it by getting married early, to try to hide it by becoming a professor early, none of that works. No community is worth anything. You can't accept them; you can't feel the community until you've gone through that healing.[19]

The wound that Bly describes apparently prevents the "boy-god" from participating fruitfully in a community, or being compassionate and supportive in the sufferings of others. The boy-god syndrome that Bly described in his essay persisted in different ways until Bly began to come to terms with the wound, and affirm both the community of other poets and his decision to become a poet.

The University of Iowa 1956

Though Bly consistently criticizes contemporary writing programs he rarely mentions his own experience in Iowa's Writer's Workshop in 1956. It is therefore difficult to surmise his experience there. As the shaman poet, apart from the values of academia, Bly can idealize the period of solitude and isolation that he experienced in New York, contrasting this experience with the domestication of the workshop writer:

> The solitary pain [of the poet] with no one to relieve it, is typical of the wild animal writer. The workshops take away some of that pain by having someone there to encourage you.... I found out recently that one of the stronger labors of my life has been the labor to avoid unpleasant emotions —pain is probably one of these.[20]

Elsewhere in his writings, Bly's concept of the "wild animal writer" is not unlike his description of the shaman poet, connoting a certain primal freedom and purity of instinct. Here, however, solitude is linked to an internal pain, rather than representing the aloofness from society that keeps one untainted by its values. The confusion of definitions reflects Bly's own conflicting views on the issues of solitude versus community. Is Bly, in his last remark, referring to his own need for encouragement, to his decision to enter a workshop after the years of frustration in New York? If so, his decision to go to Iowa was probably a very difficult one, as the stringent code underlying his definition of a poet, his criteria for legitimacy, was based on solitude.

Though Bly does not discuss his experience at Iowa, the poems of his M.A. thesis reveal something of early creative and critical development. They do not foreshadow his later meditative poetry or his political poetry. Their technique conflicts with some of his principal critical tenets set forth in his magazine *The Fifties* and *The Sixties,* recalling his earlier book review in the *Harvard Advocate.* The thesis is divided into three parts: 1) The

Book of the Monkish Life, 2) The Book of Pilgrimage and 3) A Description of the Misery of the World. The language of many of them is archaic in places: "The gale, shearing stone from stone, / Rendeth bark from tree." Perhaps most surprising in light of his later criticism (though not if one considers most of the poetry being written at the time) is the iambic pentameter and rhyming stanzas.

There is one poem, however, in his Iowa collection that addressed the conflicts that Bly had been experiencing, and led toward an acknowledgment of the wound, which until this point had been identified only as an "instinct" to be alone. Bly later said this poem was written in New York; it is the only one of his early poems to be published later (in his first book of poems, *Silence in the Snowy Fields*). Though Bly claims that he could not write poetry about the wound at that point in his life, the poem reflects a dim awareness of certain symbols which would provide him with the creative material to understand it. Appropriately, the poem is called "Where We Must Look for Help."

> The dove returns; it found no resting place:
> It was in flight all night above the shaken seas;
> Beneath the ark eaves
> The dove shall magnify the tiger's bed;
> Give the dove peace.
> The split-tail swallows leave the sill at dawn,
> At dusk, blue swallows shall return.
> On the third day the crow shall fly;
> The crow, the crow, the spider-colored crow,
> The crow shall find new mud to walk upon.
> *(Silence in the Snowy Fields)*

In the Babylonian version of the ark myth, Noah sent out three birds to discover land. The first two, the dove and the swallow, returned with nothing. The crow, however, came back with mud on its feet, giving Noah the sign that the flood had receded. Later, Bly would describe this poem as the first hint to him of the importance of the "dark side of the personality" as a way to creativity. The dove, as a symbol of divine intervention and purity, becomes inappropriate, suggesting the beginnings of the eclipse of the boy-god.

> It was the first time I realized what the myth said, the first time I ran into the idea of the dark side of the personality being the fruitful one. And it wasn't until ten years later that I read that in Jung. But it says the same thing. The dove is OK if you don't need anything important done and the swallow is nice. I believe the swallow is like Adlai Stevenson, or Eugene McCarthy; they're very graceful but they don't persist (when you need him he resigns from the Senate). What you need is the crow.[21]

Bly had transcended the "maddening cheerfulness" of his high school days. Yet at the time these meanings and intimations existed only in his poetry, which many critics complained of as needlessly obscure. Bly himself would only be able to articulate in ideas many years later the shadowy feelings this poem suggests.

In 1956 Bly received a Fulbright grant to translate Norwegian poetry into English. This was to prove an important event in the development of his creative vision as well as provide him with a discovery which would inspire the publication and critical cause of his magazine, *The Fifties*, in 1958. By this time the dryness of the academic poetry would be renounced in favor of the surrealist and "deep image" imagination.

The Trip to Norway

Despite his Norwegian ancestry Bly did not know Norwegian before he went to Norway. Though he was interested in Scandinavian poetry, his proposal to translate Norwegian poetry was more of a pretext than a scholarly intention. Bly said later, "I went there because I'm of Norwegian ancestry and I wanted to look up my relatives." Though Bly did learn Norwegian by going three months early, his greatest finds were the South American poet Pablo Neruda, the Swedish poet Gunnar Ekelöf and the German poet Georg Trakl. These poets were to have a profound effect on his own poetry and his critical ideas. Finally, these discoveries provided the impetus for the publication of *The Fifties* and, for Bly, the evidence that American letters were "isolationist."

When Bly talks about his visit to Norway he stresses the importance of these poets in terms of his work and his critical philosophy. Yet his search for his Norwegian ancestry was also successful. Bly's side of the family had gone to America in 1855. In 1956, one hundred and one years later, Bly drove up to Vigliek Jacobson Bleie's farm in a Volkswagen, the first car ever to have entered their yard. Bly remembers entering the house and being met by Vigliek Bleie who held in his hand a book of Norwegian poetry by Nordall Gieg. As Bly describes this event it seemed as if he had indeed found his Norwegian "roots." He stayed at the farm for a little while and came to be very fond of Vigliek Bleie; he mentions him in a very recent poem called "The Ant Mansion."[22]

In Bly's description of the farm and the traditional work habits of the Norwegian farmer, he provides another association between his own life and his Norwegian-American ancestry. The pace of life on the Bleie fruit farm suggests the timelessness of farms that have been in the family for a thousand years.

> At 7:00 they'd go out and rake grass and put it under the trees, and about a quarter to eight they'd come in and have coffee for about a half hour and then they'd go back out and do a little more raking and about 10:00 they'd come back in and have mid-morning lunch. Then they'd go back.

This relaxed way of life was strikingly different from the fast pace of American farming with which Bly had grown up. The Bleie farm, like all Norwegian land, goes only to the oldest son, and is never divided. The "two to three hours of work a day" were not the privilege of all Bleies.

> They were really tough on that. That's why the Norwegian farmers remained independent, because the farms were never split up. [So the younger sons] became hired men on other people's farms and they couldn't even have a woman. The women wouldn't even accept them. And so the younger men would live as hired men and celibates and the only other choice would be to get a woman who was strong and say to her, "Do you want to go up to the mountain and make a farm?"[23]

"Making a farm" was something like homesteading. The younger son went to an uncultivated area and staked out about forty acres for his farm, cleared it of stones, and with extreme effort provided a subsistence life for his family, the whole process taking thirty years or so.

Bly is the younger son in his family. After World War II, his father sold the old farm, and bought three smaller farms, keeping one farm for himself. The remaining two he gave to James and to Robert. When Bly returned from Norway in 1958, he let his brother work his land while he and his wife lived in the farm house and he continued his work with poetry. Yet in a very real sense even when Bly decided on the literary profession he did not become a "hired hand" academic. Rather he chose to make his own "farm." Though he chose not to work the land, his ambition in 1958 was to encourage a new imagination in American poetry. Bly's roots were not those of the first-born Bleies who lived peaceably on their thousand year old farms. Bly was anxious to turn over the soil and transplant himself, both in the tradition of his Norwegian-American ancestor farmers and in the tradition of Walt Whitman, who spoke for the American, not the British, language in poetry. In doing so he would also dig up some of the "rocks" that had accumulated in American poetry since the war. The Fifties Press would be his plow.

Olai Bly, Robert's paternal grandfather, in Minnesota, circa 1920.

Making a Farm: The Fifties Press

In 1958 Bly and his wife Carol returned from Europe and settled on the farm in Madison, Minnesota. That same year Bly and William Duffy published the first issue of *The Fifties* magazine. This magazine of "poetry and general opinion" was to be renamed *The Sixties, The Seventies,* and now *The Eighties.* He began his long critical war with the New Critics and their poets with the pronouncement: "The editors of this magazine think that most of the poetry published in America today is old-fashioned." Bly took charge of all the stages of production apart from the actual printing. He and several friends managed the selection, the writing, the translations and the design. His wife worked with him on the distribution to subscribers and bookstores. From the farm, Bly was able to keep up a steady stream of translations, articles and criticism as well as chapbooks and broadsheet manifestoes. The format was very simple, without the elaborate production and professional distribution of the typical literary quarterly.

The emphasis on rebellion against the prevailing literary standards was a consistent aspect of the magazine. Articles satirized and ridiculed the reigning poetic idols and literary critics. One feature was an award called "The Order of the Blue Toad." In one of the early issues Bly granted the decoration to Robert Penn Warren and Cleanth Brooks, for the fifth edition of the poetry anthology, *Understanding Poetry.*

> This book was really written by Joe Friday. When discussing poems if a poet shows any sign of generous feeling or whimsy, the authors say in a flat voice: "We just want the facts ma'am." They want to know the meter, the authorized symbols, and the rhyme scheme.... The authors are very humble. Behind this humility, however, is a steady acceptance of all the fashionable clichés of the time, including the cliché that the most important thing about a poem is its form. [They

maintain of one poem] "The meter is largely responsible for the richness and concreteness this poem has." To encourage another man to write a better book, the authors are awarded "The Order of the Blue Toad." The toad, wearing A.E. Housman's moustache, is painted on a scarlet background. It is turning a meter machine with its left foot and correcting term papers with its right. Above its head is the motto *The Ghosts of Criticism Past* and under the toad's feet a banner that reads: Vote for Calvin Coolidge.[24]

Bly's enthusiasm for younger poets such as Louis Simpson and James Wright was complemented by a gleeful willingness to identify and bury the sort of poetry championed by the *Hudson Review* or *The New Yorker*. The section entitled "Madame Tussaud's Wax Museum" was intended to identify bad poetry, even when written by respected poets, and point out the symptoms of the "dying language." Thus Bly maintained in his first issue that poetry goes dead unless it utilizes "images." Lacking images, poetry is forced sooner or later into a dependence either upon four-letter words (referring to the poetry of the Beats) or classical references. Of the latter tendency Bly stated that the use of classical references was "not an isolated quirk but part of a general attempt to make a dead language more interesting. However since Zeus and Troy have . . . no emotional meaning for us at all, they work as a sort of open sluice to drain all the sincerity and emotion out of the poem in which they appear."[25] In other places Bly dismissed the fifties use of iambic pentameter and rhyme as emotionally torpid.

Poetry was only one object of the magazine's satire and critical scope, albeit the major one. The government, *The New York Times* and eminent literary historians also came under attack and contributed to the cult popularity of the magazine. The panoramic scope of Bly's critical vision was an appropriate start, not only for the clearing of America's literary terrain to make way for his favorite European and American poets, but also for the mobilization of a new imagination in all corners of the American cultural and political experience.

These features, plus an occasional parody of a poem by an establishment or academic poet, recalled the acumen of H.L. Mencken. Yet Bly's purpose was not simply that of an iconoclast, but also to introduce unknown European poets (or his translations of them), to publish and discuss the work of significant American poets, and to redefine the traditions they worked within. Thus the cantankerous "Crunk" was also a regular feature of Bly's publication. The signature of Crunk appeared below critical essays on contemporary American poets, and was a transparent mask for Bly's own views and critical standards. These long essays, unlike the short and satirical pieces, seriously studied the work of poets such as Louis Simpson, Denise Levertov or James Wright, poets whose poetry had shown a more dynamic vision than that of the academic poet. Crunk might point out, too, the similarities between such a poet's style and that of a European or South American poet, or suggest that the poet under review read a particular foreign poet to gain an alternative critical insight to the American poetry scene.

This relationship between the new American poetry and the poetry that Bly imported from Norway is a significant and unique feature of *The Fifties* and *The Sixties*. In an interview in 1966, Bly claimed that he started the magazine after his discovery of the South American poets Pablo Neruda, Cesar Vallejo, the Spanish poet Juan Ramón Jiménez and the German poet Georg Trakl in the Oslo library in Norway, and that it was this influence that led him to found a magazine to inform other American poets on the work of the European and South American imagination.

> It became apparent to me how isolationist America was in relation to European and South American poets. These poets were well known in Europe, even in little countries, but totally ignored or unheard of in the United States. It became apparent that a good service could be done and that

would be to start a magazine publishing some of these poets in translation. I felt avenues opening up into kinds of imagination that I sort of dimly sensed somewhere off on the horizon, but I had never actually seen in English.[26]

The magazine was intended primarily for American poets who, Bly imagined, would share his enthusiasm and interest in the more dynamic qualities of these foreign poets, some of whom had been writing since the twenties and thirties but had received little attention in England and America. By far the majority of the poems Bly published were translations of poets from Czechoslovakia, Rumania, France, Norway, Germany, Spain, Sweden, Denmark and South America.

This discussion of foreign poets also led Bly to reconsider American poetry since 1900, seeking continuity with earlier achievements of American poets. He was careful to distinguish the best elements of the specifically American approach to poetry from the more ethnocentric and formal concerns in British poetry. In the first issue of *The Fifties* Bly explicitly affirmed the achievements of William Carlos Williams, T.S. Eliot, Marianne Moore and Ezra Pound, labeling much of the poetry that followed these writers as a regression towards the English rules of order in verse. He described the poetry of the thirties and forties as direct responses to the Depression and the war, but saw the imaginations and terrors undermined by persistence of the old form, the iambic line. It was the task of the new generation of the fifties to pick up the threads of the imagination in the works of these earlier American poets. Bly had described this imagination as a ''magnificence of suggestion and association.''

With this introduction Bly presented the achievements of the foreign poets in terms continuous with his definition of the American poetic tradition. This, then, was the place to notice the achievements of European and South American poets during the thirties and forties.

If we look around we see some astonishing

landscapes: the Spanish tradition, for instance, of great delicacy, which grasps modern life as a lion grabs a dog, and wraps it in heavy countless images, and holds it firm in a terrifically dense texture, in which there is Pablo Neruda, a great poet ten times over...; in the Swedish tradition, Ekelöf, in the French, Char and Michaux, in the German, Trakl and Benn—all of them writing in what we have called, for want of a better word, the new imagination.

Bly's critical command was to throw off the metrical constraints of the thirties and forties. He noted the greater profundity of association of these foreign poets by redefining the poetic term "image" with the now famous declaration:

> To Pound an image meant "petals on a wet, black bough." To us an image is "death on the deep roads of the guitar."

This new means of association was called successively the "deep image" poetry, "naked poetry," or surrealist poetry, and would provide a new vision in American poetry. Bly concluded his essay on the five modern decades of American poetry with his manifesto.

> What we need now is not men of the 1910's but something different. The men of 1914 suddenly raided modern life and brought back large portions of it—chairs, paintings, artifacts even people into their poems, but often, as with Eliot in the Waste Land, one large raid, and it was over. The single raid was so astonishing it amazed, even petrified with amazement, even themselves, so they did not continue opening the doors of their work to filling stations and mass deaths in the trenches. We need poets now who can carry on a sustained

> raid into modern life, and. . .carry on the green
> and vigorous waters of this profound life.[27]

Bly's emphasis on foreign poetry helped to distinguish his magazine from the many poetry magazines and small presses appearing all over America during the sixties. By the middle sixties the "mimeograph revolution" had created a large flood of poetry magazines, fed by the aspiring bohemians and coffeehouse poets. The seriousness of Bly's critical voice redeemed the unprofessional format of his magazine.

The attention Bly lavished upon his chosen poets was another aspect of this seriousness. Bly described Crunk's critical attentions as a direct communication to the poet rather than a sacrifice of the poet to critical theory.

> We embarked on the criticism of the younger poets. . .at that time the poets such as Robert Creeley and [Louis] Simpson were only thirty or thirty-two years old, but we published an essay on them as if they were seventy or eighty years old and tried to discuss what they had done so far in their work and tried to make criticisms that would be of real value to the poet himself.[28]

Though Bly speaks of "we," for most of the magazine's lifetime he was the sole editor. The relationship between Bly and these poets is important. The reader gets the sense of Bly monitoring and directing the concentrations of the new movement and setting it up in its historical and critical context. Though the poets went off in their own directions, the magazine was almost chemical in its effect, and for the moment Bly's comprehensive criticism and foreign poetry translations were the strongest alternatives to New Criticism.

Poets Against the Vietnam War 1966

In 1966 Bly began his first important activities in the political sphere. In February of that year he participated in a public reading in New York against the war. About forty prominent literary figures read a piece of writing, either their own or by others, expressing dissent against the United States military presence in Vietnam. Inspired by this event, Bly sent a letter ahead to David Ray, a poet at Reed college where Bly was scheduled to read the following week. Together they founded "American Writers Against the Vietnam War." Ray convinced the college to provide airfare for poets Lawrence Ferlinghetti, Louis Simpson, Robert Peterson, George Hitchcock, and James Wright. Galway Kinnell, Kenneth Rexroth, and William Stafford gave support or sent poems to be read. When Bly arrived in Oregon, Portland State College and a peace group at the University of Washington also showed enthusiasm for the idea of an anti-war reading. Within a couple of weeks Bly had scheduled readings through May in Milwaukee, Chicago, Philadelphia and Minneapolis, and at Harvard, N.Y.U., Columbia and Cornell.

The Portland readings were an impressive beginning. The caliber of the poets attracted the attention of national television, and *The New York Times* carried a lengthy article on the initial readings in Portland. The purpose of the readings, Ray maintained, was to "encourage both writers and students to stand up and take a public stand on the Vietnam War and to encourage read-ins at all the major campuses in the United States."[29] At the time Bly described the readings as a stimulant to make the students think both about the war and the relationship between poetry and large national issues.

Bly's evaluation of the effect of these poetry readings on the student movement against the war reveals much about his idealization of the role of the poet. In an interview that took place a few months after the read-ins, Bly described the enthusiasm the readings had received and how quickly the idea had spread; colleges were planning their own readings, organized with local poets. Yet in an interview given five years later, in 1971, the importance and significance of the poets' coalition had increased. Bly figured that at the start approximately 10% of the students supported the read-ins and the other 90% were against the poets, "booing, screaming and howling." Until these readings,

Bly maintained, discussion of the Vietnam War had been limited to colloquiums with "professors talking in modulated tones about burning babies." As a result of the poetical lead in the protest the percentages had reversed themselves.

> We don't do so much of it anymore. We may do
> a few in the South where they still throw rocks at
> you.[30]

These two versions reveal an essential ambiguity in Bly. In the first interview, Bly saw himself as a catalyst in the chain reaction of student protest; the unrest was present but had found no means of expression. In the later interview, however, Bly rewrote the history, described it as a time not of coalition but of confrontation. This revision suggests that while the turmoil of the times provided Bly with a community of shared political ideals, he remained apart, a man whose powers were best sparked in open conflict, whether it was with the New Critics, the military-industrial complex, the government, or the students.

A stringent sense of moralism is very apparent in some of the poems he recited at the readings. These political poems would appear later in *The Light Around the Body*, Bly's second book of poetry, published in 1968. The tenor of Bly's poetry changed drastically from the poetry in *Silence in the Snowy Fields*. In his first book Bly was able to exclaim in carefree exultation,

> Oh, on an early morning I think I shall live
>   forever!
> I am wrapped in my joyful flesh
> As the grass is wrapped in its clouds of green.

In the poems read at the Portland readings, Bly was far more darkly sober.

>   the boy
> Tortured with the telephone generator,
> "I felt sorry for him,
> And blew his head off with a shotgun."

These instincts become crystals,
Particles
The grass cannot dissolve. Our own gaiety
Will end up
in Asia, and in your cup you will look down
And see
Black Starfighters.

>> "Driving through Minnesota
>> During the Hanoi Bombings"

Here the results of American military atrocities rain down on the same Minnesota landscape that Bly meditated on in his first book. This suggests a projection of Bly's own wound onto the political realities of the times. The sufferings of the Vietnamese become a rebuke to the superficial gaiety of the American culture. Here Bly expresses an intense empathy not only with the Vietnamese, but also with the guilt of the soldier as it filters back in radioactive effect to a Minnesota evening. The boy-god aloofness and cheerfulness of his early life are discarded and forgotten. Both in the time he spent alone in New York and in his identification with the tragedy of the Vietnam war the wound reappears.

His personal identification with the American destruction in Vietnam is more compelling than the more didactic moral outrage that Bly would also express in this same period. In didacticism, the boy-god aloofness would persist in an unstable coexistence with the poem's more sincere effort at compassion. In late 1966, the Sixties Press published a collection of political poetry both to recall the Portland readings and to make available material that other poets at other colleges could use at their own poetry readings. In the introduction to this book, Bly recounts journalists' and soldiers' descriptions of American atrocities and the horror of warfare with the anger of a manifesto.

> One repulsive novelty of this war is the daily body
> count. We count up the small boned bodies like
> quails on a gun-shoot. The military people would

feel better if the bodies were smaller, maybe we
could get a whole year's kill in front of us on a
desk.[31]

Because Bly was still active as an editor, he felt he had a responsibility to outline a new approach to poetry that would incorporate a concern with political issues. In doing that he chal-
lenged many poets and critics who feel that poetry dealing with
political subjects is propagandistic by nature. The relationship
between the challenge of political content and the earlier chal-
lenge of the New Imagination is noteworthy because Bly now
formulates a critical theory to support both concerns in poetry.
This was to be the beginning of his comprehensive aesthetic and
would later be articulated fully in his books *Leaping Poetry* and
News of the Universe. On the surface, surrealistic poetry and the
subjective poetry of the "deep image" appear to be at odds with
political content. Yet Bly's most treasured poets of South America and Spain, Lorca, Vallejo, and Neruda, wrote excellent political poetry that does not abandon the surrealistic vision; and their
example convinced Bly that political poetry is indeed possible,
and even a natural responsibility of the poet. In his essay "Leaping Up into Political Poetry," Bly described a new locus of poetry, above the depths of the individual consciousness.

> The life of a nation can be imagined not as some-
> thing deep inside our psyche, but as a psyche
> larger than the psyche of any one living, a larger
> sphere, floating above everyone.... [With a
> strong sense of his own interior] the poet can leap
> up into this other psyche.[32]

Clearly, Bly's effort to establish a clear critical directive on the
precise nature of political poetry is inseparable from his own
evolving ideas concerning the role of the poet within society.
The poem already quoted, "Driving Through Minnesota During
the Hanoi Bombings," presents a tentative reconciliation between the events of the outward world of suffering and oppression

and the poet's interior world, describing how the image of violence committed against the Vietnamese is reenacted on the American psychic landscape. This "larger sphere" of the nation's conscience which Bly tries to understand is described in different and conflicting ways in his poetry, suggesting the conflicts Bly was experiencing within his own "interior psyche," specifically in his acknowledgment of the wound.

This is particularly clear in the early version of "The Teeth Mother Naked At Last." Here the causes of the Vietnam War are attributed to a national death-wish, or suburban greed, "The Marines use cigarette lighters to light the thatched roofs of huts / because so many Americans own their own homes," or the result of a technological superiority complex, "because the milk trains coming into New Jersey hit the right switches every day the best Vietnamese are cut in two by American bullets that follow each other like freight cars." In these lines Bly displays the anger of the activist who wades through the political rhetoric of the left rather than attempt to transcend ideology and jump into the "larger sphere" of the national psyche. The vacillation between the polemic of these lines and the deeper sorrow and bitter compassion expressed in "Driving Through Minnesota During the Hanoi Bombings" reflects Bly's larger conflict: the insistence upon the shaman's withdrawal, expressing both an offended anger and a longing for detachment while at the same time experiencing a sincere identification with the national tragedy.

The Light Around the Body:
The National Book Award 1968

The differences of opinion over the possibility of political poetry became most apparent in the reviews of *The Light Around the Body,* when it was published in 1968. The critics could not help but contrast this newer poetry with the earlier pastoral work: quiet, mystical, contemplative and solitary. *Hudson Review* judged the book of political poetry an "honorable failure."

Long before the Vietnam War, Bly, like Virgil,

preferred peace and isolation...[but now] Bly is
unhinged by the cruelties inflicted on the Vietnamese people by America's military arsenal and
moral indifference. His mind is haunted by images of ruin, waste, fallen houses, burnt bodies.... A man of moral absolutes, Bly exempts no
one from the collective guilt.... Consequently,
there is no forgiveness for America, no mercy, no
prayer.[33]

The *Atlantic Monthly* described Bly as a "pungent critic, an
undaunted...moralist, a hackled dissenter, a sworn enemy of
worldliness in the conduct of life and the conduct of poetry."
The advice to Bly was to lay off the political poetry and bring his
"powerful native voice" to his overly meditative poetry.[34]

Despite this critical reception, *The Light Around the Body*
received the National Book Award for poetry in March 1968.
Typically, Bly described the award as a "fluke." At about the
same time, he participated in the draft card turn-in at Washington the day before the Resistance march on the Pentagon. Initially, Bly thought of turning down the National Book Award
(he had turned down two previous awards); instead he decided
to make a public donation of the thousand dollar prize to the
Resistance for draft counseling. The government had recently
declared that counseling against the draft in public was a pun-
ishable crime. An editorial in the *Nation* described the ceremony at Lincoln Center.

The most electrifying moment at Lincoln Center
came when Robert summoned Mike Kempton
(later identified as the son of *New York Post* col-
umnist Murray Kempton), of the Resistance
movement and counseled him "not to enter the
US Army now under any circumstances." ...Bly
asked that [the money] be used to "find and
counsel other young men to defy the draft authorities and not destroy their spiritual lives by participating in this war."[35]

Donald Hall and Theodore Weiss, in the citation for the book, described the book as an appropriate address on the state of the nation. In his acceptance speech Bly lauded the men who had acted in the tradition of Thoreau by their acts of civil disobedience, while castigating the book industry, the Catholic Church, and the Metropolitan Museum of Art for not doing the same. "I am speaking for many American poets when I ask this question: since we are murdering a culture in Vietnam at least as fine as our own, do we have the right to congratulate ourselves on our cultural magnificence?"

David Ignatow later described Bly's speech at the National Book Awards ceremony as Bly's finest hour.

> ...for me the moment meant a complete and overwhelming affirmation and vindication of all that Robert stood for as a crusading, visionary figure in the literary world and in the politics of our nation.... It was Robert's finest hour and we who were attached to him through admiration, faith and common goals were affirmed through him and made to feel our significance before the world.[36]

Bly had transcended his role as a missionary to American poets to become missionary to the nation itself. This one act fulfilled Bly's ideals of the role of the poet in society and renewed the moral example that his father had set before him in Minnesota by defying the imposed authorities and reaffirming the human community. Yet the poet's achievement was larger, politically, embracing a community of souls that extended beyond the small Minnesota town where he grew up and identifying a community that included the Vietnamese.

It was this commitment that Bly was to bring to his poetry. In the poems of *Silence in the Snowy Fields,* the associations between images, though irrational, seem to have an emotional logic of their own: by sinking into the depths of solitude, Bly could find his purest images among the cornfields and landscapes of Minnesota. In these poems Bly discovers his creativity while retaining his isolation. Bly's political poetry was a significant movement outward, but at times his intimate relationship with his lands would be lost in an abstract vision of America with its death wish and its reptilian heads of state. The rendering of people and human relationships borders on bitter caricature. The stridency of his moral vision implied a degree of estrangement, not only from the behavior of his country during the war but also from the more stringent demands of empathy.

Bly's political actions were resolute, his commitment is reflected in the new themes he brought to American poetry. The question remained, however, as to how one could bring an authentic political voice to poetry. The wound that American society opened through its participation in the Vietnam War was as painful as Bly's own wound. His most moving political poems involved an acknowledgement of this shared wound; his least were those that obscured it in preaching.

The Seventies

The early seventies can be described as a fairly private period in Bly's life. The family had moved an old schoolhouse to the property and Bly used it as a study. He also kept a cabin about thirty miles from the farm in Madison where he tried to go a couple of days a week to work and think by himself. His wife Carol also took a couple of days a week to work on her own writing, leaving Bly to take care of the four children, Mary, Bridget, Micah and Noah. (Her book *Letters From the Country* was published in 1981 by Harper & Row.) The Bly family was also involved in community activities. Carol Bly established a Prairies Arts Center in Madison and worked in the church. During the winter Bly gave lectures in the basement of the church such as "The Discoveries of Freud and Jung and How They Apply to Life in Madison." He also gave seminars on fairy tales and read poetry. During this period Bly left home, as he still does, for two to three months a year to read poetry at universities and give workshops in order to make a living. Following his meditation studies in Scotland under Trunpa Rimpoche in 1968, Bly had become increasingly influenced by meditation. Meditation, he later maintained, was an important influence on *Sleepers Joining Hands,* citing particularly the "Winter Privacy Poems" in the beginning of the book. Though Bly published a portion of the poem "Sleepers Joining Hands," he is still revising it and trying to come to terms with a much longer version (about ten thousand lines) that he wrote during the early seventies.

Bly was also studying Jung intensely at the time he wrote *Sleepers Joining Hands.* Apart from poetry readings he also gave lectures at Jung Institutes throughout the country. Inspired by Jung's work on myth, he became interested in fairy stories and began giving seminars titled "Fairy Stories for Artists," "Fairy Stories for Lovers and Married People" and "Fairy Stories for Healers." He plans to publish a book called *Fairy Tales for Men.*

The seventies were also a period of extraordinary achievement and recognition for Bly. Apart from his numerous translations he wrote eleven books of poetry, among them *The Morning Glory* (1970), *Sleepers Joining Hands* (1973), *Point Reyes Poems* (1973), *This Body is Made of Camphor and Gopherwood: Prose Poems* (1977), and *This Tree Will Be Here for a Thousand Years* (1979). *Sleepers Joining Hands* had an electric effect on the American literary audience; the prose piece at the center of the book spawned intense critical debate. In one sense *The Fifties* and *The Sixties* had poets to promote or causes to uphold and this tended to distract Bly from the concentrated seriousness he would bring to both his poetry and his criticism during the seventies. In 1975, *Leaping Poetry: An Idea With Poems and Translations* came out after having been published as the first and last issue of *The Seventies.* In *Leaping Poetry* the Spanish poets were Bly's principal source of confirmation for his aesthetic. Yet the ideas he articulated here revealed a larger understanding of his critical direction, reaching beyond the Spanish surrealists movement and into the accomplishments and future of the American poetry he had encouraged and elucidated throughout the career of his magazine. Bly can also be credited as being the first American critic to make use of scientific research to support his critical claims.

An important aspect of Bly's literary aesthetic is its comprehensiveness. His attempt in *News of the Universe: Poems of Two-fold Consciousness* (1980), to give a new critical context to western literature fulfills Eliot's dictum that a poet must maintain a consciousness of the past, the historical evolution of sensibility, in order to realize the demands of the conscious present. Here, Bly's concern for criticism and his wide angle view of many literatures and traditions is finally brought to bear upon American poetry. Bly provides this panoramic view, not only upon the traditions of western literature, as Eliot and Pound had, but also upon the nature of human consciousness itself. Doing so he reevaluates an ancient, pagan past providing new pathways of association, pathways that reached back into the clutches of Grendel and reemerged in Bly's own Teeth Mother.

*

In June 1979 Carol and Robert Bly agreed to a separation and divorce and went into equal parenting. In August they both moved to Moose Lake in the North Woods of Minnesota. Though maintaining separate households the Blys live within the same school district so the children are able to spend time with both parents. In November 1980 Bly married Ruth Ray who had lived with the Blys in Madison from 1973 to 1977 with her two children, Wesley and Sam. It is possible that the personal upheaval and divorce from his first wife made him face the responsibilities of a parent and accept the sorrows and grief that such a decision involved for both of them.

Bly's move from Madison also involved difficult decisions. He had spent his whole life in Madison, as had his father and grandfather before him; he had raised his own family there. But there is also a sense of relief when Bly speaks of the move to Moose Lake.

> In a way it feels wonderful to be out of Madison.
> I had carried my grandfather and my father too
> long. Up in the North Woods it is a lot like

Norway. Both Carol and I wanted to move further
north.

Moving from his father's shadow Bly also feels a release from the
heroism he strove for during the sixties, though he says he still
feels a "longing" for such a role and is trying to wean himself
from it.

> Heroes were needed in the sixties. I offered to be
> one which was very generous of me. But you can't
> do that for very long, it's not quite human. The
> hero always tries to solve things.... I've just be-
> gun to discover the dark side of my father and ad-
> mit it to myself, and to discover my own shady
> side. As for my mother's dark side, any mother's
> dark side, well that is about twenty-five miles
> wide... and deep.[37]

In poetry readings Bly has mentioned that the sixties were a
very exhilarating time for him, but that there was also something
"fakey" about them. The seventies, he feels, were a time of
grounding.

> There were many separations and breaks and part-
> ings but I felt a kind of grounding in my grief. I
> came down. It is as if in the sixties we kept look-
> ing at the dark side of the U.S. which pulled peo-
> ple into heroism and narcissism but in the seven-
> ties I looked at my own dark side. The seventies
> were a kind of filter; it takes two hundred yards of
> earth to filter water. Hopefully in the eighties we
> will be able to experience the truer Dionysian and
> Apollonian energies. It will be more truthful, the
> water will come through clear.[38]

This hopefulness at the beginning of the eighties is a long way
from Bly's apocalyptic political poems such as "The Teeth
Mother Naked at Last." Still, it is far from a world-weariness.

The children: Biddy, Mary, Wesley Ray, Sam Ray (with dog), Micah, Noah.

Bly's untiring efforts for the cause of poetry during the seventies and, in the beginning of the eighties, the rejuvenation of *The Eighties* magazine, reveal the fertility of the ground he now stands upon.

Conclusion: New Mud to Walk Upon

The largeness of Bly's moral ambitions during the sixties may have temporarily defeated him in his search for a community with integrity that was not defined by righteousness and moral indignation but by personal affections and commitments. It is this community that Bly began to discover during the seventies.

> I do know that community in the U.S. is very hard to come by and I've come to have more and more respect for the community of poets. In the beginning one kind of apologizes for being a poet, you think you ought to have been a truck driver. . . . But it isn't so. In the community of poets. . . that community is just marvelous in its support for me. And I've become more and more willing to consider myself a writer. You have to be willing to do that and it feels good to me. So when I get up and talk about my writer friends, I'm not apologizing for their being literary people. . . . Do you understand that? I'm learning something of that now.[39]

At the memorial reading for James Wright at the Donnell Library in New York in March 1981, Bly spoke movingly of Wright both as a poet and as a man. His respect for Wright reveals an acceptance of the poet in Wright, apart from any explicit political role he may have had. In accepting the support of other poets and in offering his own support, Bly sheds the habit of his boy-god aloofness and the elevations of a shaman mask.

During a recent conversation, a friend of Bly's suggested that he tried to run away from his poet friends by settling in Minnesota. Bly responded with a description of the wound and the long process of recovery through solitude. The three years in New York were only the beginning.

> The wound is about 10,000 years old. It says, "What is this fast kid here? Trying to get through in three years." I couldn't write about my wound. You can gather a little bit in the crow poem...''Where We Must Look For Help." "The crow shall find new mud to walk upon," but notice the word "shall." It does not say the crow *has* found new mud to walk upon. I knew that the crow would. And it's the mud between the toes that I didn't have.[40]

The discovery of this new ground has different implications than Bly's apotheosis as a political gadfly. Finding new mud to walk upon involves accepting the value of being a poet. This statement also suggests the importance of a new poetic vision, unfettered by the traditional expectations of academic poetry. Although Bly began his career writing traditional poetry, the discovery and translation of the poetry of the surrealists and "deep image" writers had for him wide implications, both for his poetry and for his life.

Bly's recent willingness to talk about his life, his biography, is one aspect of this acceptance, and like his political concerns in the sixties, brings new themes to his poetry. Recently, Bly has set out what he calls the six powers of poetry. The order in which he names them corresponds roughly to the order in which he arrived at them. The first two powers, those of "image" and "psychic weight," are the powers of his earlier poetry. The third power that Bly entered had to do with spoken language, of colloquial speech.

> It took me until I was forty-five to get those three in. And it was the pitches and the spoken chords that were the hardest. In *This Body is Made of Camphor and Gopherwood* I had all three in at

With son Noah at the Mother Conference in Maine, 1978.

> last. It had taken ten years each for the first two
> and about five years for the third one and so well,
> I said, I felt good. I felt I had gotten about half-
> way to the great poem.[41]

Bly has recently begun to work with the power of narrative or
"character." With narrative he is able to discover the people, relationships and human events in his life, as in his prose poems.
He has just finished a series of poems on his father. Bly's redefinition of the powers of poetry, emphasizing two powers, sound
and rhythm, which he had ignored or dismissed earlier in his career, reveal not only Bly's creative growth, but also a new awareness of the importance of personal relationships and communication.

Perhaps they also suggest Bly's acceptance of his place in the
poetic community. Among the six powers he does not now specifically mention political issues or the necessity of setting a moral example. Now Bly's integration into the poetical community
comes both as a result of the change in his own perceptions, his
willingness to consider himself a poet, and also as a result of the
changes he affected on that community. His own poetry, his
translations redefined the boundaries and geography of the
American literary landscape. It is only by understanding the
changing relationship between Bly and this community that one
can come to terms with both his life and his poetry. Just as Bly's
exposure to the poets he found in the Oslo library freed him to
express the political or "surrealistic" realms of experience, so the
new-found openness to his poet friends may help him to express
the human relationships within his life.

Similarly, Bly's willingness to talk about his life, to be more
candid in his presentation of himself as a poet, a writer with no
foreign poet to promote or political cause to champion, has also
had a corresponding influence on his latest poetry.

> Since Pythagoras died, the world has gone down a
> certain path, and I cannot change that. Someone
> not in my family invented the microscope, and

Western eyes grew the intense will to pierce down through its darkening tunnel. Air itself is willing without pay to lift the 707's wing, and for that there is no solution. Pistons and rings have appeared in the world; valves usher gas vapor in and out of its theatre box twenty times a second, and for that there is no solution. Something besides my will loves the woman I love. I love my children though I did not know them before they came. I change every day. For the winter dark of late December there is no solution.[42]

Bly's career has shown exuberant energy and creativity. Despite his reticence in talking about his personal life he has, at odd times, acknowledged his masks and self-doubts. It is perhaps these self-doubts that have kept his career and thought dynamic and unpredictable. He still does not have the tone of an establishment figure. Because of his commitment to growth and change in his personal life and poetry, he will remain rooted in the field of American poetry and a difficult figure for the next generation of poets to uproot and plow under.

Notes

[1] Chester G. Anderson, ed. *Growing Up in Minnesota: Ten Writers Remember Their Childhood.* (Minneapolis: University of Minnesota Press, 1976), p. 206.

[2] *Growing Up in Minnesota,* p. 218.

[3] Robert Bly, "Growing Up In Minnesota," *American Poetry Review.* (January/February 1975), p. 4.

[4] Interview with Deborah Baker, March 26, 1981.

[5] *Growing Up in Minnesota,* p. 211.

In Columbia, Maryland, April 1981.

[6] *Growing Up in Minnesota,* p. 212.

[7] *Growing Up in Minnesota,* p. 207.

[8] *Growing Up in Minnesota,* p. 213.

[9] Paul Froiland, "Of Shamans and Solitude: Robert Bly On the Meaning of Words," *TWA Ambassador.* (December 1980), p. 33.

[10] Interview with Deborah Baker, March 26, 1981.

[11] Interview with Deborah Baker, March 26, 1981.

[12] Interview with Deborah Baker, March 26, 1981.

[13] Robert Bly, *Talking All Morning.* (Ann Arbor: University of Michigan Press, 1980), p. 48.

[14] Robert Bly, "New British Poets—An Anthology," *Harvard Advocate.* (Spring 1949), p. 20.

[15] *Harvard Advocate,* p. 20.

[16] Interview with Deborah Baker, March 26, 1981.

[17] *Talking All Morning,* p. 14.

[18] *TWA Ambassador,* p. 35.

[19] Interview with Deborah Baker, March 26, 1981.

[20] *Talking All Morning,* p. 291.

[21] Interview with Deborah Baker, March 26, 1981.

[22] Robert Bly, "The Ant Mansion," *Harvard Advocate,* (May/June 1981), p. 53.

[23] Interview with Deborah Baker, March 26, 1981.

[24] *The Sixties,* (Fall 1961, vol. 1, no. 5), p. 91.

[25] *The Fifties,* (1959, vol. 1, no. 2), p. 48.

[26] *Talking All Morning,* p. 79.

[27] Robert Bly, "Five Decades of American Poetry," *The Fifties* (1958, vol. 1, no. 1), p. 39.

[28] *Talking All Morning,* p. 49.

[29] *New York Times,* March 6, 1966.

[30] *Talking All Morning,* p. 74.

[31] *Poets Against the Vietnam War,* (Sixties Press, 1966), p. 5.

[32] *Forty Poems Touching on Recent American History,* (Sixties Press, 1966), p. 12-13.

[33] Herbert Liebowitz, "Questions of Reality," *Hudson Review* (Fall 1968), p. 555-557.

[34] *The Atlantic Monthly,* (February 28, 1968), p. 141.

[35] "The National Book Awards," *The Nation* (March 25, 1968), p. 413.

[36] David Ignatow, "Reflections On the Past with Robert Bly," *Poetry East* 4/5 (Spring/Summer 1981) p. 205.

[37] Interview with Deborah Baker, July 28, 1981.

[38] Interview with Deborah Baker, August 13, 1981.

[39] Interview with Deborah Baker, March 26, 1981.

[40] Interview with Deborah Baker, March 26, 1981.

[41] Interview with Deborah Baker, March 26, 1981.

[42] Robert Bly, "Eleven O'Clock at Night," *Poetry East* 4/5 (Spring/Summer 1981), p. 23.

Annie Wright

Joining Hands With Robert Bly

I heard many stories about Robert Bly long before I met him. During the winter of 1967, before my late husband, James Wright, and I were married, I heard about James' visits to the Bly farm in Minnesota, the work he and Robert did, and the fun they had.

I knew about the chicken house where James had stayed, and about the day Robert locked him in so he was forced to finish a long overdue translation. I heard about the barn where Robert and Carol built a stage, and the plays they gave there. I knew about David the swaybacked palomino, and Simon the big shaggy dog. I heard about the children: godchild Mary with hair the color of a new penny, and Biddy, who liked to climb on James' lap, hiking herself up by the hair of his beard. When Noah was born, I was with James when he sent Carol a bouquet in honor of the birth.

After we married, I finally saw it all for myself as we went to the farm for a delayed honeymoon. Robert met us in Minneapolis where we were staying with Roland Flint. He arrived at Roland's house after a fishing trip. My first glimpse of this tall, sunburned man with mosquito bites all over his arms, was watching him bend over Roland's freezer to ease in a huge plastic sack of fish caught on the trip. When he saw us, he gave a great shout of joy, hugging us both at the same time.

That night we went to the Guthrie Theatre to see an incredibly poor performance of a Greek play. When it was over James and Robert called out, "Bad! Oh, bad!"

The next day we drove to the farm, Robert and James talking all the way. Robert's strong deep voice had a strong deep Minnesota accent. He peppered his conversation with the query, "How does that grab you?"

He thought and acted on impulse. Out of nowhere came the joking compliment to James. "If you keep publishing poems about illegal fishing nets, James Wright, I'm going to have the game warden after me."

Noting a fruit stand by the side of the road, he brought the car to an abrupt stop, leaped out, bought a watermelon, cut it up for us with his jack-knife, and drove on. We ate the slices, quenching our thirst in the August heat.

Robert had prepared the schoolhouse for us to stay in. It was an old, country, one-roomed schoolhouse bought at an auction. The Blys had brought it back to the farm and set it in a small grove of trees down the hill from the field where the big house was. Robert and Tim Boland, a young writer staying on the farm, had cleaned and arranged some furniture in the little building. It was a pleasant room with a beautiful old bed of carved wood at one end and some easy chairs and a writing table at the other.

At an appropriate distance was the outhouse. Robert told us when three young writers came for a visit he set them to work digging the foundation for the outhouse. He grinned ferociously adding, "They left pretty soon after that."

Robert showed me all around the farm. David and Simon had long since gone. The chicken house was now a study for himself, but in another grove of trees was a screen house for guests.

The main house that James knew from the days he lived in Minneapolis had been enlarged by adding another house to it. Robert showed us the new rooms. The extra kitchen was an office for *The Sixties* and Odin House publications. There was an L shaped room for Mary and Biddy downstairs and two little rooms for them upstairs. As we passed the open door of a store-room on the second floor, Robert pointed to a big fishing net on the floor.

"That's the very net, Annie. That's the illegal fishing net."

Carol and the children were away during the first few days of our visit. Robert and Tim worked most of the morning and early afternoon. Then we all went into Madison to do the grocery shopping. While I prepared dinner, the three men talked in the living room. After we ate, we went for walks along the deserted highway.

One evening as we walked towards an enormous, lone cottonwood tree, Robert told us how the farmers really hated trees. Although each farm had a grove of trees planted in careful rows, it was only because the government would pay for them that they existed.

"Come on, Annie and Jim," Robert would call out just before we reached home again, "we're going to lie down and listen for animals."

We would lie in the high grass of the ditch beside the road, listening. Robert would whisper about the rabbits, or mice, or owls we might hear. We never did though. We only heard the hot summer breeze blowing through the wheat.

After our walks, we gathered in the chicken house to listen to records; folk songs, symphonies, or The Fugs. Robert might read us a crank letter sent to him as editor of *The Sixties*. He and James read aloud the translations of the Spanish poets they loved. Often Robert read something he was working on.

When Carol and the children came back, we went swimming in the late afternoon with Mary and Biddy. Robert would buy candy for them, although they weren't supposed to have it. At meal times, the table was full and we were loud with laughter and conversation.

One day the living room was covered with piles and piles of papers. "We're getting out *The Sixties*," explained Robert.

He and Tim sifted through heaps of manuscripts and letters. By the end of the day selections were made, papers were arranged in tidy stacks, and Robert was typing letters of rejection and acceptance.

"Here's my answer to this one," said Robert holding up a poem typed out in the form of a Coke bottle. "I hate light verse! How does that grab you?"

During our visit, people dropped by constantly. Lois and David Budbill stopped for a night. Fred Manfred came over from Blue Mounds bringing his sleeping bag with him. Hardy

St. Martin flew in for a long stay. When Hardy and Fred were there, we had a big fried chicken, potato salad picnic at Lac Qui Parle, spending the day swimming, eating and talking.

The entire visit was filled with expansive conversation. My head reeled with the talk of poets and poetry, old stories of the farm during the fifties and sixties, tales of Robert's childhood on his parents' farm, visits he and Carol had made to Norway and England.

Robert would make outrageous statements and judgments.

"I think he," referring to a mutual friend, "is like an omelette without eggs."

"The reason we have three different races on this planet is because each race came from a different place in outer space. Annie, how does that grab you?"

We were all glum when the visit came to an end. As Robert drove us to the airport he commented, "I feel so sad."

We saw Robert many times after that. He, Carol, and the children, stayed in New York for a few months in 1968. We often went to their rented apartment. Sometimes we would have dinner there with the Simpsons, or Galins, or Ignatows. Sometimes, we just went to talk in the afternoons after work. Mary and Biddy came to the nursery school where I was Director. Robert might arrive at the school to pick them up, stunning all the children with his height and warm laugh.

That was the year Robert won the National Book Award. We were in the audience cheering and stamping when he read the acceptance speech we all knew by heart.

Over the years, Robert swept in and out of New York City. He might appear at our house, dressed in his Mexican serape, with a group of fans and a bottle of Scotch. He might come alone. Once Layle Silbert came with him to photograph Robert, and ended up taking pictures of both him and James wearing the rubber masks Robert had used for his readings.

Sometimes he stayed over with us. He always brought a present: a roast chicken, a bouquet of flowers, a book, once a pair of golden earrings for me.

We never knew when we might get a call urging us to come

with him to the Kinnell's, or to join a group at Bobo's in China-town, or to see Mary when he brought her.

It was always exciting, always a time filled with people, food, long conversations and great warmth. Each time we saw him, Robert had new ideas. He talked of Jung and the multitudinous levels of consciousness. He discovered new books by new poets. He talked of his Great Mother Conferences, or new foods, or how some stones could speak, but we might not hear them for a thousand years. He continued to be outrageous with funny stories and comments.

In the spring of 1970, we made one more trip to the farm. It was bitter cold, even for March, even for Minnesota. The small groves of leafless trees, surrounding barns and houses like islands in a flat white sea, looked pitiful and forlorn in the cold.

Carol had sold a story and used the money to have a fireplace built in the living room. We read and talked in front of its warmth. The fish net was still in the storeroom, but there were changes. Mary and Biddy could read, and Noah could walk and talk.

Our schoolhouse was now a place of meditation for Robert. Concerned that we might miss the atmosphere of the first visit, he offered to set up the carved wooden bed for us, even though it was stored away in the barn.

We continued to see Robert when he came to New York. During all the years of their friendship, James and Robert corresponded. Sometimes James didn't answer letters and sometimes Robert didn't. While it wavered from time to time, the correspondence never stopped. Their lives had changed from the time on the farm when James went out in need of quiet and friendship. Their ideas, so similar in the fifties, were now quite different in the seventies. But their feelings about each other were just as strong.

Last winter Robert came to see James at the hospital. Earlier in the fall, after a long lapse, their correspondence had been re-newed. Robert came into the hospital room quietly, taking James into his arms i.v. tubes and all. Although James could not talk, he wrote notes to Robert on a yellow lined legal pad.

Robert talked and James answered him in writing. James was alert and responsive in a way he hadn't been for some months and rarely would be again. After Robert left, James wrote me a note saying:

> I was afraid Robert was gone for good.
> I'm so relieved he's not.
> Today was good.

This winter Robert Bly came into New York. I saw him at a party given by Saul Galin. His serape has been replaced with a vest in an elegant pattern of roosters, and a flowing black tie. When he saw me, he pulled me into the kitchen so I could see our godchild Mary, now a freshman at Harvard.

During the party, Robert urged old friends to meet new friends. He was excited about Jane Kenyon's translations of Anna Akhmatova, reciting some of them accompanied by one of his two dulcimers.

As always with Robert there was conversation, music, poetry and friends. As he joined hands with James long ago in Minnesota when James needed comfort and companionship, as he joined hands with me on my first visit to the farm, so he joined hands with all of us at that gathering. Joining hands is one of the special gifts of Robert Bly.

Michael Clifton

Interview with Robert Bly

This interview took place at Indiana University in Bloomington, on November 16, 1979. After Mr. Bly's reading the night before, I discussed briefly with him what I referred to as "American poetry's shift towards the nonrational" that started in the late '50's, and that Mr. Bly had urged along in his poetry magazine. I wanted to talk with him about it, and particularly talk about the literary and cultural events that led to the publication of *Silence in the Snowy Fields* and James Wright's *The Branch Will Not Break*. Mr. Bly kindly agreed to an interview. When I arrived at his room the next morning to talk about this poetic shift towards the nonrational, and the elements in (or lacking in) our culture that made the shift necessary, Mr. Bly remarked that he and Wright had made, in essence, a regression in order to go forward. I set up my recorder and the interview continued.

MC: *In what sense were you and James Wright going through a regression?*

Bly: If you think of poetry as a part of the advancing edge of civilization or culture at any time, then the conscious mind often takes the lead. Poetry advances sometimes with the conscious mind out in front and that means that the poet is often moving through a countryside of ideas. The poet may move through a landscape of irony—Eliot does that—or through a countryside of structure, which Eliot finds in John Donne's work. The poet may travel in a countryside of cultural references well understood, clearly understood. He or she is perceiving, well, in a way a little like a graduate student: picking up more and more material which the psyche is consciously digesting; and the one that goes ahead is the consciousness, or the conscious mind. That works all right for Eliot, it works all right for Pound. The First World War did show that there was something the matter with the habitual advance the conscious mind was making in Europe all through the nineteenth century, because the First World War amounted to an enormous collapse of civilized values. The trenches had a primitive mood, pre-eighteenth-century, even pre-Roman. Robert Graves understood it and said "goodbye to all that." But after the war, later, the drive picks up again, this conscious advance, and it picks up again with Eliot, it picks up again with Fitzgerald, and Cummings—you see the conscious mind advancing again. In the thirties it slows down. Rexroth realizes it: there's something the matter. The troops are too far out in front and the supplies are not arriving.

That's a nice way of putting it.

Rexroth for his part moves to California; and that is a movement from the east to the west, where he can be alone and try to figure the whole thing out. Rexroth found some food in Chinese literature, whereas Roethke went crazy. That's another way of regressing. His madness and my idea of it are a little melodramatic, but his madness still saved him from the dryness that overcame many other poets of his generation. There were a lot of poets in his generation that we don't even know about anymore, because they dried up. Elizabeth Bishop went to South America and remained partly wet.

I didn't know that.

She went to South America, lived in Brazil. It's very interesting. So by the time my generation got out of college, around 1950, the whole literary scene was dry. None of us knew anything about what we wanted to do. Robert Creeley's early work states that confusion well. The literary culture felt dried up; there was only the *Partisan Review*, it seemed, and all the poems in the *Partisan Review* were square. They were rectangles, which means that the English idea of form had taken over again. Whitman laboriously tried to pry people free from iambic pentameter, but they creep back in the box again. The iamb had come back again. It means the English form returns whenever consciousness is out there in front, when the conscious mind is trying to go ahead. Then we bring back English forms, because in them one can use irony and, you know, all those things. It was apparent by 1950 that irony had won again, and the victory increased the dryness. Everybody felt terrifically dry, way too far out, way too—I don't know what you can say. As a person one felt out of touch with the sources of life; as a writer one felt used in the same way that the point men are used in Viet Nam to go on ahead, or something like that. It seemed that if you wanted to be a point man and write with irony the generals would let you be famous: you could go ahead and print your books. And Lowell accepted the position.

He forged ahead with the conscious in poetry.

Yes. And the whole cultural baggage—everything. And it's kind of wonderful. Wilbur did too. But Lowell—I heard him once, and I felt very sad about it—Lowell said to an audience: "I was a free verse poet, and then on my honeymoon I pitched a tent on Allen Tate's lawn, and within two weeks Allen Tate had made me into a rhymed iambic poet." Apparently, Tate and Ransom were the ones urging this forward motion of the conscious mind; it was all right; really that was *their* generation's job; but Lowell got sucked in as a younger poet to do their work. And Lowell felt resigned about it. In effect Lowell said, "I found a father better than my father." But I didn't have good feelings about hearing what he said. It's like a—to put it blithely—it's like a chicken describing to you how it once was wild and then it went straight and this nice farmer put it in a cage. That's not fair as a metaphor, but it carries some of the fear we felt. So the question for my generation was "Do you want to be in a chicken cage, connected with the rational mind, or. . . ." We'll have to drop that metaphor now, it's getting out of hand. Let's restate the idea: "If you want to be out in the front of the movement, then that kind of dryness that's associated with the iambic pentameter and the sonnet will be with you, because it's all a part of the same thing." So what did we do, we were just kids: we said OK. Our agreement was called *New Poets of England and America* and was published in 1958. Almost everything in it's written in iambic pentameter.

At that point you said "okay."

We said okay. What did we know? I was in Harvard three years; no one mentioned the name "Pablo Neruda" to me. I never heard the name. My teacher was Archibald MacLeish: he was a wonderful man, but somehow the South American poetry wasn't real to him. So we all said okay. Among the Harvard and Columbia people, Don Hall said, "Fine," Adrienne Rich said, "Fine," Louis Simpson said, "Fine," I said, "Fine"—we all just said, "Fine." What else? We didn't know anything else. I wrote my first book in iambic pentameter; I didn't publish it. Jim Wright published his, Louis published his, Don published his, Snodgrass published his. At last it got to be 1958: *New Poets of England and America* came out; and in that same year I brought out the first issue of *The Fifties*. I knew there was something wrong with the poetry of the men and women my age, because it wasn't flowing somehow, or it didn't penetrate downwards. I didn't feel touched by it, I didn't feel tied in with it. Ginsberg mentions that sensation too. I didn't feel tied in to it somehow with my soul: one knows inside when things aren't going right.

Yes.

On the inside front cover of *The Fifties* it said: "All the poetry published in America today is too old-fashioned." I sent that to everybody that was in *New Poets of England and America*.

That's wonderful.

I didn't know any of them except for Don Hall. I got lively and insulting letters back from some. Anthony Hecht wrote me a really angry and aggressive letter. He was furious because I had suggested that it might be possible in this century to write in some other way than the English way.

But at that point you still didn't know what.

No, but I knew that Whitman had something to say, and I knew that we just couldn't go on with the English mode: it wasn't containing or embodying the post-World War Two experience. I didn't know what could, so I didn't have any clear suggestions.

I remember Anthony Hecht enlivened his letter by saying: "You're just a Captain Bligh pissing up a drainpipe." And he went on on that vein, so to speak. And Allen Tate, I think, made a comment on it; he said, "Of course you can write something besides iambics; you can walk on your hands, too, if you want to." So a lot of anger surrounded that issue. The first article I did was on Louis Simpson's work in *Fifties* #1. I didn't know him, but I sent him the article. He wrote back and said, "I'm very disturbed by the critical things you say. . . ."

He was disturbed?

. . .Yeah, well, one always is. He said something like this: "I'm pleased by the things you find to admire and disturbed by your criticism, but in general I'm glad to have someone take my work seriously, and the issues that I know it involves." So we became friends. One day he described to me the shock he had when he just read *New Poets of England and America* all together; he had helped edit it, but saw it in fragments. He thought to himself when he finished reading it, "The major experiences of my generation are not there: the brutality of the war, the grandeur of it, the grief of so many dying, our private lives, so desperate." And instead there are poems about childhood, about graduate school, about marriage—those experiences are written about, but not the *other* ones, not the—I don't know what you'd call them— the unruly experiences, or the mad experiences—whatever you'd call them. Not *those* were there.

Not the things that the poets were actually having to suffer.

That's right, what they were living every day, underneath. Perhaps their disastrous relationship with their father wasn't there, because it didn't fit into iambic pentameter—no one knew how to do it. Louis is a terrifically intelligent man, and when he aims, the arrow often goes straight to the mark, to "the white" as the Spanish say. I thought about what he said. About this time I found Trakl's work; it carries experiences of *dis*integration: what the conscious mind can't hold together. His wonderful line says it: "Oh, my brother, we are blind minute hands, climbing toward midnight."

I've missed that.

Another poem begins:

> The dark eagles, sleep and death,
> Rustle all night around my head:
> The golden statue of man
> May be swallowed by the icy comber
> of eternity.

The poem ends:

> Look, a precarious skiff is sinking
> under the stars,
> under the silent face of the night.

Looked at negatively, the last image means that the conscious structure of the civilization is failing, and individual psyches are sinking or disintegrating. Looked at positively, it means that contemporary psyches are being immersed in water. A boat is nice, but its wood holds you away from the water.

So either way...

Either way is all right. To return to the first issue of *The Fifties:* when he received the issue, James Wright wrote me a long letter, very touching, talking about his grief and the resolution he had made to stop writing that same week. He said something like: "I don't want to be a writer if all we can do is write light verse. I don't want to be a poetaster. If I can't write poetry, I'd rather forget it." He said that *The Fifties* gave him some hope there might be a way out. And he went on: "I've never heard anyone else in this country mention Trakl." He asked if he could come to see me. He did, and we became friends right away. It turned out that Trakl was crucial—a wholly new road for him. When he was in Vienna as a Fulbright student, he wandered into the wrong classroom one day. (He tells this story in his essay on Trakl.) He saw a thin, elegant man talking intensely. He sat down. The man was an old friend of Trakl's who was teaching a course on Trakl's poetry, and even with his imperfect German, Jim could feel the images resonate in the room. And he realized that the images were utterly new to him in some way. In contrast to images in John Donne's work, Trakl's images were free of the symbolic structure of the rationalists. All through his schooling Jim had experienced mainly images tamed by a symbolic structure or system. Trakl had freed his own images. It felt as if each image were coming nakedly toward the listener.

So you discovered Trakl on your own and then Wright wrote to you...

Yes.

...and this mutual finding of Trakl was purely accidental.

Yes, that's right.

He said, "I've discovered this amazing poet."

That's right. Jim remarked, "I saw Trakl's name in your magazine, in its first issue, and I thought to myself, 'That's strange: I've never seen that name written down in the United States.'" When we met, he told me an interesting story. Jim, you know, believes in teaching. He believes in the value of teaching, as I do, and he got his Ph.D. not in creative writing but in Dickens. And he teaches Dickens. He refuses, wisely, to teach creative writing; his subject is Dickens. He respects the study of literature and the world of the university. At the same time, he knows how paranoid and—how can you say—self-centered, somehow, English Departments can be. And he told a story: just before he left Washington, where he did his Ph.D. work, he was wandering about at an English Department party in Seattle. I suppose about 12 o'clock when well drunk, he got up his spirit and recited a Trakl poem in German. It seems everyone became embarrassed.

It was an incredible faux pas.

It was the wrong thing to do.

Why? Why so much the wrong...

I don't know. It was what he *felt*. From one point of view, their hostility was a projection of his. Some may not have responded because they didn't understand German, and others because the whole sort of poem was new to them. But he felt something else —a coldness or rejection. And he felt them saying, "Jim, get back in the cage. Come on, what are you doing? Get back in our old English cage. Stay there!''

You think that recital was his announcement: "I'm breaking out"?

Yes. It was an announcement: "I know something else. I know something else: I can't integrate it. I know something else, this is what it's like, and that's all I know." No one there came forward to help him integrate it, to say, "That reminds me of John Clare," or anything like that. Nobody said anything. They just said, "Well, hm hm." (laughing) Louis Simpson, about 5 years later, while he was teaching at Berkeley, wrote me a funny letter on this subject. And he said, "Robert, it's very strange out here," he said, "because the English Department doesn't seem to talk much about literature. When we all get together at a barbecue, the Milton man and the Pope man, for example, don't argue; or the Keats man and the Dryden man. The mood is: you don't knock my man; I won't knock yours. They're a little like the Ford man and the General Motors man who live across the street from each other and don't knock the other's product. But they're all against those little foreign models you're bringing in!" To return, Jim and I became friends partly because we both felt something deep and strong in Trakl.

So he's far less your disciple than the legend goes.

Oh yes.

He knew Trakl already.

Yes. And he knew German better than I did. And so he and I then worked together on those Trakl poems, and that was our first work together. *Twenty Poems of Georg Trakl* was the first book of European poetry the Fifties Press published. We felt such excitement when we saw the book!

We began this interview by talking about regression. I think Jim Wright learned from Roethke that certain forms of overly-civilized behavior are, as they say, counter-productive. It's important to go back. It's important to return: go back to the roots, go back to the greenhouse. Roethke knew that that greenhouse stuff wouldn't interest Allen Tate at all. In the greenhouse poems there are no references to Catholicism, to the history of the Roman Empire. It's not there. Lowell did all his work in that history to please Tate: he did that whole *Lord Weary's Castle* to please Tate. He wasn't even a Catholic! As a Lowell he was a Protestant. He became a Catholic to please Tate, and of course Eliot, by extension.

I never knew that.

He did become a Catholic.

I accepted it on faith that Lowell was Catholic his whole life.

No, Lowell means old Protestant. Way old Protestant. Tate said to him in effect: "By becoming a Catholic, you inherit the whole of Western civilization. As a Protestant your roots go back to 1517 and no farther." That's not true. I don't think it's true, because many Protestant concepts go back to Meister Eckhart and mystics even earlier; and Jacob Boehme, who is Protestant, goes back to the ancient alchemists. But anyway, it was a convincing argument, and Eliot, who dominated the whole feeling scene, was Catholic. And one seemed to hear the whole history of Western civilization in his poetry. To me, Lowell's Catholicism is somehow not trustworthy. And I know some priests who don't trust Tate's either, because it had been accepted, in one sense, for cultural reasons. None of us know the truth of all that. But it is clear that Roethke didn't follow Tate's path. Roethke says, "Aw, I'm not going to do that. If I have to do that, I'd rather go back to the greenhouse. In fact, I think I will! I'll go back to water and womb-images and 'Dada is coming,' and 'Ordnung,' and all that stuff. It may sound a little elementary and you probably won't like it, but it'll help me." Jim learned how to do that from him. Jim told me an interesting story. I heard Jim say one day, "Well, hell." I said, "What was it like to be a student of Roethke's?" "Aw, he was wonderful. I'd want to talk to him about poetry, and he'd call up and say, 'Hey, Jim! C'mon, let's go to a boxing match tonight!' So we'd go." During the fight Roethke would scream, "Kill 'im! Kill 'im! C'mon, kill 'im!" And then they'd go home: that was the poetry lesson for that night. Jim, then, has shrewdness and a love for certain intensities, not historical, that Roethke encouraged. Do you understand me?

Yes.

Poetry results from all sorts of experiences, not literary.

His recent prose reminds me of Roethke's prose.

Does it? Ah ha. Well, there's a little of Jim's background: he had Roethke, who understood the present tense, and intensities that were not historical; he had Trakl, who understood images; and each of us had a little Rilke.

So we became friends, and remain friends. Each of us felt that in our personal life, and in our personal poetry-life, if one can make up such a phrase, either each of us found a source of wetness or we were finished. If the boat would not sink—finito, finito!

Rilke didn't work as well because he consciously carried the culture with him?

I think so, a little bit, yes. I still feel a little uneasy with his carrying, especially in the *Duino Elegies*. He's carrying too much culture with him. I've been translating him for over twenty years now, and I'm going to bring out a selection of the translations soon. He is a great, unbelievable poet. He's almost the same age as Trakl. In a way he's a much greater poet than Trakl; and yet in Trakl the substance appears almost naked: it's coming right up from the unconscious. Rilke knew that. He said: "In Trakl's poetry, falling is the pretext for the most continuous ascension."

That's good. Trakl's images really are striking.

His images are not images exactly. "On Golgotha God's eyes slowly opened"—whew! What *is* that? It's bigger than an image, I don't know what it is. You'd have to make up a phrase for it: "visionary appearance," perhaps. "An image that opens like a seed." You know images can be trivial. "A sewing machine lying on an operating table"—was that Breton's line? The two objects joined make an image, but it doesn't carry anything with it of the psychic past; by contrast, almost every image in Trakl carries thousands of years with it. . .Even of life before Catholicism. I don't know what you call that.

But it's human experience: actual experience, not the culture.

Yes. Another way to put it occurred to me the other night. Paul Carroll gave a party in Chicago at the studio, and people were chattering happily. A man suddenly said, "Why is it that memory is called the mother of the Muses?" So I said, "God, I don't know." I'd been talking about memorizing poems, but that's just practical advice. It's very heavy, the statement the ancient Greeks made: "Memory is the mother of the Muses!" So a friend of Paul's, a very smart man, said, "Well, the fact is that they're not using the word 'memory' the way we do. By 'memory' we mean our power of remembering, and remembrances that go back to our childhood." The confessional poet, it's true, often remembers an amazing number of details from childhood. From the Greek point of view he or she has no memory—"because by 'memory' they mean something going back to the DNA. *That* memory is the mother of the Muses." He's right, it's a different thing.

A few months ago I heard a lecture by Michio Kushi, who introduced the whole grain diet in the United States. He described the shape of the DNA chains, interweaving, motioning with his hands, how they cross so beautifully. And he said, "Now here in the center is where memory is stored. What is stored there are ancient memories, from the time we were mammals, even from the time we were fish! Now I will tell you something disturbing: in people of industrialized countries born since 1945, many have a diminished store of memory. That is because eating of sugar, in prepared food, has increased tremendously since 1945, and also taking of drugs has risen tremendously. Both tend to wipe out those 'knots' in the DNA that store memory. We have a number of persons coming into positions of power now who have a diminished store of memories. It is difficult for them to make decisions, because you need all these memories every time you make the simplest decision."

Uh oh.

Yes, bad news.

I was born in 1949.

(laughing) Michio Kushi says that, and it's interesting to me. But Trakl's got the old memory, yes?

Right. So you and Jim are looking for the primitive—that kind of memory that goes many eons back—not reaching for something more superficially primitive, like, well, Jerome Rothenberg and Technicians of the Sacred.

Yes indeed. Absolutely. Boy, Jim Wright always—you ought to hear him on that subject. He just hates Sitting Bull imitations.

I would love to.

Sure, just go and see Jim.

I want to.

Go to New York and see him. Trakl, then, carries a lot of this ancient memory, without starting a school. I mean, you start to translate his poems and you're stunned by what one could call the presence of that kind of memory. And it's the same kind of memory that's in Homer: "Many men run up the hill making cries. They resemble the cranes when they fly from the north in large flocks, giving out harsh cries and flapping their wings." Whew! Wow, *way* back. The listener does not lose touch with the soldiers, and yet he or she is also way back. And it's that kind of memory that English poetry doesn't have, much. In our Midwestern way, Jim and I tried to, and still try to, write poems that will contain some of this memory. And an interesting thing happens inside: one feels oneself going into a sort of regression. It is not the regression experienced in mental illness, or in drugs, or in helplessness, which tends to weaken the ego. Rather, it could be described as "a regression in the service of the ego." By its immersion in ancient memory, slowly and carefully encouraged, the ego ends up strengthened, and the person has brought it more material.

Well, the poetry has to help you to live.

Yes. But the ego prefers to control *all* areas of our life. And when you go into a literary regression you're not *denying* the ego, you're just saying to it, "If you'll be quiet now, I'll go back and find some stuff that'll really interest you"; and then the ego has to say, "Okay, okay, okay, okay. I'll let you go, but be sure to come back.'' (laughing) The work of art is written on the way back. We succeeded sometimes and failed sometimes, still do. But the responses to those early poems surprised us at times. Some readers and critics understood very well what we were doing—John Crowe Ransom was one of them—but others felt anger. Some did not see the work as a turning away from cultural memory in order to face deep memory; they saw it as turning away from the intellect and going into emotion. More than once a person said to us with a sneer, ''What do you want, *feeling?*'' as if feeling were something disgusting. Often in universities the unspoken sentiment was, ''You people are barbarians, because you don't respect the intellect.'' I recall that Jim in the mid-Sixties read in the California Circuit, which included four or five universities who accepted two poets a year invited by the circuit organizers. At Stanford, I believe, two people showed up. The reason was that the head of the English Department had put a note in the graduate students' box and the English Department boxes saying, ''Don't go. This is a Romantic,'' or words to that effect. Sometimes people would bring up the Nazis, who meant to them men who abandoned the intellect and went into emotion. Sometimes a man would stroll up at a party and say, roughly: ''I hear you gentlemen have rejected the intellect.'' And Jim would roll his eyes and say, ''Aw, shit, here we go again.'' It's a general fear of feeling. You understand how that mistake could be made?

Yes.

And partly it's because neither Jim or I wanted to set out in detail what we were doing. And no one else did, so it was never clear, at least not to some.

But you did write...

Yes, I wrote a lot of criticism.

You were ''Crunk.''

Yes, that's right, but even there I didn't talk about this sort of thing, somehow. That was all right, because we didn't want a whole lot of people, I mean—we didn't want a school. Early on, editors—the editor of *New World Writing* was one—kindly offered us a number of pages if we would write up the philosophical underpinnings, set those up, so to speak, lay out a manifesto, and create a school of writing. I decided against it. I said, "You want to do it, Jim?" He said, "No, people are too greedy for schools."

To return to memory, Paul MacLean's discovery of the two "animal brains" folded inside the human skull—"the reptile brain" and "the mammal brain" as I call them—helps to visualize what ancient poetry does. It draws material from all three brains. It visits the memory storehouse of each brain. Homer is an example, so is Dante.

Yes, in that Harvard Advocate *interview you mention Charles Fair's book* The Dying Self *and brain research. I read Charles Fair's book and thought it was a fascinating idea.*

Yes. So one can talk about it in terms of the complicated brain. A third way of talking about it is how to release poetry in English from the results of the Norman Conquest. When the French, or Bretons, took England in 1066, the "politeness" of French culture entered, along with the civilized iambic meter, and the court atmosphere. Nouns with a Latinate base became the nouns for ideas. A layer of abstraction entered the language. Gradually, the poets lost contact with the old Viking material. In my twenties, I heard Ransom give a talk on this point, reading "I am sick, I must die" in the old pre-Norman way, with the emphasis on the starting syllable. So what I have tried to do is to reestablish contact with the old North European mood of poetry before the Conquest.

You know this now. You didn't have any idea that that's what it involved in those days.

That one I was clear about even in college. My closest teacher, John Kelleher, was and is a great Celtic scholar, and we had many talks about this. John loved the ancient Celtic material, and I would try to learn something about ancient Norway from its connections with ancient Ireland. The Irish recognize that the English language blocks them from the ancient Irish material with a sort of iambic pentameter wall—made of plastic. The literary Irish are rebels against that; John Kelleher stood for that rebellion, and there I was, a sort of American rebel against the English. Yet it's only very recently that I've been able to *do* anything about it—that is, make a link with ancient Celtic or Norse poetry. When I'm doing the sound poems, which I call "ramages," I'm doing work related to what the old Norse poets did. They're an elementary form of Norse sound-form. The Vikings dealt with sound in a deep way. It's very difficult to go that deep in iambic pentameter lines or in any "lines" we know.

Yes, I've seen translations.

In a translation one can't bring in that amount of sound. So no one knows, really, what the Viking stuff sounds like. The first poet I ever translated was Pindar, and Pindar has similarly astounding sound work. To this day no one is sure what meter Pindar uses; scholars have been studying his poems for two thousand years and no one is sure, because our ears are not delicate enough to hear the gradations of sound and sound-length that Pindar works with. Latin sound-work is rather elementary compared to the Greek. So early on I was aware of a certain sound-knowledge in the Celts and the Greeks.

We've talked about regression a little now, mainly regression culturally. One could also talk about personal regression. That means that instead of thinking about the present and the future all the time, one goes back to early experiences, early moods. That involves going back to early, early griefs, I think. I'm still doing it, or just beginning it. Suppose the subject is your father or grandfather. You can write such a poem out of the relatively balanced psyche which you now have—if you do that the poem comes out nice in the workshop, and everyone's satisfied—instead of that...

It doesn't do anything, though.

...No, I agree—so instead of writing the balanced poem, the poet can regress to a time when he or she was more hairy, so to speak, and more unbalanced, and had a lot more grief; the psyche goes back and lies down there. Now, Jim did a lot of that; those painful poems about Ohio: all that grief he pulls out of his childhood—"Jenny, either you come up to me, or I'll go down to you." He's a genius at that, and he helped me tremendously, by teaching me how to get near that material. He has more guts in that than I did. People in his family talked with each other more than they did in mine; and I was, so to speak, trapped in the present. And he taught me again and again and again and again: "You don't have to stay in the bland present; you can go right back to the source of the grief, and what'll come out will be a mournful kind of song, but if it's true, what the hell: who cares?" So in that way I'm his student, and it's taken me a long time to learn. You remember those little things I recited last night, a couple of those little grief poems I did last night?

Oh yes.

I heard that cry in Jim Wright first. And I had to wait and do it in my own way.

That's not a connection I would have made.

(Laughing) I didn't make it either, until just now, talking, because I think of the grief as a natural fruit of my own life, and so on, but I can see it's absolutely clear that I—you see, in many ways *The Branch Will Not Break* was a better book than *Silence*, because it got into areas of ancient grief that I didn't get into. From another point of view, *Silence* had a certain layer of joy on top of it, which *Branch* doesn't have.

That's interesting: that you come to the grief; in his later poems he's come to the joy.

That's right. And both of us knew, by studying Chinese poems, that the true poem has them both. Well, the body is the only one that can do it.

Once you knew there wasn't any help in English poetry. . .

Or in *most* English poetry.

Okay. Did you, then, simply start shopping?

Yeah.

Just looked to see what you could find?

It's true.

And. . .

And it happened that I went to Norway on a Fulbright in '56, and I was still in despair. In 1956 I was thirty years old, and still in despair. While there I read my first poem of Jim Wright's in some little American magazine, and I said [makes a clicking sound of approval]; I knew that as a poet he was awfully strong, even though the poem was in relatively conventional iambic pentameter. But I heard the power: I heard something in it. A few months later I was reading in the Oslo library and I picked up a book by Neruda and I read three lines. I didn't need more than three lines to realize—wow!

You had to go all the way to Norway. . .

Yes!

. . .to Oslo. . .

That was the easy part. That was the easy part.

. . .to read a Chilean poet.

That's right. I found him there. That experience just amazed me, and I went home stunned, because—and of course, there's a link with my own continent. In Oslo I also read Trakl—I think that I brought Neruda to Jim, and he brought a lot of Rilke and new Trakl to me. So that's right, I mean, and you look around. A year or two later I found Pasternak, and I know there's something in Pasternak. . .but I still haven't been able to get near it, because the translations are so bad and I haven't learned Russian. I *know* there's material there as hairy as in Trakl and Neruda, but I can't find it in the translations. But in the first issue of *The Fifties,* on the back cover, I listed Pasternak along with Trakl and Neruda as poets we wanted to translate and study. Just for fun I sent a copy to Pasternak at Peredelkino. I didn't send a letter, but I think both Carol and I signed it. Pasternak knew by intuition where we were literarily and what we were longing for. He wrote a lovely letter back in purple ink. "My dear Carolyn, and my dear Robert," he said, "I have your magazine and I like it very much. I like especially your 'Poem in Three Parts.' And I like your translations of Gottfried Benn, just as translations"—I think he meant he wasn't too crazy about Gottfried Benn—he went on, "As for your desire to bring me into your magazine, please don't bother yourself with me. Don't save any space for me. I've deviated from my former path, and I've become out of date. Very sincerely, Boris Pasternak.''

That's amazing awareness and honesty.

Isn't that amazing? He meant that this search—if one uses the terms I've suggested—for ancient memory, which he had been involved in through Symbolist poetry, he had given up. During the Second World War he felt the necessity to become a national poet. It was a necessity. And he did that. And so he felt that he was no longer a part of the old search for ''the unknown.'' Isn't that something?

That's remarkable.

That's something, it's really, really something. (sighs) Well, Mari's down there waiting. Anyway, we got a little bit done, huh?

WILLIAM STAFFORD

Thomas McGrath

Totems (I)

In the fall
Feathers appear in the tassels
On Robert Bly's serape.

Without his knowledge or consent
His feet start a heavy dance
Like the dance of a prairie chicken.
All at once he is spinning
Like the reel of an old fanning mill,
Glowing in many colors as his phases change.

Lifting light as a top
He lofts up onto a fence post
The soles of his shoes smoking
In a smell of burning cedar.

Slowly geese appear in the sky.
He leaps up to join them,
Laughing and honking south.

Thomas McGrath

Driving Toward Boston I Run Across One of Robert Bly's Old Poems

1.

Tonight we are driving past Lac Qui Parle toward
Boston.
When I think of the Boston ladies I am suddenly
galvanic with joy!
I see them lying there, pale with Love...like
flowers...like palimpsests!
On which we can still make out a few marginal
words...
*Wampum...rackrent...pui ine o dromos sto
horyo, asshole!*
Ah—the lemon ladies and the lime-green ladies
of Boston!

2.

The parlors of those houses on the road to
Boston are full of salt.
These ladies have taken the sea to bed just once
too often...
And the men— ah, here the Cabots and the
Lodges and Lowells are dozing
(Dreaming of rum and molasses, dreaming of
Sacco and Vanzetti)
In an oily torpor, like the sleep of ancient
Cadillacs...
Alas! John Adams: desuetude has entered the
timing-chains of those enormous engines!

3.

Driving toward Boston we pass the Stuffed Ski
    Surf Shop—
And then the Stuffed Ski Surf Shop—again and
    again!
Perhaps we are not driving toward Boston after
    all...
Waltham flies by, full of mysterious time
    zones...
I know Boston is on the Post Road someplace in
    the nineteenth century.
The wind is whistling a snatch in the puritan
    winefield.
I speed forward, confident, thinking of the
    Boston ladies;
A little of last year's blue blood dreams and
    screams in the ditch.
Comforted, I press on—and on—perfectly
    happy.

4.

Whether or not we *are* heading toward Boston
(And even the question of whether I'm *perfectly*
    happy)
I leave to another time—a time full of lakes—
    and crickets!
Meanwhile I drive past Waltham again, gaining
    more time,
Somewhere on the road to or away from
    Boston...
Thinking of the Boston ladies I have a powerful
    erection!
High as the Dakota mountains! High as the
    great mountain near Fargo!

Patricia Goedicke

The Leaper Leaping

The voice is high, flat, a narrow Middle Western twang. Nasal, metallic. Faintly unpleasant? And the torso, unencumbered by the familiar poncho, is surprisingly stiff, the satin-looking blue pinstriped vest outlining the awkwardly elegant instep of the spine. Where is the hushed, primordial hum I have been hearing in my head all these years, reading Robert Bly's poems for myself?

He is about to give a reading, in New York, and from what I hear I am afraid I won't like it. After all these years swimming underground, in the miraculous silences of those poems. But he begins, and I settle down. I am prepared for large dance movements, the swooping Sufi gyrations friends have described to me. But at first there is only a slightly irritable tapping, on the lectern, of long bony fingers. Then the hands lift, begin to weave a little, in small tight circles, pretentious maybe, self-conscious? But then, suddenly, not. As the poetry takes hold—this time it is James Wright's poetry; the occasion is a Memorial for Wright—the hands take hold with it, then the whole stiff torso relaxes, expands, begins to breathe; the business-suited man with the corona of white hair turns into a sleek horse, then into a gangling giraffe rearing and swaying, up there like a motionless wind on the stage.

No doubt I exaggerate (and the motions at this reading were restrained! Probably because he was reading Wright's poems, not his own). But the performance was remarkable. What happened to the voice? I forgot it. I understood, I "knew," I rode with the poems only. And at the end the dulcimer came out. For the last poem, Wright's "Milkweed." Little pieces of the spirit blew over the auditorium, small tufts of seed on the winged metal notes of the dulcimer.

So. No real singing, then. Only, at the last minute, the dulcimer—and then the body movements, the big body tip-toeing, lunging, swaying. Why so much movement? It seems to me that it may have begun long before the actual physical movements, with those famous associational leaps Bly found and talked about, first in the Latin American poets, and then began to use himself: the random movements of the psyche leaping freely from one image to another, a slow *hasapico* of the spirit not unlike the exact, unexpected dartings of a Greek dancer moving from one archetypally perfect response to another, from one cluster of words to the next, a bridge over—what? The unconscious, the non-verbal. Sheer movement, a still unexplained leaping over the mysterious synapses of the brain. It is these jumps, shiftings, apparently accidental choices of the mind that excite us, offer us the tail end of a glimpse of the non-rational, spontaneous, almost physical gestures of the human psyche at its deepest possible level. As Bly says, in a poem which seems to me to refer to these same processes ("November Day At McClure's"), "Inside us there is some secret. We are following a narrow ledge around a mountain, we are sailing on skeletal eerie craft over the buoyant ocean."

And then there is the "purely" physical part of it; besides these mental maneuvers, small fish leaping in the sea of the mind, also there are the hands weaving, the real dancing on a real stage, the outward and visible manifestations of an inner spiritual condition, the ecstasy of the Chassid and the whirling dervish alike. Besides demonstrating an awakened spirit, besides *showing* us the priest-poet possessed, given up to the powerful unconscious forces his poetry is meant to invoke, such movements are also intended to wake us to the inner life of the world around us, rouse us, make us feel the motions of the dance ourselves. Feeling is the key; feeling in, with, at one with all nature, in unity with the world, not separated from it by the divisive condescensions of the weighing, judging, analyzing, invincibly "superior" powers of the rational spirit that has ruled Western thought from Descartes on down. And it's easy, too. We sleepers can join hands in the dance effortlessly; after all it's just a step away from us, up there on the stage or, sometimes, circulating down here among us in the audience.

The Way

How can we know the dancer from the dance? Not a real question. What matters is "the way," a way that Bly continues to point out to us in everything he does, whether dancing up on the stage or quietly, in the pages of his own poetry, in poems so full of consciousness of the world of rocks, trees, water that it seems impossible to pick even one that is not entirely grounded in it. That world—the "unknown dust that is near us," the joy that is near us, the light around the body that is "like a November birch facing the full moon / And reaching into the cold heavens" is wide awake in Bly's poetry, and reading his poems one can't help but be moved by it, reminded of how, ridiculously enough, our very skin does indeed "see far off, as it does under water."

Moreover, if Bly's poetry does seem sometimes to contain echoes of the poetry of others, those echoes are the not surprising partners, it seems to me, of a voracious reader and feeler who is determined to pass on the news—the good news—to his fellows. His achievements as a translator—and who can forget his description of Neruda's slow, bottom-of-the-sea, crab-like movements—the many articles which have followed the enormously influential "Looking For Dragon Smoke," the various editions of the *Fifties, Sixties,* and *Seventies,* and most recently, the beautiful "ecological" anthology Bly did for the Sierra Club, *News of the Universe: Poems of Twofold Consciousness*—in all these activities he has been indefatigable in his attempts to waken us to the life of the purely physical, the non-human world of nature and the body.

And he has been successful, too—no doubt about it. In person and in his poetry, he moves people. The impression he made on the many young people present at the Wright reading was obviously a very powerful one. He makes us change, he reminds us of parts of ourselves we have forgotten. For with Bly, the body re-enters modern poetry, but this time seriously, full of the portentous gravity we—poor mortal animals that we are—have always known it to possess. I know I am not alone in feeling whenever I read Bly, Jacobsen, Machado, Neruda, Tranströmer (the list is very much longer!) at least a slight "unfolding" of the left side of my body. And then too, there is the huge increase in our modern sensitivity to the archetypal image and the poetry of association (connotative poetry, Stevens would say) that Bly has certainly encouraged, to say the least. Bly has his imitators— many of them bad, too; what innovator can avoid the bad ones? —but the new life he has injected into the modern imagination, the deepening and broadening of the whole *corpus,* is worth it all.

The Body And Its Movements

It's something I've been thinking about a lot lately, this business of the role of the body in poetry. I have always believed, with Stanley Burnshaw, that "poetry begins in the body and ends in the body," and taken the statement as spiritually and emotionally as I do physically, but recently I have become more and more aware of a kind of "leaping" of the body which is untied to any identifiable idea, and physical in a way that is quite different from the effects of imagery as they are usually understood. What happens is that, talking to a student about a poem he or she has just written, I become aware suddenly that, quite separate from the intellectual or emotional impact of the poem, it also seems to have a kind of purely physical aspect; it is a strangely "thick" poem, let's say—and the poem is much more about this "thickness" than it is about anything else it *seems* to be saying or doing. When I try—incoherently, you may be sure, for just how *does* one find the words to express a sensation of this sort—to express my sense of this to the student, almost invariably he or she is delighted; yes indeed, that was precisely what was most important to them, the stratum of the poem that was the foundation of everything, and they are so pleased to have that recognized! Or, I am trying to express to the student the way a particular enjambment moves (or does not move) an image along, and suddenly I find myself swinging my arms around, chopping or stroking the air, wagging my head and torso, anything to show the sense I have, *in my body,* of what's happening. Most often of all I find myself, in the middle of talking with a student about his or her work, jumping up, stamping around my office, walking, running, putting my body into all sorts of contortions trying to express my feeling of the whole shape of the poem at hand. I know exactly what Valéry was talking about in the passage where he describes his twenty minute seizure by a kind of musical rhythm that was nothing but pure rhythm, for it seems to me he must be talking about this same, basically kinetic sense I keep feeling when I'm reading or talking about poetry. Valéry's analogy between walking/dancing and prose/poetry is well known (though I think some poems walk as well as dance!); what is more helpful to me in trying to understand this curious kinetic sense—which I feel constantly not only in Bly's poetry itself, but also in everything he says *about* poetry—are statements such as this of Valéry's, from *The Art of Poetry:*

> Each and every word that enables us to leap so
> rapidly across the chasm of thought, and to follow
> the prompting of an idea that constructs its own
> expression, appears to me like one of those light
> planks one throws across a ditch or a mountain
> crevasse and which will bear a man crossing it
> rapidly.

which goes on to suggest that we not *rest* on the planks for fear they will break, but rather continue onwards, for, he says,

> We understand each other, and ourselves, only
> thanks to our *rapid passage over words.* [Italics
> Valéry's]

The suggestion here is, for me, that movement is everything —a description of the ultimate nature of reality with which modern physics, in its inability ever to locate a fixed resting place for the endlessly moving particles under its purview, seems to be more and more in agreement, and that connects most interestingly with the strange osmotic fluidity with which the poetry Bly is most fond of moves from spirit to matter and back again, in and out, inside those veins where, as Bly says,

> . . .there are navies setting forth,
> Tiny explosions at the water lines,
> And seagulls weaving in the wind of the salty
> blood.

T.S. Eliot carries the description further in his introduction to Valéry's *The Art of Poetry* when he speaks of Valéry's discussion of

> Particularly deep states of disturbance or emotion which give rise to inexplicable bursts of expressive activity whose immediate effects are forms produced in the mind, rhythms, unexpected relations between hidden points in the soul which, although remote from each other until that moment and, as it were, unconscious of each other at ordinary times, suddenly seem made to correspond as though they were parts of an agreement or of a pre-established event. We then feel that there is within us a certain Whole of which only fragments are required by ordinary circumstances.

Human / Non-Human

Bly too wants us to experience a "Whole," but the whole that Bly seems ultimately to be referring to is the human interchange with the non-human, with the whole of the organic and inorganic world. For the next step in Bly's thinking is from the non-rational body to non-rational nature, all of it. It is a quintessentially natural step, but for Bly's audience it has meant an enormous widening of horizons. In Bly's world the imagination, leaping from the physical to the transcendent and back again, seems to move everywhere: North, South, East and West, but also above and below, permeating all of the varied intra-cellular and molecular substances of the whole non-human world. It is a world we have always been dimly aware of, but never as emphatically as this, never cloaked in quite the same dark authority (he even dares to take on science, sometimes, in the quasi-scientific terminology of some of his essays) Bly has given it.

Yes, Bly has indeed "taken on" science, or at least that kind of thinking we insist on calling scientific. He is afraid of what rationalism, the mind operating all alone and all by itself, has done, not only to the world but to us, and he wants to make us conscious that we are not the only beings present in this universe, that there is another consciousness which we must make contact with or destroy ourselves. And the body—not the mind—is mankind's surest route to that other consciousness, that communion with nature that will save us. For too long, Western man has written "the poetry of condescension"—poems which assume that man, because of his rationality, is superior to nature. What Bly wants now are "transparent poems," visionary poems, which exist chiefly as windows, openings, passageways from man to the "other" consciousness which surrounds him, in animals, trees, rivers, mountains, water; all the various structures of the natural world. One starts by looking inward, but not inward at one's mind; inward rather at those pre-verbal movements and sensations that are our one infallible and closest link with nature. Furthermore, one does not *rest* in the inward-meditating posture. After the "centering in" comes the reach outwards, the "leaving the house," the looking out beyond ourselves to a unity with the whole of the over-arching universe.

The Dream

It is a deeply moving thing, this call to forget ourselves, our own petty concerns (that "pettiness" which separates D.H. Lawrence from the mysterious majesty of the king snake that visits him), and it is true, as Bly suggests, that involvement with the perfectly reasonable but basically petty ethical and moral concerns of humanity will do very little good for us "in the grave." "When I write of moral things," Bly says,

> the clouds boil
> blackly!
> By day's end
> a room of restless people,
> lifting and putting down small things.

When he sees "Oval / faces crowding to the window!" he turns away, "disturbed—"; for, in this essentially romantic view of the world, the danger is certainly in human voices, a fear of mankind which is, given the events of the past century, understandable. It is a basically misanthropic view—a not uncommon concomitant of the pastoral position—and Bly carries this pro-nature, anti-social stand to perfectly justified extremes in the powerful anti-Viet Nam poems of *The Light Around the Body* and *The Teeth Mother Naked at Last*.

For Western man's reliance on reason alone, on the one attribute, finally, which *separates* him from nature, is what has led mankind to the terrible political, economic, and ecological plight we now find ourselves in, hovering on the edge of—the push of a single button away from—total ruin. Thus, Bly's attack on the situation is two-pronged: first to cry out against what he calls "the Old Position," and second to keep reminding us, over and over again, of what Gerard Manley Hopkins called "the dearest freshness deep down things," the restorative powers of the non-human world, the call for men to give up trying to rule, to impose our own will on nature, and instead be quiet for a while, lie back and listen to what *nature* has to say—possibly something quite different from what we expect, something that will surprise and save us all.

A foolish, utterly impossible dream? Possibly. Certainly there are many who think so. And certainly there are many dangers implicit in a belief which seems to suggest the abnegation of those rational powers we have always thought were one of the chief glories of mankind. Perhaps Bly does not mean us to give up reason entirely—surely he does not, and is, rather, concerned only to emphasize the very real evils of a reliance on reason alone. There is one trouble here, though—his powers are such that the position he champions seems almost absolute. Perhaps this is only a result of Bly's exceptional ability to move and persuade. But it seems to me, even though I'm sure it's unintentional, that there's a touch of demagoguery in those powers, a touch of the charismatic mystic, the guru-fanatic—particularly as he affects the young. The response to his work is usually either [1] fierce denial (sometimes even ridicule), [2] an overwhelmingly passionate "Yea," or [3] a very strong "Yes" followed by an almost equally strong "But." It is this last response that this paper espouses. I feel attracted but cautious: I say "Yes," but I immediately want to name some of the dangers that seem to me inherent in this "New Position" of Bly's, at least if that position is carried to its logical conclusion.

Well, what are the dangers? They seem to me to involve two interrelated areas: first, the possible obliteration and turning away from all the exciting diversity and individuality of humanity, and second, the risk, in the abandonment of reason, of encouraging philosophical and political totalitarianism. Bly seems to be aware of both dangers, and tries several times to come to grips with them, especially the second, but Jonestown and Auschwitz are ever present specters, and I am still worried by their undeniable connections to the kind of anti-rational feelings Bly is talking about—all the more so because I am in such profound agreement with his overall views.

Each Mortal Thing

Inasmuch as the position Bly is championing is a romantic one, it also involves, at its very deepest core, a reclusive, anchoritic, ultimately anti-social stance. (As Bly has Tao Yuan-Ming say, in his translation of "Two Drinking Songs"—but proudly, not at all in any kind of bid for pity—"An aloneness gathers around the soul that is alone.") For to really merge with nature, it seems to me one must turn one's back on man, and that posture is impossible for most ordinary human beings to sustain. Walt Whitman, whose love of grass never precluded—indeed it overwhelmingly included—his love for man, expresses it most poignantly, perhaps even a trifle sentimentally but still most powerfully, in his "I Saw in Louisiana a Live-Oak Growing," where, after describing how, "Without any companion it grew there uttering joyous leaves of dark green," finally what he thinks of when he looks at this natural creation is "manly love," and he concludes,

> For all that, and though the live-oak glistens
>   there in Louisiana solitary in a wide flat
>   space,
> Uttering joyous leaves all its life without a
>   friend or lover near,
> I know very well I could not.

Moreover, not only does absorption in the non-human threaten us with the kind of cosmic loneliness Whitman is describing, it also threatens to flatten everything, to blur man into a kind of wonderfully ego-less but finally vague, soft-edged, anonymous communal soup. To lose one's rationality in non-verbal communication with nature is certainly to lose all trace of that deplorable ego-centeredness which has plagued man from the very beginning, but what about that marvelous individuality which is one of the most exciting things, not only about nature, but also about mankind? The consciousness of trees, rocks, water is one thing, but human diversity is another, and even though Bly himself would not, he says, want to imply too great a unity in nature's consciousness, it seems to me his position ultimately runs the serious risk of stripping mankind of that very quality—his rationality, alas—that makes him different—and difference is not *necessarily* an evil—from the rest of the world.

It is a problem Gerard Manley Hopkins, like all religious people, struggled with also; for the desire to submit oneself utterly to the will of God, to abandon the Many for the One, seems to run completely counter to that mad rejoicing Hopkins finds in "All things counter, original, spare, strange; / Whatever is fickle, freckled (who knows how?)." And Hopkins' passionate delight in the world is not confined to the "dappled things" of nature, either—one has only to look at a poem like "Felix Randall" to see that, for Hopkins, man himself, in all his "manly"-ness, is just as gorgeous an object of contemplation as any Binsey Poplar. Hopkins confronts the problem most closely and most successfully in "As Kingfishers Catch Fire, Dragonflies Draw Flame," a wonderful sonnet about how it is possible for the One to speak in and through the Many: ". . . For Christ plays in ten thousand places," ". . . To the Father through the features of men's faces," and

> Each mortal thing does one thing and the same:
> Deals out that being indoors each one dwells;
> Selves—goes itself; *myself* it speaks and spells,
> Crying *What I do is me; for that I came.*

True, this is a distinctly Christian position, but it seems to me perfectly reconcilable with the kind of consciousness of the "other" world that Bly seems to be talking about, and important to remember when one wants to protect the dear particularity of mankind against the powerful suasions of egoless unity with nature.

A Confession

Besides that, we *like* Felix Randall. We like reading about Lear too, and Cordelia and Caliban *and* Ariel, and Hamlet and Horatio and even Titus Andronicus, not to mention Falstaff and Touchstone and Bottom. And I, for one, would hate to lose them; vital as it is to recognize man's relatively insignificant position in the universe (the exact inverse, it appears, of his power to harm it), important as it is to accept the non-human world, I confess I am still interested in the human race—and interested in it just as much as (certainly not less than!) I'm interested in trees. Yes indeed, "human voices wake us, and we drown," not into a salutary sense of acceptance, of identification with the silences of the snowy fields, but instead into the great shallow babble of hundreds of different voices: children screaming, the insurance man muttering, the politician ranting. . . . Yes indeed, the faster we lose our age-old beliefs in God, Fate, the Ground of Being, Something, anyway, greater than mankind (and the ecologist's view of space-ship earth is but another in the long sequence of such beliefs), the more dangerous, trivial, and superficial humanity seems to become, the more we see Personality, the Cult of Personality—whether the Superstar is a rock singer or a scientist—taking over everything.

But still. Are we not, in all our diversity, all our incredible multiplicity, just as much part of the universe as a Binsey Poplar? Hopkins surely thought so, and so did Keats, with his grand description of how Shakespeare was able to contemplate all kinds—villain, hero, fool—and keep them in balance, never banishing any one of mankind's characteristics—not even his reasonableness—from the stage of his imagination and our lives.

Twofold / Manifold

But Bly speaks of a twofold consciousness, and even as I understand and applaud and even sigh in agreement with what he and Blake mean by the phrase, I am slightly troubled by the restrictiveness of the number. Bly is of course referring to what goes on between the "I" and the universe: the self's perception of consciousnesses other than its own, which exist outside itself, in trees, animals, waterfalls, stones, etc. But what about our consciousness of other *human* consciousnesses? In *News of the Universe* Bly, trying to define what he means by the statement, "There is a consciousness in trees," does use as an example a situation in which a man feels "desire energy" for a woman, but he only uses it as an example of a non-human "force." The real thing, the most important thing he wants to say, is aimed at the non-human world entirely.

Now, I agree emphatically that there is most likely a presence in the non-human world that we should—we must—be responsive to and responsible for. But I believe there are other, *human* consciousnesses all around us that we must also acknowledge. If it is true that "inside the 'human consciousness' there is a small bit of 'tree consciousness,' " then surely there is inside me (and surely Bly agrees, and is only emphasizing trees for the sake of waking us up)—not only a bit of Hamlet consciousness, but also a bit of John Doe consciousness, of Abraham Lincoln consciousness—even, odd though it seems, a bit of Ronald Reagan and Alexander Haig consciousness! And believe me, I feel myself often—almost always—just as separate from such consciousnesses as I do from trees. Of course, being a human being I "know" Reagan and Haig by definition in a way I cannot "know" non-human beings, but the real trouble, I believe, is that I don't know them—or myself—*well enough*. If we did really and truly understand each other, surely the world would long since have resolved its problems and come to terms with itself. Certainly we must learn to respect the non-human world; but equally certainly we must learn to respect the human world —yes, even our enemies. In any case it seems to me that the little knowledge and respect we human beings do have for each other—our love for each other—is all that has so far kept us from destroying ourselves utterly and taking (not incidentally, I agree with Bly) the whole of the rest of the world with us. So, I believe, if a *little* knowledge of each other has been this helpful, more would be even more so.

The Sole Self

But the negative side of the romantic position is very negative indeed, and involves not only the whole of mankind but the life of each individual in its dark toils. For to turn one's face away from mankind, to join oneself with nature only, is finally to commit a kind of suicide. To yearn for the silences of the snowy fields only is to deny one's rationality, one's own humanity in the name of the ultimate romantic folly, that not-so-disguised death wish whose recognition led even Keats, as Robert Pinsky reminds us in *The Situation of Poetry* (and as Bly also recognizes in *News of the Universe*), to call a halt to his yearnings, to stop just short of following his nightingale into death, into the existence of "a sod." Forlorn though he felt to return to his "sole self," Keats did return—as all living men must return—to the humdrum, difficult, ego and anxiety-wracked world of men.

Even worse, however, than the possible loss of a poor romantic fool here and there (to alcohol, LSD, whatever is the latest substitute for nightingale music as a means of escaping the self), is the danger the romantic position poses for the whole world. As Marvin Bell says in an article in *Field*, "The notion that man's brain is superior to a tree will lead to the premature end of civilization. But so will the notion that a tree is superior to a brain. At least the tree, as far as we can tell, is too smart to think so." We tyrannize in many ways, but most of all, and most dangerously, I think, when the tyranny consists in the suppression of— it's been said so often!—the many and possibly dissenting voices of reason. When reason walks out, folly walks in, and sometimes folly wears jackboots, and carries a Luger, or owns three-fourths of illiterate El Salvador.

Keeping the Balance

We can castigate and deplore and criticize reason as much as we want to. God knows in reason's scientific and technological and industrial clothes it has accounted for much, maybe even most, of the horrors of the present century. But the voice of reason is good for something, and what it is good for, I believe, is the fact that its voices are so multiple, so different, each and every one, from the One. In society—that contract we make to learn to live, somehow, with each other—what they are after is the will of the many; a compromise position, the setting up of a balance which will not, man being a creature of the mind as well as of the body, ever be achieved by letting only one aspect of the neuro-physiological continuum of his makeup hold absolute sway over the other. It is right and proper and profoundly necessary that we attend to the voice of the unconscious—as a psychiatrist's child I have witnessed this truth all my life—but just listen to what happens if you turn Freud's famous "Where Id was, there shall Ego be" around! It's all very well to listen to the primordial hum of the universe, but what if the hum should, as my friend Stephanie Strickland suggested, suddenly turn into the growl of a leopard and eat you up? What is to stop the unconscious, the non-human, once it is given full dominance? Once you give in to the passional, romantic, hugely seductive drama of a necessarily ego-less Nature, you'd better be certain that Nature is Good; otherwise who knows how many others—besides yourself—may wake up one day in the equivalent of a concentration camp?

The assumption behind Bly's view must be that nature is good, or at least that in man's contemplation of *both* the good and evil in himself and the non-human world, ultimately the good will win out. However, even though he approaches the problem several times in *News of the Universe,* he never really settles it satisfactorily, to my mind anyway. Instead of trying to define just what this "consciousness" of nature *is,* he sidesteps, goes on with the dance—the *process* of the dance, anyway—

readdressing himself over and over to the problem of the desperate need for an interchange between man and nature.

Still, even though it would be wonderful if Bly were a little more sharply aware of the danger of letting loose the ungoverned forces of the Id, of laying ourselves totally open to the possibly red tooth and claw of the non-human, what Bly seems to me desperately concerned with is to remind us that there is also much that is good in the unconscious, much that is nourishing and necessary in the tooth mother's other maternal and succoring side. Furthermore, it is only because rational man insists on ignoring her—repressing her, in Freudian terms—that we find ourselves at the mercy of the woman scorned of our own unconsciousness of ourselves and the non-human world both. It is a view of mankind which is Jungian as well as Freudian, and it certainly seems true of the mechanisms of human beings. But even though there is a strangely moving section in *News of the Universe,* "Leaving the House," where Bly describes the gradual healing, the coming together of both the good and the evil in man, he presents no real evidence for such a potentiality, and his belief in the possibility of such an outcome seems finally not much more powerful—to me, anyway—than a beautiful but more or less wistful dream.

Still, all along, in *News of the Universe* anyway, Bly's chief aim has been mostly simply to administer a corrective dose to Western society's insistence on stressing rationality as All. Reminding us constantly that there is another side, that the non-human world is just as important as any other, he keeps warning us that it is the rationalist position, by shutting off access to those other, speechless consciousnesses, that has brought earth to the brink of disaster, has laid waste to the human and non-human resources of the planet as thoroughly as any Hitler.

However, even though it seems to be Bly's aim only to emphasize the existence of the non-human world and its importance—not, in addition to waging war on "single vision," *also* to speak for a balanced equation of Id and Ego, nevertheless, the enchantments and persuasions of the romantic, ultimately Eastern position being what they are nowadays, I feel I must sound a small warning. The world of the non-human *looks* so calm, so soothing, so "Whole"—but what if it is not? What if the Id/Ego equation *were* reversed?

Neither way of putting it is right, but after all it is balance, finally, that keeps us from falling, that saves us just as we are about to topple into the abyss. Much as we may long to give ourselves up to nature, I fear what saves us is precisely our inability to settle down, on one side or the other. For that's what equilibrium is, really, the eternally moving still point between one extreme and the other, the necessity for each extreme always to listen to the other; not the All suppressing the tiny One, but the Majority responsive to and responsible for each individual member of the Minority.

Human Voices

What really saves us from the growl of the leopard? Alas, I fear it is the voice of reason, alone or in company. For if man is—and surely he is—different from the rest of nature—how can we possibly achieve anything by entirely ignoring that fact? To throw rationality out the window isn't the answer: rather we must incorporate it into the equation, naturalize it, so to speak. The voices of reason may seem quarrelsome, dangerously arrogant, terrifyingly trivial and vicious towers of Babel, but they have been called sweet for a reason, and that reason, I believe, is that it is those voices that know how to compromise, make agreements, perform and arrange for the great balancing acts that make society—peaceful human society—possible. That peace will be a noisy one, of course, full of differences, full of the loud voices of men and women trying to drown each other out, calling over and over again for Order, Order, but it will nevertheless have in it at least the *potential* for a peaceful settlement of disagreements.

It is a moot point, of course, the idea that it is man's rational powers alone that distinguish him from the non-human—after all, there is some evidence that chimpanzees can be taught to "reason"—but what seems at the moment most indisputable is that man alone, of all beings on earth, has the power of speech. And it is through speech that, using the dictionary as the great common denominator, the great compromiser between what I mean and what you mean, we build up the great repository of language, the treasury out of which some of the most intricate, most complicated, and most important social agreements have been arrived at. Human beings speak to each other, and not just in order to give each other directions to the next clover patch. We speak to each other of things that are not: of the past, of the ever vanishing present, and of the future. We speak to each other of hope, of dreams that we may one day realize, not just for the salvation of humankind, but also for the salvation of the whole earth, the kind of dream that makes it possible for an eminently practical ecological group like the Sierra Club to join forces with and to understand, even to appoint as its spokesman, a poet as ultimately mystical as Robert Bly.

For besides listening to the consciousness of trees, water, rocks, Bly obviously also knows that we must listen to each other's voices—and that is why he continues to be a poet. If he had given himself up totally to recognition of and unity with the non-human, he would have no need to express himself in language—and furthermore, he wouldn't care. His essentially mystical position has been criticized often; what hasn't been recognized enough, I think, is the fact that for all his advocacy of the non-human, Bly has never once shown any sign of turning his back completely on the human, has always tried, through his poetry and indeed in all his writings, to bring the two together. It's true that there is little or no sense of the ordinary speaking voice in Bly's poetry. Plenty of bardic hum, the roar of silence, whispers of the ocean; sometimes, as in *The Teeth Mother Naked at Last,* the screech of anger, but very few ordinary human beings speaking to each other. None of the real people Richard Hugo writes his letter poems to; none of Dave Smith's marvelous "roundhouse" voices; none of Hayden Carruth's jazz musicians and tough New England characters—and these are not, incidentally, only poets "of the people"—Carruth especially is extremely sensitive to "The Signature of All Things," and has written many great poems of deep consciousness of the non-human.

Goat-Foot and the Text Beyond the Text

But Bly himself is aware of the necessity for poetry to unite itself with human speech. In an article in *Field* on the image he speaks of the spoken language as the second of some five or six major "powers" of poetry, and even remarks that learning to use the spoken language was one of the most difficult things for him as a poet.

Furthermore, Bly goes on to describe another of the "powers" of poetry as being the sounds of language—not only the "resonating interior sounds" of words, but also sound structure as it is related to rhythm; Donald Hall's Goat-Foot, which Bly calls the drum beat of poetry, and is modest enough to remark that he finds little of it in his own poetry. But he is aware of it, that disco rhythm, that dance, that movement of words—as we all are, even as we think of words as the chief agents of the rational, chief separators of ourselves from the rest of the world.

For even as we use such scientific abstractions as the computer as a model for the workings of the brain, we are aware of a certain physicality in the very mind itself (the rhythm that almost swept Valéry off his feet? Certainly the planks he sees being thrown across the ditches of the mind); that feeling George Steiner described (in a recent interview with Bill Moyers) as present whenever we're looking for a word we are certain is "on the tip of the tongue," a sense of *spatial* relations in the brain, as if *something* were actually searching, weaving, wandering, moving through rows of bookshelves, looking for just the right piece of the puzzle. The point here is, of course, not the similarity to the retrieval system of a computer, but rather the feeling of physical movement that seems to be inherent even in the most intellectual, the most abstract, of human mental processes. Nietzsche and the structuralists may argue that there is no reality beyond the text; that one text generates and is generated by nothing but another text—but what *is* this kinetic feeling, then, this utterly inescapable sense we have that words are rooted in the physical world of the body in all its strange, unknown relationships to a larger world around it?

The Dancer and the Dance

Well, this kinetic sense seems to me highly suggestive, at the very least, that there is indeed a reality beyond the text, and it is this sense I have of Bly particularly—the ideas, the poetry, the man himself—that finally makes me believe in him, beyond all my caveats about the logical extensions of what he says. He speaks of the non-human—the strong possibility that there is indeed a world, another reality somewhere "out there," maybe even a good one!—in every movement of his body up there on the stage reading his poems. The language in which the poems must be couched is itself a compromise, a bow to the rational that the structuralists might seize for themselves, but the body movements insist that there is more—and besides, it is in the very nature of poetry itself to remind us constantly of the "seamless web" that is woven between man's intellect and the physical world around him.

For where do words come from, after all? To ask that is to ask a question the linguists have recently been addressing with ever-increasing passion, ever increasing recognition that the answer rests on nothing less than a redefinition of what it means to be human, but for the moment what seems to me most clear is that words, like all the best poetry, at least *begin* with the body. It has been noted from earliest times: the metaphors embedded in words are testimony to the fact that each one comes from some kind of leap between the known and the unknown, from the body to the outside world and back again, by means of a word that stands for and somehow compares the human to the non-human we are trying to understand. Ordinary people, especially young people, do it all the time, in the new words, new images, the slang they make up . . . and poets do it most consciously of all. Whatever position they may seem to come from to begin with, ultimately all poets seem to me to be about the same business, the preservation and renewal of the absolute interconnectedness of mind and body, human and non-human, man and nature, the word and the flesh.

So Bly on the platform, perhaps hearing in his head the thinness, the fallibility, the weakness of his own, unadorned human voice, lends to that voice first the power of the image, the "deep image" he championed way back in the fifties, and now, more and more, the physical power of movement. He may want mainly to write poems for meditation, transparent poems, membraneless mediators between the self and the universe, but he knows the necessity for demonstrating, acting out, making the word incarnate manifest. So he gives himself to the movement, the bridge, the vibrating waves that link one "desire energy" with another (in Bly's case, man's consciousness with the consciousness of trees, water, rocks, but for me the consciousness of other human beings as well). To the natural movements of his own body he adds the more passional movements of ecstatic dance, and to that he adds the music of the dulcimer: voiceless sounds, vibrations blowing the words of the poem out over the auditorium, music adding its power to poetry's to remind the audience that the mind, language, reason, are only one part of the natural world. It is a dance we all feel all the time; it is poets like Robert Bly who bravely dramatize it, exhibit it even for those who wish to laugh at it, the ceaseless motion of molecules moving moving moving, searching through the vast compact library of the brain, whirling in every line of poetry, whispering and breathing thickly in every word we utter as in every leaf that falls, every paw that prints itself on the ground, every blade of grass a human being picks up and whistles through.

Richard Hugo

Letter to Bly from La Push

Dear Robert
            Lots of whales cavort and spout
three hundred yards offshore. The danger
of them there, high waves and cold winds mean
we cannot swim. I'm still not in my country
though fishnets dry and hostile eagles scan
our country's enemy, the empty gray.

It's green here, black green mostly, black
against dark sky—all pines are silhouettes.
Even the sun is solid, and red memories
of better runs, of bigger kings, of jacks
that tore the gill nets in their futile drive.
We have to lie or be dishonest in our tears.
Some days I almost know how tall brown wheat
goes gold against dark sky, the storms
that hate our wheat, the thunder
that will come for wheat, evangelistic anger.

My fish is trout. I hear the long jawed pike
can smile you dead when hooked. My symptoms
never die. I've been away ten years, and spray
has killed four houses I remember and the church.
Birds are still fanatic. The shore is raw.
That last rock fist: the void still makes it stick.
The whales are closer and in colder wind
I send warm regards as always,

                                    Dick

Reprinted with permission from *31 Letters and 13 Dreams*, Poems by Richard Hugo © 1977 by W.W. Norton & Company, Inc.

Bill Zavatsky

Talking Back: A Response to Robert Bly

In his own poetry, his many translations, in his magazines, anthologies, essays and interviews, and in his public talks and readings, Robert Bly has given more to American poetry in the last two decades than any other writer who comes to mind. Beyond his considerable literary influence, the issues to which he has addressed himself—the unconscious, the masculine and the feminine, our relationship to animals and growing things, our search for a spiritual center, war—place him beside those very few of his contemporaries who have persisted in affirming the union of the poetic and the moral in our time. When he handed over his thousand dollar check for the National Book Award in 1968 to a member of the Resistance, an anti-draft group, Bly literally put his money where his anti-war oratory had been. It was an electric moment, and provided many of my generation with an example of conduct we shall never forget.

Bly's concern has even led him to encourage criticism of his work, something I can remember no poet ever doing publicly, and in the following pages I have taken him up on that invitation. My hope is that the affection I feel for him and his gifts has found its way into my words. If Bly—with whom I am acquainted mostly by mail, and whom I sometimes address as Robert here—had not first articulated many of these issues, I would have no ground on which to stand to criticize him.

The "Object Poem"

"In the last sixty years, a wonderful new poem has appeared. It is the object poem, or thing poem," Bly wrote in *News of the*

127

Universe. Why no mention of Imagism, still warm in the grave as a movement by 1920 but powerfully influential in American poetry far beyond its heyday? An important part of the Imagist project seems to have been the reconstitution of the object. All those tiny poems about an oriental fan or billowing waves or faces in a subway station—Imagism was a miniaturist's art and the emphasis was on close-ups of objects. It's surprising that Bly can praise Rilke's many poems about things and forget the many that William Carlos Williams wrote; and if Williams didn't go to school to Rodin, who sent Rilke to observe the animals in the Jardin des Plantes, Williams did sit at the feet of the photographer Alfred Stieglitz, an artist with no mean eye. What I am pointing out is that there is a parallel between Rilke and Williams, however much their work differs. It was Williams who unfurled the banner which read "No ideas but in things." It's essential to read Rilke, but it's also important not to bypass huge pieces of our own history, and Robert is often running off to Europe at the expense of the lessons to be learned at home. Finally we must struggle on our own ground. Nobody paid Williams' bills for him or put him up in castles to wait for the angels of inspiration. Maybe it's easier to see visions when you know where the rent money is coming from. The whole question of writers and economics is one that Bly hasn't addressed publicly, and maybe he ought to.

But I want to talk a little more about Imagism. Let's say that Imagism was an act of father-consciousness—the violent stripping-away of the "feminized" rhetoric and idealized subject matter of the Victorian period. Everything that Imagism's chief theoretician, T. E. Hulme, demanded from poetry suggests the masculine: that poems possess a "hard dryness," that their language be "a visual concrete one." He called the new mode "neoclassicism," a label that fits one kind of father-mind perfectly.

In rescuing the object from the ornamental excrescences of Victorianism, Imagism also whittled away most of the traditional subject matter—much of it novelistic—of poetry. ("Whittled" is too gentle a word; "hacked" would be more appropriate.)

Even narrative was sacrificed so that the object could be seen more clearly. Once the demolition and removal operations had been performed, poets like Pound wanted to begin building long poems again. The modernists had a new set of tools at their disposal: free verse, permission to use the rhythms of ordinary speech, the image, and—perhaps most important of all—the technique of collage juxtaposition. Using it in *The Waste Land,* Eliot jumped the reader from past glory to present despair in the space of two lines. But Eliot finally abandoned the technique, maybe seeing before Pound that it was a blind alley, suitable for ironic effects but trapped in the fragmentary—basically a poetry *of* despair, of the impossibility of making connections between things. "A bundle of broken mirrors," Pound called *The Cantos,* and his harsh self-judgment seems just. Long poems were impossible because the narrative glue had been thrown away. That is why neither *The Cantos,* nor the works made in its image —*Paterson* and *The Maximus Poems*—cohere, but instead offer themselves as selections of beautiful passages, glittering images.

My idea is that narrative is essentially feminine, that it creates connections between things, draws objects and people and actions together in a web of relationship. Storytelling was originally a communal event, though today it is something we think only children should experience. But the poetry reading has been doing its work among us over the past fifteen or twenty years, and the reader-audience relationship has begun to shape new attitudes in the poet towards his work and new audience expectations. So have the poetry in the schools programs, where obscure or intellectualized poetry simply doesn't work. At the root of poetry reading and teaching is the I-thou affiliation, and the same forces that have created them are changing the shape of our poetry, pushing it, I think, toward narrative.

The Prose Poem

Robert has said that "the prose poem appears whenever poetry gets too abstract. The prose poem helps bring the poet back to the physical world." *(Talking All Morning)* I agree, but see the prose poem as the beginning (or return) of something larger. I believe that the hunger which created the prose poem and which has deepened our appetite for it in the last ten or fifteen years is the hunger for story.

The prose poem was born in the middle of the 19th Century as the novel began to tear ever greater chunks of territory away from the poets. In poetry itself a philosophy that saw art as a mode sealed off from everyday experience was in the ascendant. The prose poems of Baudelaire and Rimbaud are a kind of rearguard action, a symbol of the split in consciousness then occurring between poet and novelist, a refusal to give up narrative at the very moment when these poets were creating an esthetic that pointed towards the Beyond.

So the prose poem began as a kind of vestigial organ which has been growing larger and larger over the past hundred years, sprouting eyes and limbs; it has been crawling and staggering towards the lost half of what poetry used to do: tell stories. It has unconsciously been constructing a back door to poetry and teaching itself how to open that door. Puzzled because it is a creature of the unconscious, it doesn't even half know where it's been going. But by now it is apparent that the prose poem is another means by which narrative, however surrealist-oriented at the moment, is re-entering the poem.

Narrative

"The narrative poem has disappeared," Bly said in *Talking All Morning*. "This doesn't mean that nobody can tell stories anymore, but it means that the narrative is not really useful now for describing what has been found out." Or does the loss of narrative represent a loss of wholeness on our part? Has our poetry been, in fact, short of an expressive organ it cannot do without?

Let's assume that my comments about the prose poem are correct, and that there is a hunger today on the part of many poets for story-telling. We can't leave the reader out of this, either; maybe one reason most people don't read poetry is that the poems are too difficult to follow, too confusing. Maybe most poets don't really *care* whether anyone feels or understands their work. To me this is a sad state of affairs, and finally we poets are going to have to take some responsibility for what we have done, rather than blame the "Philistines" for not comprehending our modernity. This is an incredibly difficult area to approach, because poets (and, for the most part, their critics) have done nothing but congratulate themselves about the breakthroughs into collage and fragmentation techniques and, generally, only reactionaries have criticized those techniques. Seeing what is narcissistic, boring, obscure, self-indulgent or uncommunicative about our poetry means trying to see with the blind part of our eye. How can we take a clear look at the developments of literary modernism that will be both critical and affectionate? In short, I'm suggesting a theory that says that for every advance in technique, something must be given up; collage gained new ground for poetry, made new expression possible—at the price of narrative.

If my hunch about the connection between narrative and the feminine has any merit, more feeling ought to be coming back into poems and more characters will appear in them as poets begin to tell stories again. We will have a poetry that will leave readers touched rather than feeling stupid, charged with energy about the possibilities of poetry rather than feeling they ought to get a Ph.D. to understand the allusions. Instead of just having a head, poetry will begin to grow a body with a heart in it; it will belong to everyone, not merely to an elite. The poetic image itself will probably have to give some ground, for it has become too identified with masculine consciousness, but after the torrent of imagery we have experienced during the last twenty-five years, a lessening of the flow will be welcome. Perhaps if we are allowed to space out our images more, we can concentrate on finding the ones that really contain feeling. As we quiet ourselves down, we will also begin to ask whether the writing we are doing really communicates, really makes our readers feel and think. That interplay between writer and reader is also part of what a devotion to the feminine can bring to our work.

The Feminine

One of the meanings of the title of Bly's 1973 book, *Sleepers Joining Hands*—the book which contains "I Came Out of the Mother Naked," his major statement on mother culture—is that the relationship-making aspect of the feminine would *like* to make connections but is still unconscious to them, "asleep." The image suggests two, or perhaps endless ranks of "sleepers" (those devoted to the exploration of the unconscious hence committed to the development of the feminine) closing ranks in a manner which could be either affectionate, militant, or both.

But for all his discussion of the feminine, we have nothing in Bly's work that resembles a real woman, and only lately, in the prose portrait of his father in *Growing Up in Minnesota,* have we had anything like the portrait of an actual man. (In the poems Creeley becomes a crow, Voznesensky a wood animal, Rusk a bomb—all to some degree caricatures.) There are a couple of charming poems in which one or more of Bly's children appear, and those poems count, but I am here talking of work in which some kind of interaction is depicted, and that happens most fully on the adult level.

The model of the feminine that Bly puts forth in the mother essay is basically that of the Good Mother/Bad Mother—the fecund, loving, nurturing mother and her opposite dark side, the Teeth Mother who devours her young. For all its usefulness, this model is an abstraction, an idealization that needs to be grounded in flesh-and-blood women to come alive. Bly's goddess is a nature goddess; the poet was raised a farm boy and still lives in the country, so this shouldn't strike anyone as strange. If J. J. Bachofen, an early thinker on this question, is right in saying that all great nature goddesses contain two levels of maternity—"the lower, purely natural stage, and the higher, conjugally related stage" *(Myth, Religion and Mother Right)*—Bly seems to incline towards a more primitive feminine psychology. Bachofen calls it the "hetaeric stage" of the matriarchies, a "swamp stage" which "follows the prototype of wild plant life." The more sophisticated values of Demetrian matriarchy—which most importantly include the primacy of human relationship—have yet to fully enter Bly's work; he is still more concerned about how we relate to trees and animals.

Oddly enough, the male American poet who most deeply shows the impress of the feminine in his work is one whom Bly has mostly avoided. I am talking about William Carlos Williams, whose work from the beginning is filled with portraits of women and flowers (another form the feminine can assume). His poetry moves towards two amazing late poems, *Asphodel, That Greeny Flower,* a poem of reconciliation directed toward his wife, Flossie, in which Williams acknowledges his infidelities and begs forgiveness as he declares his love; and "For Eleanor and Bill Monahan," which invokes the Virgin Mary and where the poet cries out

> The female principle of the world
> is my appeal
> in the extremity
> to which I have come.
> *O clemens! O pia! O dolcis!*
> *Maria!*

Of course the whole poem—in fact all of the final three books, *Pictures from Brueghel, The Desert Music,* and *Journey to Love* —have to be read to see the deep feeling and acceptance out of which those lines pour. It would seem that the series of strokes which Williams began to experience in the late 40s hastened his openness to the feminine, or at least to a more direct and simple expression of it.

One of Williams' last books, out of print for twenty years, furnishes us with a document extraordinary in all of American poetry and unique in the light it sheds on how a male writer is affected by the powerful influence of an anima-figure, his mother. The book is called *Yes, Mrs. Williams* (1957), and while it ostensibly records the fragments of her reminiscence and his reflection as they translated a Spanish novella by Quevedo, it in fact commemorates and celebrates her as one of the major inspirations in his artistic life.

Elena Williams had what the Jungians call an "animus problem." That is, the development of her "male side" had been crushed when her hopes for a career as a painter were ruined after her father suffered a financial reversal and was forced to take her out of art school in Paris, where she had studied for three years. Elena never adapted to the small New Jersey town to which her husband took her, and we know from *Yes, Mrs. Williams, The Autobiography,* and other of her son's writings how moody and difficult a woman she was. She passed her problem down to her son, who shared her mercurial temper and irascibility—indeed he had to fight it, to find a way to use it in his life and art or be wrecked by it. The anima isn't one-dimensional, however, and along with the negative anger and moodiness came the creativity.

Williams was by temperament what Jung called a "sensation type." His ego oriented itself to reality basically through eye, ear, nose (he wrote a wonderful poem called "Smell!" which celebrates this sense), mouth, and hand. His physician's training undoubtedly strengthened his sensation function, and this is why the physical world comes to us so powerfully in Williams' writing. For him the real struggle was

> the virtual impossibility of lifting to the imagination those things which lie under the direct scrutiny of the senses, close to the nose. It is this difficulty that sets a value upon all works of art and makes them a necessity. ("Prologue" to *Kora in Hell,* in *Imaginations*)

This passage expresses the dilemma of the sensation function poet: how to sort out the flood of sense-impressions. Elena Williams' great strength lay in her feeling function—the ability to make judgments, to decide what is important and what must be discarded—a faculty Jungians have identified with the feminine and which her artist training must have enhanced. By observing his mother Williams learned two things: how to make value-judgments about his experience, and the lesson of persistence. He probably arrived at an understanding of this by the late teens. (*Prufrock* appeared in book form when he was writing the "Prologue" to *Kora in Hell,* around June of 1917; Williams was thirty-four.)

Williams' obsession with the Demeter-Kore myth shows how fearful he was that his own creative nature would suffer the same fate as his mother's. (Kore or Kora, daughter of Demeter—she is also called Persephone—must spend the winter months underground with her abductor-bridegroom, Hades, according to the myth, but is "freed" in spring and summer, when the crops under Demeter's power grow again.) We can see that for Williams, Kore represented his own anima as projected by his mother. In psychoanalytical terms, *Kora in Hell* could be called *My Creative Life Trapped Inside Me.* The subtitle of the book, *Improvisations,* shows that Williams pulled every trick he knew to try and free himself.

Williams refused to "bury" his feminine side. He needed his own springtime as an artist to survive the cold Jersey winters and the pressures of a demanding medical practice. In the "Prologue" to *Kora,* probably his most important esthetic statement, he holds up his mother as the model of what he calls his "broken style" (actually a form of free-associational writing). In the jagged course of his prose poems (and this holds true for his poetry) Williams imitates the leaps in his mother's thought and behavior—she teaches him how to "follow his feelings" as he writes. We can say that, for him, imagination was the sorting-out work done by the feeling function applied to sense impressions. This realization freed Williams from being an imitator of Keats and Pound and allowed him to develop a method of composition founded upon an attention to the twists and turns and leaps of his anima. To be in touch with the anima is to listen to one's own heartbeat, and despite his later preoccupation with what he called "measure," and his prescription of the "variable foot" for American poetry as a whole, I think Williams really meant that each of us had to find the pulse of his or her own work without falling back on a dead tradition.

I go on about Williams and his relationship to his mother, first, because the relationship was of tremendous importance to him, and secondly because it supplies us with a living example that takes us one very important step beyond the abstract models Bly has brought to our attention. Often it is easy to have an intellectual understanding of the anima-role, particularly if one is male, but difficult to translate it into personal terms. Williams' experience shows the dangerous and beneficial aspects of anima-involvement, and underscores the importance of human interaction for artistic survival. I bring it up, too, because in his essay, "Being a Lutheran Boy-god in Minnesota" (in *Growing Up in Minnesota*), Robert describes himself as a "typical 'boy-god.'" The *puer aeternus* (and interested readers should consult Marie-Louise von Franz's study of that name, just republished by the Sigo Press) is the product of a mother-complex. So that when Bly only tells us that his mother "was and is a good mother, without envy or malice, affectionate, excitable, living with simplicity and energy—one of the servants of life," I am a little suspicious. Either he doesn't fully understand the part the mother plays in the creation of the *puer,* or he is passing over it for reasons of his own. I hope, when he is ready, that he will give us more than the few pages of probing analysis we have in the essay. The problem of the *puer aeternus,* a protracted state of adolescence which makes "growing up" almost impossible and even undesirable, is one of the deepest psychological afflictions that besets us in this century.

"Confessional Poetry"

In attacking "confessional poetry" Bly equates "confessional" with "autobiographical." (As for "confessional," a useless term, couldn't we substitute the phrase "personal crisis poetry"?) Does it need to be said that not all autobiographical writing is crisis material? Or, from the opposite angle, that it need be goofy or trivial?

Bly takes the "confessionals" to task for lack of specificity in their work, but the figures of the human he puts forward in his own poetry (few as they are) are just as vague, just as idealized. Why should our images of nature be detailed and those of the human be blurry?

Robert's idea that Berryman, Plath, Sexton, and others were killed by the kind of poetry they wrote doesn't make sense. They wrote out of crisis situations in their lives—the wound preceded expression of it, and to think otherwise is to substitute cause for effect. (Bly himself has said that the writing of poetry often begins in the hope of healing a psychic wound.) If these writers had written a different kind of poetry, would they have lived? I think, instead, that had their lives been happier, they would have written another kind of poetry.

Perhaps because these writers faced their dark side, writing out of what Jung called the "shadow," we want to turn away from them. It's never pleasant to glimpse what is broken or incomplete in our being, or even in the lives of others. In a 1976 article Robert praised the classical moderns for the amount of "shadow work" they did, and maybe it is true that as the shadow emerges, we can begin to move along the path of spiritual regeneration. Certainly Jung believed that we had to face what was negative in us before we could begin to heal the damage. That so many writers from the "Brahmin" class of American letters faced the darkness and were swallowed up by it at the same time that their social class was losing its long-held grip on our society hardly seems a coincidence. Maybe the lesson that the experience of the "confessionals" holds for us has something to do with the bankruptcy not only of the class system in America but with organized Christianity, which long ago stopped looking for its own shadow. American writers who had a deep involvement in the shadow-side, like Poe, Hawthorne, Melville, or Dickinson, lived lives of terrible suffering, perhaps because a burnt-out Christianity left them nothing but darkness to face. One can't confront the shadow alone; that's why Dante had Vergil by his side for part of the journey. But without that confrontation our work has no depth, no weight—like Peter Pan, who lost his shadow and the ability to live a real life in a real world.

And so, when in one of the interviews in *Talking All Morning* Robert claims that the richness of the "interior animal life" which he sees in Lorca "cannot be expressed with images...of curbs and broken bottles and the objects with which Williams hoped to express it," I see him pushing away a realization of the shadow (and again favoring the European over the local, as if nothing of spiritual importance could happen here). American shadow is going to look different from Spanish shadow. Williams saw it reflected everywhere, in trash, in broken chips of glass, in the bums, even in the dog-droppings of the Rutherford and Passaic streets—the sense of inadequacy, of failure, the holes in our being. Williams doesn't turn away from this ugliness; rather, he embraces it. Perhaps Robert had realized this by 1976 when he wrote the essay to which I've referred (the interview dates from 1971; the article is called "Wallace Stevens and Dr. Jekyll" and is in *American Poets in 1976*).

Bly can praise the Eskimo shaman who "takes on illnesses, visits other worlds, reminds each person he or she meets of the night side," but these activities also describe, at least to some extent, the poets of personal crisis. If nothing else, let's distinguish them from other poets whose work, as Robert says, is "concentrated on the human," poets like Williams, Reznikoff, and Ignatow, who don't point towards self-destruction.

Perhaps Robert's "problem" is that he doesn't want to face the shocks of the human in his own work—that is where his own shadow-area may lie. His rural upbringing makes it easier and natural for him to emphasize the land and animal life over people. The surrealist poetry he has advocated, written, and translated, and whose influence he has brought into American poetry has moved us closer to the unconscious, to the feminine, and has been of incalculable value. I don't mean to disparage his love for trees and animals. But a surrealist poetry isn't well-equipped to deal with everyday experience, particularly the poetry of relationship. Surrealism is an ecstatic mode, and a poetry written out of moments of ecstasy leaves much of life untouched. Maybe there are disadvantages to leaping around; that is what the *puer aeternus* does, after all, and he never develops relationships or stays to live his life in one place.

Rather than one kind of poetry—"leaping poetry"—being suitable for all that happens, I am suggesting that at least several kinds of poetry are necessary to capture the variety of human experience, and none of them is "better" than the other.

In *News of the Universe* Robert writes: "This book asks one question over and over: how much consciousness is the poet willing to grant to trees or hills or living creatures not a part of his own species?" Is this really "the" question? What about granting consciousness to other people? We have so many poems with things and trees and rivers and hawks in them, but so few that really bring us what it is like to experience another human being. A poet like Robinson Jeffers loved the land and the wildlife while exhibiting a consummate contempt for people. Does Bly think that we will automatically grant respect and affection to women and to people of color if we grant them to trees and animals? I think that leap is a much more difficult one, and in our poetry we ought to be teaching ourselves how to make it.

Mark Rudman

New Mud to Walk Upon

Most of us have seen Robert Bly working out his inner struggles publicly, from poetry readings to the Bill Moyers show to his most recent book, *Talking All Morning*. This is mainly a collection of interviews—an amalgamation of modes of discourse: autobiography, social and political commentary, advice, and literary criticism. In a way, amidst the welter of subjects it roves over, it is a short course on modern poetry (more specifically, American poetry). In a few pithy sentences Bly can illuminate and clarify exceedingly complex territory, matters that concern every poet and everyone interested in poetry. For example, in response to a question about his "generation of 1962," he says:

> the poets of my generation, it seems to me, have a
> curious unfinished quality which is deep in them.
> Their first books were no good. They began very
> slowly. Like children putting blocks together,
> their first buildings were not castles, just huts.
> Poets like Eliot and Moore and Lowell somehow
> inherited a massive amount of usable ideas which
> acted as transformers to turn their psychic flow in-
> to literature. Wright, Stafford, Merwin, Hall,
> Kinnell, on the other hand, started slowly, and
> only by the age of thirty-five or forty did they be-
> gin to write well...the poets of the 1947 and
> 1917 generations had already written stunning
> books in their twenties. So it's a generation that's
> learned—a learning generation. It is still learning.

The key sentence, in whose wake we are all swimming, is the one about "the poets of the 1947 and 1917 generations" who "somehow inherited a massive amount of usable ideas which acted as transformers to turn their psychic flow into literature." This is something that Bly has been trying to come to terms with. Its geniality and generality to the side, this is literary criticism of the highest order, the kind of thing academics write books about but never actually say.

In *Talking All Morning*, he makes a case for the necessity of criticism: "The younger poets, in failing to attack Merwin, or Rich, or Levertov, or me, or Ginsberg, or Simpson, or Hall, or Ed Dorn, are not doing their job. They're not making a place for their chicks." I want to respond to this by suggesting that the erosion of the critical spirit has as much to do with the fact that Bly's generation, in his own words, "is still learning," as it does with the buddy system spawned by M.F.A. programs. Maybe it's less a question of individual poems or books of poems than cultural attitudes on the part of both generations. Before it's worth your energy to "attack" another poet's work you have to respect it, revere it, perhaps want to have written it and, above all, love it. The ferocity of Bly's attack on Robert Lowell's *For the Union Dead*, for example, is fueled by disappointment and is directly proportional to Lowell's eminence and ambition and to Bly's expectation of him.

Bly is perpetually curious, receptive to new ideas, and able to say things that sound absurd if taken literally: "If plants wrote poetry, they would write prose poetry." But behind this statement is Bly's way of thinking about a major problem of poetry: the problem of organic form. His way of solving it is to equate nature (natural growth) and language (poetry). According to this line of thought, the form of the prose poem evolves organically out of the mind, like plants out of the soil; verse, or poetry in lines, is torn from its natural root because the mind has imposed form on the substance and once again this inhibits us from perceiving the mystery of existence.

But the paradox is that when Bly writes prose poems he is prone to similes which are too often a product of his intelligence. This immediately disrupts his own desire for organic form. "The Dead Seal near McClure's Beach" is a powerful prose poem with enough bad writing to sink a lesser vessel.

> Walking north toward the point, I came on a dead seal. From a few feet away, he looks like a brown log. The body is on its back, dead only a few hours. I stand and look at him. There's a quiver in the dead flesh. My God he is still alive. A shock goes through me, as if a wall of my room had fallen away.
>
> His head is arched back, the small eyes closed, the whiskers sometimes rise and fall. He is dying. This is the oil. Here on its back is the oil that heats our houses so efficiently...

The sentence containing the phrase "A shock goes through me" is unnecessary and trite. And the simile is forced, dull, an act of will rather an act of transformation. And yet I'm not sure the poem would be better without it. Look how intense it would become if Bly moved directly from "My God he is still alive" to "His head is arched back...."

The very syntax of "The Dead Seal..." shows Bly working at making similes. "The flipper near me lies folded over the stomach, *looking* like an unfinished arm"; then, still groping for comparisons, "The seal's skin *looks* like an old overcoat."

The best argument against this method is found in Mandelstam's "Conversation about Dante."

> Dante's comparisons are never descriptive, that is, purely representational. They always pursue the concrete task of presenting the inner form of the poem's structure or driving force.... The force of a Dantean simile, strange as it may seem, operates in direct proportion to our ability to do without it. It is never dictated by some beggarly logical necessity.
>
> (*Mandelstam: The Complete Critical Prose and Letters.* Ann Arbor: Ardis Press, 1979. Ed. Jane Gary Harris)

The awkwardness of Bly's similes is transparent. But then—jackpot: "Suddenly he rears up, turns over, gives three cries, Awaark! Awaark! Awaark!—like the cries from Christmas toys," is an absolutely terrifying image that recalls the terror children feel when something that's supposed to be funny isn't—sounds of lost souls risen in rubber bodies. I'm tempted to say that this works because its aptness is in the hearing of it, but that doesn't explain everything. It's here, not where Bly tries for verisimilitude, that the seal's presence is made present in the poem. If Robert Bly in one of his gray rubber masks were to read the poem aloud and give "three cries" we might be terrified; but as a poem on a page it's the simile "like the cries from Christmas toys" that breathes life, that is death, into the poem.

Bly, like many strong poets, is most moving when he isn't trying so hard to perform a feat. Melville's harpooneer starts out of idleness. And Bly is best as a poet of idleness, idleness in the Keatsian sense: "I was led into these thoughts, my dear Reynolds, by the beauty of the morning operating on a sense of Idleness...and the thrush said I was right—seeming to say—

> O fret not after Knowledge—I have none,
> And yet the Evening listens. He who saddens
> At thought of idleness cannot be idle,
> And he's awake who thinks himself asleep.

When Bly says, calmly, "Here on its back is the oil that heats our houses so efficiently," the effect is wrenching. The sentence has an almost Shakespearean doubleness. The impartial brutality of the world outside the privileged moment, enacted in the poem, provides the context for tragedy. "He is dying...He is taking a long time to die." For the duration of this poem Bly is in deep communion with this seal. He is shaken to the root of his being and the feeling comes through. Even what I've called the blatantly "awkward writing" is connected to the amount of dread involved in this confrontation between animal and man. Bly reveals more about his theory of the feminine (the "Teeth Mother" and the "Great Mother") in the next lines than in all of his more explicit statements on the subject. The seal is a "he" who becomes androgynous—a link between the sea and the mother. "I am terrified and leap back, although I know there can be no teeth in that jaw." This is the "vagina dentata" which so terrifies the male of the species.

And just so that we shouldn't miss the point that the speaker's fear of the seal is commensurate with his fear of women (and equally bound up with his fear of death and his death wish or desire to return to the sea/womb) Bly, in another awkward and loaded passage (in which comparisons are once again forced and the connections hammered into place) says the seal "looks up at the sky, and he looks like an old lady who has lost her hair." (Compare this with Keats' line Bly quotes in *Sleepers Joining Hands:* "with horrid warning gapèd wide.") The seal has been transformed into a hag. The treatment of the subject may be labored but the content is heavy, like lead, the alchemical base of creation. The seal is even the color of lead, and that leads me to a poem of his that I love and from which I derived the title of this brief essay.

Where We Must Look for Help

> The dove returns: it found no resting place;
> It was in flight all night above the shaken seas;
> Beneath ark eaves
> The dove shall magnify the tiger's bed;
> Give the dove peace.
> The split-tail swallows leave the sill at dawn;
> At dusk, blue swallows shall return.
> On the third day the crow shall fly;
> The crow, the crow, the spider-colored crow,
> The crow shall find new mud to walk upon.

The repetition in the last two lines signifies a letting go. The tremendous energy and tension in this poem, which begins in such a quiet, stately, and formal manner, is released in those last two lines which, I confess, I have often said aloud or chanted to myself when I felt particularly buoyant and joyful. "The spider-colored crow," in this context of darkness and silence and mud, is another lead-based image that Bly has been able to transform: to give it wings. It signifies an explosion of joy that can only come after a long immersion in "wet streets soaked with rain / and sodden blossoms..." with the body giving way to "washing, continual washing," the inner ear hearing "cries, half-muffled, from beneath the earth, the living / awakened at last like the dead" ("Awakening" *Silence in the Snowy Fields*). All that had to be experienced before the crow could find "new mud to walk upon."

Both of these poems represent stages on life's way, in the life of the spirit, something of which Robert Bly has never lost track. His courage and tenacity to work through the lead and transform it has helped create new ways of thinking about and writing poetry—new mud to walk upon.

The Need for Poetics:
Some Thoughts on Robert Bly

1

Why does poetry matter? Is it important? If poets do not feel and think passionately about poetry how shall it be redeemed? Poets must write those essays about poetry that only poets can write: those in which blood is mixed with the ink. Keats' letters are an inexhaustible source of nourishment and guidance to young poets, to people beginning the enterprise and life of poetry. But poetry must be reaffirmed and reinterpreted by poets in each generation. Ezra Pound did this with his *ABC of Reading* and his essays (especially "A Retrospect" and "A Few Do's and Don't's of an Imagiste"). T. S. Eliot did likewise when he published "Tradition and the Individual Talent" in 1919. In regard to Eliot, it is interesting to note that shortly thereafter he began his own magazine, *Criterion,*

> the purpose of which was, he tells us, to create a place for the new attitudes to literature and criticism, and to make English letters a part of the European community.
> Northrop Frye, *T. S. Eliot: An Introduction*

The poet's role as reaffirmer and reinterpreter of the worth and purpose of poetry has declined since the great Moderns, but the strategies of that role—the essay, the magazine with a purpose—remain the same.

A critic can tell us what a poem means, but not what poetry means. The ethos of poetry is in the keeping of the poets in each generation, in each historical period. And not just as it is embodied in the best poems, but as the life of poetry is rendered in the intense and thoughtful forms of the essay, the statement of poetics, and the manifesto.

*

Why did so few American poets in the fifties write in the essay form about poetry? Perhaps in part this was a legacy of the New Critics, whose marvelous instruments of analysis too often left the poem in neatly sorted and labeled piles of sinew and viscera. Were the best poets cowed by these critics, rendered so self-conscious they ventured few and modest claims for their art?

> Most American poets of my generation were taught to admire the English Metaphysical poets of the seventeenth century and such contemporary masters of irony as John Crowe Ransom. We were led by our teachers and by the critics whom we read to feel that the most adequate and convincing poetry is that which accommodates mixed feelings, clashing ideas, and incongruous images. Poetry could not be honest, we thought, unless it began by acknowledging the full discordancy of modern life and consciousness. I still believe that to be a true view of poetry. . . ."
>
> Richard Wilbur, *Poets on Poetry,*
> ed. by Howard Nemerov

Perhaps the poets of the fifties experienced that sense of social displacement that gives an undertone of insecurity and resentment to the lucid intelligence that animates Randall Jarrell's best essays. One might also think of the poets of that period as having suffered too much history, as in Louis Simpson's wonderful poem, "The Silent Generation," that rhythmically enacts the psychic disintegration it describes:

> When Hitler was the Devil
> He did as he had sworn

With such enthusiasm
That even, *donnerwetter*
The Germans say, "Far better
Had he been never born!"

It was my generation
That put the Devil down
With great enthusiasm.
But now our occupation
Is gone. Our education
Is wasted on the town.

We lack enthusiasm.
Life seems a mystery;
It's like the play a lady
Told me about: "It's not...
It doesn't *have* a plot,"
She says, "it's history."

from *A Dream of
Governors,* 1959

*

What the act and art of poetics demand is a form of intense,
naïve enthusiasm. By naïve, I simply mean that a poetics must
be an unexamined intellectual and emotional energy flowing
outward; as such, it is opposed to logical analysis and critical
thinking: it cannot be balanced. It's a crystallization in essay
form of heart truths. But it's a crystallization: it has form and
structure, involves vision and revision just as a poem does. In regard to form and structure, it might be interesting to consider
the inimical influence of that form which has in the last ten years
largely replaced the essay on poetics: the interview. Too often in
interviews personality replaces poetry (something our culture
would applaud); rather than the pondered testimony of a life
lived with and through poetry, we have only the most superficial
phenomena: anecdotes, off-the-cuff opinions and prejudices.

The entire quality of the interview is at the mercy of the interaction between interviewer and poet.

*

In a time when poets seemed content simply to quietly or
emphatically write their poems and keep on with business, Robert Bly was determined to think and write seriously about how
important poetry is. We see this determination throughout *The
Fifties* and *The Sixties* and in an important essay called "A
Wrong Turning in American Poetry" which first appeared in
Choice.

A good deal has been said about Bly's translations, and it's
obvious that his efforts in this field brought about a revitalizing
of American poetry. But the same could be said about W. S.
Merwin and many others who were actively translating at this
time, and yet the impact of other translators was not as strong.
Why? Because Bly didn't simply translate, he championed the
poets and the ideas about poetry that their work embodied.
When he translated Rilke, Neruda, Vallejo, Garcia Lorca, Trakl,
and (much later) Tranströmer, he did his best to speak about
their notions of poetry.

When, in conjunction with his translating, Bly affirmed what
he called "the image" (and which has since acquired the critical
label, "deep image"), he was attempting to reunite American
poetry with the mainstream developments of Romantic poetry
as it had evolved on the European mainland: a poetry structured
by symbolic imagination and making *extensive* (Neruda, surrealism) or *intensive* (Rilke, Tranströmer) use of symbols. If we
seek a literary definition of symbol, we might well turn to
Pound's definition of "the 'Image'" as "that which presents
an intellectual and emotional complex in an instant of time. . . .
It is the presentation of such a 'complex' instantaneously which
gives that sense of sudden liberation; that sense of freedom from
time limits and space limits; that sense of sudden growth, which
we experience in the presence of the greatest works of art." (from
"A Retrospect") Although Pound defined "Image" acutely,

his own poetry was not characterized by its use—Pound's was a discursive, didactic imagination, or perhaps a musical imagination, but certainly not a symbolic one.

This notion of image which Bly repopularized is that of the crystallized intelligence of the unconscious mind, and as such it incorporates into poetic theory useful contributions from the dream theories of the depth psychologies of Freud and Jung. What Bly's talk of "the image" accomplished was a naïve and necessary affirmation of the symbolic imagination that structures lyric poetry.

If traditional symbolist theory sees the role of the image as the embodied lyric epiphany (either that moment in time that transcends time, or that which fuses and reconciles a poem's opposing forces), then another role for the image is probably at work in the politicised, anarchic intensity of surrealism from which one major aspect of Bly's own poetry is derived. In surrealism, we have a bubbling cauldron of images rather than a crystal.

2

Bly's essays, in the historical context of American poetry in the mid-fifties, represented the most intense public thinking about poetry's human importance that was taking place in English. The response to those essays, then and now, varied greatly: to many young poets, they were inspirational; to many of his peers, they were provocative; to many of his elders, exasperating and impertinent. Bly kept (and keeps) the pot of American poetics boiling. His pot is a stew: a bewildering richness of ideas and opinions—many of them contradictory, many of them seeming to be only half thought out. His intelligence is usually a moral one, occasionally a moralistic one.

I have mentioned the role of the image and the affirmation of symbolic intelligence as two lasting contributions from the early essays of Bly, but I think any attempt to locate and trace the continuity of his ideas and themes might be wrong-headed. Bly's ideas appear to arrive full-blown from the unconscious and seldom seem the product of discursive thought. In this regard, it might be interesting to quote one of Bly's favorite sources on a form of consciousness he calls the introverted intuitive type:

> The peculiar nature of introverted intuition, if it gains the ascendency, produces a peculiar type of man: the mystical dreamer and seer on the one hand, the artist and the crank on the other. The artist might be regarded as the normal representative of this type, which tends to confine itself to the perceptive character of intuition. As a rule, the intuitive stops at perception; perception is his main problem, and—in the case of the creative artist—the shaping of his perception. But the crank is content with a visionary idea by which he himself is shaped and determined. Naturally the intensification of intuition often results in an extraordinary aloofness of the individual from tangible reality; he may even become a complete enigma to his immediate circle. If he is an artist, he reveals strange, far-off things in his art, shimmering in all colors, at once portentous and banal, beautiful and grotesque, sublime and whimsical. . . .
>
> Although the intuitive type has little inclination to make a moral problem of perception, since a strengthening of the judging functions is required for this, only a slight differentiation of judgment is sufficient to shift intuitive perception from the purely aesthetic into the moral sphere.
>
> C. G. Jung, *Psychological Types*

Bly is in large part a teacher-guru of the Way of Poetry—someone to whom ideas about poetry and poetry's role in culture and politics are as important as poems themselves. He has this in common with Gary Snyder, though their styles of presentation differ. If both of them are occasionally obscured by (and

resented for) the largeness of their respective followings, we must never forget that their ideas are of utmost importance to poets and people who care about poetry.

Robert Bly has, in his time, changed American poetry: opened up new directions it might move in, inspired some poets to explore those directions, others to react strongly against such prospects. His role, stature, and style seem to me equivalent to that of Ezra Pound in the early decades of this century.

Victoria Harris

"Walking Where the Plows Have Been Turning": Robert Bly and Female Consciousness

Our epoch is filled with the resurrection of the woman. In a variety of disciplines—politics, anthropology, sociology, psychology, linguistics, literature—apartheid features of patriarchy are giving way to a spirit of *inclusiveness,* the proper context for the female spirit. In a cohesive gesture, we increasingly mend a world divided by maps, categories, "objectivity," and a strict adherence to logic. Cohesiveness results from a participation in the collapse of a defined bifurcation between masculine and feminine natures. Authentic synthesis occurs as the woman enters a previously masculine world, and the male taps internal qualities usually attributed to a woman. Increasingly, one may recognize this psychic integration in the poetry of Robert Bly. Augmenting a new era, and yet recalling an ancient one, Bly's poetry is invested with a reliance on intuition, a universe of energies, and an interest in the incorporative nature of a participatory universe. The female rises in his poetry without apartheid features: no god exists apart from me, no world exists apart from my perception and participation. Furthermore, Bly recognizes that a language structured solely by logic is inadequate to communicate intuition, vision, and spirit; that a poem circumscribed by an inherited form precludes vision that goes beyond the containment of form. In such poetry life evolves beyond its own goals. Such features suggest reception and gestation beyond intention. Thus, the female. In a departure from a history of categories and form, Bly includes intuition, empathy, and reception as bases of female consciousness. By nurturing the woman within the man, Robert Bly portrays a universe the poignancy of which results from a sense of expansion.

Female consciousness is particularly evident in Bly's recent prose poem, "Walking Where the Plows Have Been Turning."[1]

> Some aliveness of the body came to me at five in the morning. I woke up, I saw the east pale with its excited brood. I slipped from bed, and out the back door, onto the sleek and resigned cottonwood leaves. The horses were out eating in the ditch. . . . I walked down the road toward the west.
>
> I notice a pebble on the road, then a corn-ear lying in the grass, then a small earthbridge into the cornfield. It leads to the backland where the plows turn, the tractor tires have married it, they love it more than the rest, cozy with bare dirt, the downturned face of the plow that looked at it each round. . . .
>
> The light gives a cornhusk in one place, a cottonwood tree in another, for no apparent reason. A branch has dropped onto the fence wire, there are eternities near, the body free of its exasperations, ready to see what will come. There is a humming in my body, it is jealous of no one. . . . The cricket lays its wings one over the other, a faint whispery sound rises up to its head. . . which it hears. . . and disregards. . . listening for the next sound. . . .

In the poem, Bly advises that if we listen, we shall hear the earth, the female, whose felt power justifies the departure from western tradition and form, including traditional poetic and syntactic structure, and finally releases the enclosure of form itself into a universe of energy. Bly perceives, empathizes, hosts a mystical union, takes visionary glimpses of the universe, and yet tells us there is more. A close reading of this poem will reveal his universe—intuitive, integrative, perceptive, empathic: female; the path toward it—tradition and the breaking of it, perception and its expansion into empathy, traditional poetic form relaxed into a more organic synthesis, traditional syntax ignored to suggest departure from structured language, and, finally, words to suggest communion. The integration does not, however, conclude within the poem. Bly reveals, and we witness; he receives, and so do we; he creates, and so do we, a participatory universe, inclusive, female.

"Walking Where the Plows Have Been Turning" depicts a three-paragraph progression. This progression differs from "the leap" which Bly has written about and which occurs in many of his own poems. In this poem, Bly replaces the leap—a startling hurdle from natural progression to universal potential—for a different quality. The three paragraphs here seem to metamorphose into different bodies at a slower pace. In fact, this metamorphosis, like gestation, takes as much time as it needs. The paragraph structure affords a fuller sense of enclosure, while the sentences within intermingle. Without each line breaking off into space, Bly constructs both interiority and fuller development in each paragraph. I suggest that this poem is structured like three trimesters of gestation. Instead of an insightful leap into the universe—a gesture itself symbolically phallic—this poem evolves through preparation and reception, thus symbolically gestate. The three-part poem mingles centripetal and centrifugal energies until the climax of the poem occurs, when mingling itself is focused upon and even the energies themselves cannot be distinguished as incoming or outgoing. The symbolic sexuality seems both a vehicle toward and metaphor of mystical vision. Part of this mingling, indeed, involves the male's reaching female resources within and around him.

Bly emphasizes the present moment, relying on continued perception, not photographic and recordable in memory banks, but presently alert, participatory, and deepening; directing attention not only to traditional poetic concerns of imagery, rhythms, diction, and sounds but also to each turn from regular structure. Bly's use of syntax demonstrates a further effort to go beyond established patterns, suggesting the infinite, for example, by breaking finite patterns of grammatical composition. Such structurally-motivated attentiveness also constitutes part of the milieu in this poem, which at first focuses on attention and retention, but then shifts to beatific pleasure in a more encompassing satisfaction of existence that, itself, goes beyond existing parameters. The use of means (such as attention and retention) to go beyond these means (such as into the realm of intuition) parallels Bly's expansion from traditional poetic form or grammatical construction. The prose form of this poem, then, as well as its syntactic construction, is semantically significant. This poem seems to suggest a pattern, then departs from it, only to return again to the pattern. Attention, for example, leads to a sense of insouciance, then back to attention again. These departures and reentries are rhythmically part of a course that changes from models and recollection, even from the dictum of attentiveness itself, to exhilaration at the numinous residing in the physical. Then, an instant later, the numinous evades perception, but the vehicle to that luminous plateau remains.

One part of this progression, itself expansive, is from perception to reception to empathy. An energy pattern—centrifugal, centripetal, and centrifugal—changes not only in direction, but in quality; the last signals both an outward force and a release from parameters. In the first paragraph (reminiscent of *Jumping Out of Bed*)[2], the speaker tingles with an awakening that is explicitly receptive: "some aliveness...*came to me*" (italics added). His physical awakening, it will be shown, foreshadows his vision of the life of all surrounding him, and indeed, this comprises a spiritual awakening undergirding this poem. With one exception, "The horses were out eating in the ditch...," the significance of which will be discussed later, the first paragraph, written in recollection (as indicated by past tense), presents the chronology of events apparent to a receptive speaker. After the opening line of the poem, reporting both the time: "Five in the morning," and the speaker's interior response: "Some aliveness of the body," the speaker begins each subsequent thought with the pronoun "I." The words, "I woke up, I saw the east pale with its excited brood," begins the "I" series with a comma spliced construction.

Bly has done this before, syntactically suggesting that the additive nature of logic opposes a more holistic response to the universe. Here, language, rooted in logic, is shown flawed—the error perhaps existing in the structure of a sentence, but more probably existing in the reliance on a logical mode to communicate this awakening. A turn away from logic may be symbolically indicated by the speaker's position, facing the east, where thoughts need not be validated through an objectivism that serves to dichotomize reality, but where wisdom is gained through more religious sources of Buddha, or reaching the Tao, or maintaining a balance of yin/yang energies. That Bly never avoids one plateau of existence to reach another may be noticed now, when the visceral response to awakening prepares the speaker for going beyond ordinary corporeal enclosure, and when syntactic structure is used as a vehicle for departure from it. By making an unexpected departure, Bly highlights that turn of events; whatever occurs leaps beyond cognitive modes of recognition impelling more involved perception, in fact often necessitating a reception not circumscribed by intention of what is to be portrayed. Bly syntactically suggests going beyond expectation in the opening construction, containing parallel units of "I" with a subsequent verb: "I woke...," "I saw...," and "I slipped...," arousing an expectation of pattern; Bly calls attention to the change from this structure in the following image where "out the back door" is not preceded by the pattern of personal pronoun and verb. Formally arousing this expectation of further repetition in structure, Bly brings the next image into starker relief by departing from this construction. The reader not only notices lack of focus on the speaker and his action, but is simultaneously drawn into the image "out the back door, onto the sleek and resigned cottonwood leaves." This break from repetitive structure changes at the moment when the focus shifts from the speaker and his action to the surrounding scene. Here, Bly begins a centrifugal motion whereby the body does not imprison the vision—neither the corporeal form, the poetic form, nor the syntactic form. This release from formal pattern, in other words, also has semantic significance: an increased scope will result from this gesture of going beyond established boundaries. Thus, visually Bly stops the construction beginning with "I" and verb, and ventures into the scene. Moreover, as in the negative capability of Keats, the speaker noticeably increases sensitivity in his empathic vision of leaves that are "resigned." Now the speaker is not removed from the scene as subject is from object; for, as we have been told, he now is in a scene that he easily "slips" into. Indeed, the following sentence dispenses with the "I" and notes that "horses were out eating in the ditch...." The outgoing consciousness of this speaker, shifting his focus from himself to his landscape, also signifies a departure from dichotomies as suggested by boundaries. This leaning outwardly prepares the way, and, as will be discussed further, the ellipsis marks suggest that there is more in a vision than finite structure could portray. The strength of structure relents now before the powers of intuition. This power, not brutishly victorious, is a release from boundaries of tradition, rules. Such release, suggesting fluidity of energies instead of restriction of form, empathy rather than recognition, establishes a patina of associations with the female milieu. Bly seems to disregard the entire tradition of history while resurrecting the ancient modes of myth. I suggest a growth in the poet and his speaker of perceptual modes most often attributed to the woman. The receptivity beginning this paragraph prepares the speaker for his outgoing venture concluding the first paragraph.

This paragraph concludes the "I" series: "I walked down the road toward the West," and the next paragraph continues with another sentence beginning with "I." The journey, symbolic in direction: westward, and in time: daybreak, leaves the female milieu of night and dream where images are not based upon physical perception and logical intention. Change is augmented by this centrifugal push from the body-"I" outwardly toward the world. Two sentences in this paragraph that do not begin with "I" along with a change in tense establish a shift away from both physical enclosure and historic tradition. In the first sentence suggesting "aliveness" and receptivity, the speaker does not control this vitality, and really cannot cognitively prepare for it. Again, logical intention seems irrelevant here, since this preparation is of a different kind—one that does not intend a result, but one that like gestation requires preparation and time. Tense in this paragraph is indeed significant. Recollection, the mind of memory, does not articulate the source of vitality; the shift from a chronology of action does, when sequence, for instance, is interrupted only by the perception that "the horses were out eating in the ditch." This action is not chronological, but endures longer than the catalogue of events before and after this sentence. Furthermore, it implies the speaker's nascent outwardness—by interrupting the "I" sentences with a perception of other things. This gesture is a harbinger of the speaker's spirituality; his aliveness becomes a vehicle not for internalization, but for generation of empathy, and finally communion with the living world. Thus, the paragraph contains an element of life not confined to the first personal "I," and suggests that "some aliveness of the body" may become "some aliveness of the universal body"; the physical body becomes both a metaphor for and a vehicle to the universal body; reception becomes preparatory for generation. (This outwardness, then, like a birth, brings energy from the body out into the world.)

In the second paragraph, a journey occurs from the speaker's body out to a scene that increasingly becomes a female milieu. First, dichotomies are mended through a decreasing sense of enclosure concomitantly with an increase in empathy. Secondly, the female quality of mythic earth is realized: a decreasing sense of earth as a field of distinctions occurs concomitantly with an increasingly intuitive vision. First, the awakened speaker continues westward—symbolic of a world of logic and dichotomy. But this subject-object dichotomy signalled by the opening of the sentence—again beginning with "I"—relents before a unifying process. Now, the speaker explicitly leans outwardly, reaching toward the land with which he is familiar, symbolically reaching toward the earth—the great mythical mother, whose harvests are symbolically represented by this poem. While empathy grows, this leaning leads to a sense of communion, until familiar objects in the landscape transform into personified treasures, thus elevated to the level of conscious life. The magnitude of this evolution may be signalled by the change of verbs and by the change in narrative stance, from self-expression to empathic communion, thereby leaving aloofness of dichotomy inherent in history for involved relationship of ritual in the mythic present. This second paragraph, for instance, shifting from memory, as indicated by the past tense concluding the first paragraph, begins in present tense, thus relying on perception. Furthermore, perception changes from the more pedestrian sensory kind to an inseeing capacity. Thus, when speaking as a subject separated from object, the speaker says, "I notice," connoting rather casual observation by a passerby. These noticed images gain in significance when the focus shifts from a speaker noticing to those elements witnessed in the landscape. Thus, the sentence leads from "I notice a pebble on the road," to "then a corn-ear...," to "then a small earthbridge...." The series of "thens" portrays the speaker's expansion from an enclosed self-contained being, inherent in the pronoun "I," to one whose leaning and leaning draws him outwardly, into close commune with his milieu. Bly here fulfills his own hermeneutics: he has said that good poetry is not self-expression. "What is that?" he inquires. Poetry is the opposite of self-expression.[3] "Being grounded," as he states, is a necessary first step. That grounding does not preclude empathy, but is rather a preparation for having the capacity for venturing out.[4] In other words, the internal resources must be developed to the point that, as in this poem, an "aliveness" occurs allowing harmony with life of the universe. Now, the realm of intuition, the communion with living powers of earth, the release from parameters of self and other, legitimize an ancient female ambience, born again in this evolving speaker.

Such evolution becomes apparent in this series of "then" comments; indicating sequence by its denotation and repetition, Bly intensifies a departure from expectation when the "then" phrases lead not to further repetition, but to an interiority of vision increasing when the speaker seems released from a self enclosed milieu. From the casual "notice" of an insular "I," the observer transforms from one with merely sensory sight to one possessing a deeper capacity. The sequence of images is seen increasingly through intuitive vision: first *on,* then *in,* then *into* the landscape. The first image, of a "pebble on the road," would be available to any observer. Then, as the focus shifts to a field, "a corn-ear" appears lying "in the grass," thereby projecting outwardly and thus portraying less casual observation than implied by "noticing." The third image of a "small earthbridge *into* [italics added] the cornfield," represents interpenetration of elements. Not only do cornfields admit earthbridges, but the speaker leaving surface manifestations probes beneath, significantly penetrating fields with earthbridges; the earth here changes from horizontal plane into a deeper plateau; such verticality results from a capacity to see beneath surfaces. Rejecting the dichotomy of subject and object is also a symbolic departure from cultures of positivism, scrutiny, and category. The speaker intuits depths of earth, in earth, entering finally into the earth—spiritually· joining the symbolic woman.

A study of Bly's syntax also reveals interpenetration of elements as symbolically rich in this paragraph. A rush of events is implied through repetition; "I notice" is followed with "a pebble," "then" a "corn-ear," "then" "a small earthbridge." Bly changes grammatical gears, however, in this construction that ostensibly contains repetition but goes increasingly from the speaker's action to the image. "I notice" describes "a pebble on the road," the action here occurring in the speaker who notices the pebble; then, with a verbal, "a corn-ear lying in the grass," more pointedly centers on the corn-ear, and finally "a small earthbridge into the cornfield" noticeably departs from the portrayal of the speaker and of natural observation. "I notice" could not semantically be the antecedent verb of "an earthbridge *into* the cornfield" (italics added). The concluding image does not focus on the speaker or the object in the landscape. Rather it unites apparent divisions by portraying an image as invested with the speaker's intuition. Focusing on an image while leaving the source of the action has the effect of making that image more pictorial. Thus, through verb-omission, Bly offers this picture of deep interpenetration and holds this picture still for a moment.

This pause on interpenetration leads to a visionary glimpse more sublime than recordable through a grammar of logic. Grammatical inadequacy in the subsequent sentence, which contains comma splices, a fragment, and ellipsis marks implies a theory that grammatical logic is inadequate, symbolically responding to the inadequacy of an historical world that spawned such structures. "It leads to a backland where the plows turn, the tractor tires have married it, they love it more than the rest, cozy with bare dirt, the downturned face of the plow that looked at it each round...." The referent of "it" is presumably that earthbridge whose unity with the cornfield provides the vehicle for a vision into universal harmony. The comma splice following this image utilizes a grammatically incorrect connecting device. Here, the joining of two things is not as harmonious in language as it is through vision. Again, joined by comma-spliced connections, the next two images increasingly envision a speaker in harmony with his landscape at the same time that the punctuation is flawed. It appears that by this very combination, Bly portrays a vision too large for logical modes. Masculine and feminine symbolism seems appropriate here when connection is made with the earth and fault is found in the written language. And indeed the content of the lines affirms this suspicion of connecting with female forces; tractor tires mingling with the earthbridge is portrayed as a marriage; then contiguity is further portrayed as love. The landscape is not only personified, but alive with the emotion of love in union. Union is first depicted as "cozy," then Bly increases the sexuality with the image of "the downturned face of the plow that looked at it each round...." Not only has the landscape become alive with love and sexual harmony, but this sexuality may be the vehicle to an epoch of more spiritual harmony. Ellipsis marks, I suggest, syntactically represent this notion that physical contiguity-becoming-love-becoming-sexual union is preparatory for more spiritual union, and this, in turn, preparatory for a vision of correspondences. This suspicion will be confirmed later, when the implied notion of ellipsis—that there is more—increases with the depiction of the speaker's spiritual awakening, including his awareness of aliveness in the earth.

Like vision that penetrates surfaces, "aliveness of the body" seems a resource allowing this speaker to leave his body. Deadness of the body, accordingly, would lock the energy in the frame stillborn. This paragraph concludes not only with portrayal of a series of images changing from photographic to insightful, but this inseeing vision augurs an intuition of earth itself brimming with life, thus brings life into the scene. The second sentence does not begin with "I" but with "it," referring to an earthbridge. Furthermore, the speaker not only centrifugally journeys outwardly, but the "it" of earthbridges shifts from its inanimate state to one containing a more personified aspect. Earthbridges lead "to the backland," perhaps further away from sensory sight, but seen with intuitive vision, as a place "where the plows turn," and then, in combination with other natural objects, the juncture becomes marriage: "the tractor tires have married it." Union in marriage is underscored in three ways. First, the personification attributes consciousness to the farmland scene. Secondly, the marriage suggests the quality of life involved in this scene. Thirdly, Bly formally connects this image of conscious unity to "love," the emotion undergirding marriage, in a comma spliced construction. Thus, logic, the logic of syntax and grammar, is inadequate for this intuitional vision of unity; a coupling of two sentences with a comma seems merely additive, while the vision of unity requires a more integral connection. Unity of subject and object, then, becomes communion in marriage. Such communion is depicted by "I" reaching "it," thereby leaving an enclosed speaker in order to enter the living milieu. "It" becomes "they" as singular joins into plural and "they," although referring to tractor tires, is given the passion of love. "They love it more than the rest" personifies and qualifies this commingling quality as that which fosters love. The significant prerequisite, then, is unity—leaving the enclosure of "I" for a gesture of universal harmony.

Symbolically, the speaker departs from a dichotomized

atmosphere of subject and object. Bly eschews the constructions of history—its patriarchal forms of logic, grammar, and tradition —while offering the more matriarchal forms of the mother herself, receiving and bearing, intuitive and fluid. The rewards are reaped in a scene symbolically harvesting love; love fosters a "cozy" event suggestive of intimacy when joined to the next image of "the downturned face of the plow that looked at it each round...." This sexual metaphor, used to express intimate minglings, changes the more casual "cozy" into a more passionate mingling, much as the more casual "notice" changed to the more intense intuitional vision. This instant of personification reaches a visionary plateau, yet the poet implies no stopping place. Grammatically, Bly cannot depict this harmony except by portraying the inadequacy of grammatical logic. Though the mark of a visionary has been made—the tingling body, the leaving of it, the reaching outwardly, the union made—Bly leaves ellipsis marks signifying there is more. In such a fluid milieu, categorization of "what is" becomes pedestrian. There is always more; the aliveness beginning the poem and the humming concluding the poem suggest this sensitivity of body awakened by spirit. This spiritual birth is central to the second paragraph in which envisioned correspondences cannot be transmitted through logical discourse.

By the conclusion of this poem, Bly brings the reader closer to the nurturing earth, close enough to hear tiny crickets. Bly emphasizes harmony, reception, intuition, sensitivity, and sexuality, while discarding the authority of rule, logic, parameters, and tradition. It seems no accident that these characteristics clearly depict the mythic matriarchal cultures as opposed to the historical patriarchal times. Indeed, holism associated with matriarchy and myth seems inestimably more valuable than the rational dimension of splitting the universe into categories. The concluding paragraph goes beyond the natural ordering of the mind; Bly seems to suggest a setting for receptivity as opposed to selectivity. Shafts of light, for example, yield "a cornhusk in one place, a cottonwood tree in another, *for no apparent reason*" (italics added). Images perceived by the speaker seem offered by the light in a natural correspondence, unordered by will, or intention. "Apparent" takes on the same casual quality as "notice" did in the previous paragraph. Bly does not dispute whether or not a reason exists, but maintains that the reason is not apparent. Indeed, the world of appearance, afforded the objective eye, seems ordinary compared to the vision of a universe of connections glimpsed in this poem. In the following sentence, for example, temporal and eternal time join in a conception too large for logical apprehension. The additive nature of a logical mind is again indicated in syntax containing comma splice and fragment. The beginning of the sentence, "A branch has dropped onto the fence wire," is a natural, temporal image. The subsequent meditation, "there are eternities near," is a Wordsworthian response too large for logic. Since language seems bereft of the capacity for containing intuition, this line, added to the previous sentence with a comma splice, indicates not the lack of intuition but its magnitude—too grand to be contained in a grammar of logic. Indeed, the intuition is a given, presented with the certitude implied in a state-of-being construction. Intuition joins the concatenation of values revealed in this poem to suggest clearly by now that a female psyche permeates this earth.

In this paragraph, Bly goes from natural image to natural image; observation changes to vision when it becomes clear that a synthesis exists among these elements. The reader also is compelled to make the connection, one more harmonious than logically decipherable. Moreover, this harmony encompasses aesthetic response in general, the reader no longer removed from the poem as subject is from object. Thus, Bly structurally indicates logical inaccuracies at the moment when the vision enlarges, and this enlargement, furthermore, enforces the envisioned harmony by drawing the reader into the poem. Bly strengthens the poet-poem-reader relationship through intuition.

Intuition—a holy thing—is not removed from the physical being. In fact, the body may be a vehicle for intuition. With no transition from eternity to the body, Bly quickly flashes from one to the other, perhaps indicating connection through contiguity. "Exasperations" may imply petty quarrels of the physical life, such as are resolved through a vision of eternity. Thus, the body, becoming "free of its exasperations," has symbolically given birth. Intuitions are born as a release from containment. In this poem its especial interpenetrating characteristic also symbolically mends dichotomies of subject and object, memory and perception, even male and female. "Eternities are near" articulates these visionary correspondences.

Such freedom suggests evolution from restraints, and leaves the speaker "ready to see what will come." This stage is signalled again by an aliveness in his body. Now, "there is a humming in my body." Auguring a birth, the physical humming becomes metaphoric of spiritual revival. Through his use of punctuation, Bly implies that physical becomes more than physical: first, a comma splice and then ellipsis marks occur in this construction when the humming body precedes "it is jealous of no one." The antecedent of "it" is presumably humming, since humming seems to be the alert, alive aspect of the speaker, such in quality that "it is jealous of no one." Bly indicates a life (humming) not restricted to ownership (jealousy). Furthermore, there is more, perhaps too grand for language; thus, the ellipsis marks.

Bly calls upon the tiny cricket once again to indicate spirituality at the conclusion of this poem: "The cricket lays its wings one over the other, a faint whispery sound rises up to its head... which it hears...and disregards...listening for the next sound...." Again a comma splice and ellipsis marks indicate intuition bursting grammatical boundaries; just as the vision supercedes eyesight, and the humming declares more than physical body, the message requires more than grammatical logic. Thus, more is needed as is additively indicated by the comma splice insistence that this too should be said. But the essence of this perception does not transmit through one sentence, then another. The comma spliced arrangement turns out to be a redundancy of an arrangement, each, in itself, inadequate; the combination, cumulatively inadequate—a repetition rather than a clarification. Then, Bly uses ellipsis marks for opposite purposes. Sentence upon sentence suggests repetition, each in itself inadequate singularly and cumulatively. If the whole grammatical structure seems inadequate, then how could the perception be transmitted? Intuition broke the boundaries of the body; distinction of separate natural objects joined through their correspondences; limitation of grammatical logic is overcome through portrayal of its inadequacy. Now, Bly turns to ellipsis marks—a positive rejection of incapacity. Instead of silence as a response to the ineffable, Bly offers words, and then asserts over and again that there is more. A poet whose wisdom is more than words, Bly reaches into the life surrounding him and provides images, correspondences, and then teaches—saying these are the vehicles; there is more. As a guide, Bly notes humming in a body; as a visionary he describes not only the cricket's "faint whispery sound," which corresponds to this humming body, but with empathic sensitivity notes that "it hears. . .[and there is more] and disregards. . .[and there is more] listening for the next sound. . .[and there is more]." In other words, we too are "walking" and must not stop our journey.

Thus, "Walking Where the Plows Have Been Turning" is a three part metamorphosis in which through reception, expansion, and generation Bly constructs a mythology of human experience. He clearly values incorporative functions, elevating sensitivity and empathy over observation and detail; receptivity and sexuality over aggression and submission; fluidity of form over tradition and pattern; and a world of correspondence and intuition over a land of rules and order. Finally, Bly mends a world torn into parts through his construction of a more fluid ambience of interacting energies. Intuition, sensitivity, empathy, reception—usually characterizing the female—permeate this creation. We witness, I suspect, one of the creators of a new epoch, in which the mythic woman powerfully rises also within a male. There will be more to witness Bly tells us, if, receptive, intuitive, and attentive, we too listen "for the next sound. . . ."

———————

Notes

1 Robert Bly, "Walking Where the Plows Have Been Turning," *Georgia Review,* Fall 1978, Vol. XXXII, No. 3, p. 513. Revised and included in *This Tree Will Be Here for a Thousand Years* (New York: Harper & Row, 1979), p. 49.

2 Robert Bly, *Jumping Out of Bed* (Barre, Mass.: Barre Publishers, 1973).

3 Bly stated this idea at a poetry reading at Western Illinois University, Nov. 2, 1978.

4 Bly discusses "grounding" in "On Gurus, grounding yourself in the Western tradition, and thinking for yourself," *East-West Journal,* 1976 Aug., pp. 10-15.

Michael Cuddihy

Harvest

a poem for Robert Bly

I'm here to help slaughter chickens on the Bly farm, but the sun has been up for hours. I grab hold of a white-feathered cock and wring its neck, the head warm in my hand as the bird scatters down the road, a trail of feathers, ragged, unpredictable. A gate. I jiggle the latch, the yard already full of people at tables, eating, all talking at once. Carol Bly is standing near the back: "But you were supposed to be here hours ago." Then Robert, hearty, ebullient. "There are not many chickens left. How about helping us pick these apple trees!" He leads me between the rows of tables, out past the yard into the orchard. I can reach only the lowest apples from the wheelchair, but my arms are strong, gnarled and tough, like the limbs of these old trees. The apples feel like baseballs. I have to resist the urge to throw them. A moment and the three of us are at the Barn in Water Mill, where I'm staying with two older brothers. We talk excitedly, Bly paying extravagant compliments. He looks pleased.

A moon faint as a thumbprint. We are on Long Island, but it could easily be Minnesota, the air damp and cool. Now we are headed back to the Blys' in an old car. I am in front, the far right, what people call the death seat. We move down the highway, the sky unaccountably dark. The moon follows at a safe distance. Next to me, Carol Bly has fallen asleep. My brothers are walking along the road, Robert towering beside them, a scythe over his right shoulder, the faint scar on his cheek lit by the moon. There is no driver. I turn around, the back seat full of black servants, near to me now as childhood: Marge, Mr. Norse, and Annie Lee Hall, long forearms knotted in her lap. But they have been dead for years, I tell myself, wondering if this is real, or are we all part of it, the engraving Dürer finished on the eve of the Reformation, leaving his initials, A͞D, in the lower left hand corner.

Some Notes on Grief and the Image

> *My grief is that I bear no grief*
> *& so I bear myself. I know I live apart.*
> —Jon Anderson
>
> *The ocean comes to grieving men.*
> —Robert Bly

Although it must be living itself that leads anyone to *condition of grief,* it may be a poet's obsession with the Image that leads to grieving. But how so? Why? If an image is, as Pound said, "an intellectual and emotional complex in an instant of time," it is exactly that "instant of time" which passes; even though an image may reify itself many times in a reader's experience, it will pass again as well. The image draws on, comes out of, the "world of the senses" and, therefore, originates in a world that passes, that is passing, every moment. Could it be, then, that every image, *as image,* has this quality of poignancy and vulnerability since it occurs, and occurs so wholeheartedly, in time?

*

Pound's definition above gives us a limited, if nearly adequate, idea of the Image. So we have known for years that the Image is not a photograph, that it engages or can engage any of the senses, and, if we want to illustrate this, we can remember the tactile imagery of Keats in "Eve of St. Agnes" or the imagery of sound in Roethke's *North American Sequence,* or, in Whitman, all of the senses. But why, both in the popular imagination and among poets, is there this persistent fault in the way we think of the Image. Usually, people think of and remember images as if nearly all of them were *seen.* And why are so many images composed, and I would include much of the use of the *Deep Image,* for the eye itself? "Old warships drowning in a raindrop" is a visual image before it is in any way a conceptual one. I would suggest that much of our use of imagery in contemporary poetry is related to the eye, to sight more often than to smell, taste, touch, or hearing. Perhaps eyesight is the most developed sense that we have, and perhaps the very activities of reading and writing engage, too wholly, the eye. I think the problem, if it *is* a problem, may be cultural as well, however. None of us can really escape our culture, and our culture conditions us through the use of film and photography almost daily. And photographs, whether on the front page of *The New York Times* or in museums, are, *literally,* time that has been made to hold still. As such, they remind us, because they are images unmediated by language, of time itself. Perhaps, as Roland Barthes indicates in *Camera Lucida,* each photograph, but especially portraits and landscapes, are, in the "realism" slight deaths, slight catches in the breath, too, especially if they are intellectually and emotionally complex. And yet I do not mean to suggest that photography is limited to a kind of literal representationality, a total Realism of the eye. The work of Minor White and Aaron Siskind disproves this, and many of their prints resemble not what the eye sees, but what it didn't then see, at the moment when the shutter clicked. In the darkroom, after the eye has done its other work, the photograph grows into something more like a Franz Kline canvas, and less and less like a factory or a river bed. And all that is, by now, an old story: some photographers wish to go beyond the camera; some painters wish to go beyond paint; some poets wish to go beyond words. Some go beyond and do not come back. Many live and work in two worlds which are like unidentical twins. The pleasure is in the tension.

*

That image, "Old warships drowning in a raindrop" goes beyond the natural phenomena observable to the eye, and yet stays within the boundaries of what can be seen but never is really seen in experience. We call such an image surrealistic. But it is only partly so. The image never totally severs its connection to the eye; therefore, to Realism, to *imagined* phenomena. To go *beyond* in any final sense is to go mute in a final sense. One of the purest Surrealist acts, it was said, was to blindfold yourself, and to walk to a busy street corner, turn around a few times, and then to fire a pistol into the crowd. Why the blindfold? So you would not see. This makes, of course, the shooting more fair and more disinterested. You could kill a prince or a *plongeur* with equal ease and abandon. But more importantly, the blindfold kills already, inwardly, the Realist inside yourself so that the other person can be released, that "other" who fires the pistol, the one who has already left this world. The trouble with words is that they are in and out of the world. They want to be specific. They want to *mean,* even if we no longer quite want them to mean in the ways they wish to mean. Once, I was talking to a friend over lunch. He had studied in Switzerland, and I wanted to ask him about de Saussure, about *sign* and *signifier* and *signified.* Our talk eddied out, as I had hoped it would because I wanted to learn something about contemporary criticism. I finally asked him if he thought that anything held the word, or the signifier, to the thing, or the signified. His answer was simple. "Yes," he said, "desire."

*

Perhaps the Image, like a thing or an animal or a human, desires to be, to be itself eternally. The Image is like us, but it is not like us. It desires to constellate itself beyond us, and to live apart from us. It may or may not desire to fit into the fabric of the whole work of art, to be "organic" in *that* shopworn sense of the word. In truth, *we* pass, and the Image becomes more moving to us because it remains and at the same time records something that passes. The images we write hold still, and their stillness is curious because it reminds us that, someday, up ahead, at the end of the story, completion is inevitable but incomprehensible. Freud called it "the riddle of death," but a riddle is also an image, a stillness.

*

A Ramage for the Star Man, Mourning

The star man, mourning, floats among the stars
firmly, the farms beneath his feet.
How long it takes to climb into grief!
Fifty years old, and still held in the dark,
in the unfinished, the hopeful, what longs for
   solution.
As that girl there, who explains things, combing
her hair. . .the face seems alert, the body
still drifting through the ponderous farms of
   ocean.

Robert Bly

In some of Robert Bly's most recent work, the condition of grief
and mourning is what the poet hopes to accomplish. Bly longs
to be taken into something, constellated and completed. He desires to "climb into grief" and his image of it here is an attempt
to define its condition, a condition beyond time, and beyond the
merely "hopeful." Why beyond the merely hopeful? When we
witness the harrowing completeness of tragedy, we rarely think
that such art is "positive" or "negative" in its final effect, since
tragedy is in some way a machine designed to purge us and to
devour these two poles, the "positive" and the "negative,"
these two illusions. It is designed to make us "grow up." I suppose that people who truly desire only "something uplifting" in
art are adolescents. People who want only their own cynicism
confirmed by art are also, probably, adolescents. But Bly's little
poem is no tragedy, and toward its end, Bly's method becomes
uncharacteristically modest and renunciatory. An unidentified
girl, combing her hair, is explaining things. We are not told
what these are. The final line of the poem introduces evolution,
myth, and the line bores me, as does the opening of the poem.
Yet I am drawn to the human statements, the renunciatory tone
taken in the midst of the poem, its declaration, made barrenly
and without any image, of the desire for a condition of grief.
And that girl, combing her hair, so like the poet and yet so

unlike him, is the true mirror of the poem. It seems to me, then, that the ocean she is still drifting through does not complete the poem. Nothing completes the poem. It is, for now, unfinished. And that is what Bly already realizes in the poem. Completeness is the condition he longs for, and the "ocean" simply muddies the experience with its image, which is complete only in itself and which has little to do with the poem. But the man behind that image, like the Wizard of Oz behind his great machine, or like Robert Bly behind his masks at a poetry reading, is admitting here that he is, after all, only a man, and fifty, and "unfinished."

*

But at least Bly has set out here on another journey, and, as he has written elsewhere, "The ocean comes to grieving men." There is only one problem with men who grieve absolutely. They may be beyond language, or language may no longer have any real hold on them. In Fellini's *La Strada,* the circus performer and strong man, Zampano the Great, murders accidentally and out of passion, and is therefore left totally alone, and so in the last scene crawls on his knees to the sea. That is a condition of grief. There may be other conditions, but they are no longer Zampano's. The problem for a lyric poet is that he cannot grieve, in words, for himself. The artist in that last scene is, after all, not Zampano, but Fellini. The conditions of actual grief may not permit the poet to speak.

John Haines

Robert Bly: A Tiny Retrospect

I think it was sometime in the fall of 1958 that I saw a notice for a forthcoming magazine of poetry and comment to be called *The Fifties*. I was intrigued by the nature of the announcement, promising translations and new poems intended to correct the "old-fashionedness" of American poetry.

I had recently begun reading Spanish poetry, so that the notice coincided with my own growing sense of discovery. My reading then was confined mainly to the older masters, to poets of the classical age, to Becquer and to Lorca, whom I had read briefly some years before. I knew nothing of German or French poetry, and I had not yet felt the full force of the modern spirit in poetry outside that being written in English. But I sensed, even at the distance I lived then, that there was something in the air, the first faint shock of a new energy.

My second wife, Jo, had come to live with me, and a new life was beginning, built upon solitude and a unique companionship. It was to be for several years a life of considerable hardship, but it contained at the same time great space and richness. The new poetry enlarged and deepened that space; there was an unmistakable feeling of freshness—a new expressiveness and emotional depth.

Between Bly and myself there followed letters, an exchange of views regarding this new poetry that was beginning to be written. My own views were often uninformed and openly skeptical; his were knowledgeable and for the most part persuasive. James Wright was there also, seldom a correspondent, but contributing his translations, poems and occasional comments. It would be difficult to exaggerate the importance of that contact for me at the time; for someone as isolated as I had been and was still to be, that correspondence, intermittent but generous, was a rare and cherished thing.

And then the books, the poems—Trakl, Machado, Jimenez and others—the imagery succinct and resonant, compelling in its associations. Reading those poems as they came to me, issue by issue and page by page, I became aware of something brooding in the sub-arctic twilight, in the long nights; nature became saturated with something like its old spiritual vitality—a long-sleeping animal presence awakened in the cold snows and the deep timbered shadows. That time will always be associated in my mind with darkness and frost, with clarity and richness; with deep reading and the slow coming together of thought and style, of word, perception and deeply-held emotion.

I have not read those early issues of *The Fifties* and *The Sixties* for many years, but I suspect that they still make good reading. Nothing like their innovative energy has appeared in the years since. If anything, the imaginative space has been shrinking; poems tend to be longer these days, wordier, more discursive, with fewer surprising images in them, and I would say also that there seems in general to be less close observation of things.

A good deal of space might be given to discussing just why this initial energy spent itself so quickly. In a surprisingly short time, it seemed, after the publication of *Silence In The Snowy Fields, The Branch Will Not Break,* and my own *Winter News,* a second and third-hand pastoral surreality manifested itself, and all kinds of people began writing poems crowded with stone and earth images and a forced imagery of darkness. Small, tousled animals were creeping out of all kinds of castles in the oaks and maples, and from little houses in the grass. Moose were sighted in the suburbs of Los Angeles, as I recall, and wolves were baited on the rooftops in San Francisco.

It is hardly Bly's fault that we appear to have such a swift talent here for seizing upon anything innovative and fresh, turning it into an item for sale and duplication. And with all this, it may still be true that the energy and the released ideas have worked more deeply than we think, and the time may come when they will surface again in a new and needed poetry.

Robert and I have had our differences, our disagreements, and I feel sure that we will continue to have them. It is easy to disagree with him, and necessary, in my opinion, even while acknowledging the great benefit of his continuing commentary on poetry. But if, as Pound remarked once, another man's ideas compel you to take out your own and look at them, that may be as much agreement as we have a right to expect, and it can be a great deal.

I admit to being skeptical of his system of traditions in poetry, for example, as provocative and as useful as they may prove to be. His notions about consciousness in the natural world also need to be looked at with some caution. The steady contemplation of any object, whether a natural one or not, can awaken correspondences, though it may be that rocks and trees have about as much consciousness as we endow them with—which can be a great deal, but then it all depends on what we mean by consciousness. There is a good deal of fashionable white shamanship around these days, and it won't do to pass on to another generation a lot of ill-digested, half-understood notions that can become real ideas only when they have been lived and transformed into genuine poems.

Agreements and differences aside, I respect him for his untiring efforts to push American poetry further into the 20th century. We need these gadflies. Left to ourselves, we tend to withdraw into complacency and self-indulgence, into a companionable garrulousness. We are too comfortable and too safe, removed from the social and political disasters of the modern world, and our writing as a consequence often reveals a poverty, a privileged distance from the horrors in which we have participated often enough as suppliers and instigators. Then, out of a deeply-residing guilt, we see how easy it is for us to strike the pose without the content, to assume the manner without the substance. But one possible benefit to be gotten from Bly's example during the past two decades is the understanding that there is not, finally, anything that can be separated as "political" poetry; that the act of writing today is itself a political act, even if it pretends to be no more than a declaration of silence.

Whether Bly's voice as a poet will equal his influence as translator and critic, a coming generation will have to determine. He has been compared to Pound in his effect on his contemporaries. The comparison is apt, up to a point. I don't know that his influence has been as decisive, as authoritative and as lasting as Pound's; it is perhaps more special and tentative, though it resembles Pound's sometimes in its oddness and eccentricity. Nor is his mastery of verse equal to Pound's. Compared to Pound, he hasn't much of an ear. On the other hand it may be true, as much of Bly's writing suggests, that the real voice of poetry can be felt now, not as formerly in word-music and intricate verse-structures, but in some deeper and quieter manifestation of a spiritual content, in a revelation of those layers of thought and feeling all too often obscured by the noise we make as we talk and write and publish. That content has a music of its own, though it can never be separated entirely from the sounds of words and the movement of verse.

It was remarked once in connection with Thomas Hardy that what the world asks of its poets is a certain mastery of the meaning of their time, and a corresponding power to bring that meaning home to other ages. It seems to me that despite changing fashions in poetry, and the inroads made on our powers of attention and concentration by the shrillness of our competitive passions, that this is still what we require of our poets. It may be asked (though I will not attempt to give an answer) whether something like this mastery can be found in Bly's work, or in the work of any contemporary poet, as it can certainly be found in the poems of Eliot and Yeats, and to some extent in the poems of Williams and Stevens. Only a partial answer could be given at this time, but the question will be asked of us eventually, and when the hysteria of our times has given way to a quieter atmosphere we may have an answer.

For me these days, having come a long ways (sometimes I think too far) from my former darkness of mind in nature, there is more light, more understanding; the forest has lost some of its mystery, and other shapes have emerged from the shadows. But one thing seems reasonably clear: when the stage-shows have been dismantled and the personalities have been forgotten, what will remain of our poetry will be principally the evidence that among us there were a few individuals who understood the necessity of returning poetry to what the Orkney poet, George MacKay Brown, has called "its true task, interrogation of silence."

David Ray

On Robert Bly

Bly is the archetypal crank, like all of us discontent with the direction of a nation that spawned Henry Thoreau and John Muir but now subsidizes the murder of peasants and the systematic pollution of the world. Bly has helped bring poetry back to its roots and into contact with its European heritage. His poetry will outlast his own polemic and probably some of the problems he reflects in his work. When we finally learn that we have to take ecology seriously, to survive, we'll turn—or the world that follows us will turn—more to poets like Bly than to those who have narrowly defined both their perimeters and parameters of existence.

David Ray

In the Money

for Robert Bly

> "*Men who are unhappy, like men who sleep*
> *badly, are always proud of the fact.*"
> Bertrand Russell

You wouldn't think of weeping, but rage
instead, shaking that fist
that's all atremble. I stand accused
before you, of having my so-called
act together, and I'm a father
whom expert daughters curse as well
though they can't match your record
of sleeping near the tracks.
They've had to brew their own distress,
invent us monsters.
If we did not exist
they would make us up in dreams.
They sway as you do in the wind
like bitter stalks of winter
and rage their hate and bitterness.
Your heart is pure, *your* rage is fine
and pure and echoes off the tainted walls
of the sorry, sordid earth. It's the rest
of us who live
our lives of quiet desperation,
stoop to toy with words to say
something to a daughter, millionaire
or bum, though their ears
are closed as if against the wind
and each step taken is choreographed
from some foul-papers script. With envy
you stroll on, while I with envy stay.

David Ray

Travelling and Sitting Still

for Robert Bly

You think you're going someplace
When you're sailing through the sky
At five miles up, over the Pacific.
Or when you're jammed in the station
Waiting for the train to Kyoto
Or when the streetcars are clanging
Or it's shove against shove to get a table
Where you eat *sushi* or something Hungarian,
When you're filling out forms or handing
The passport over or even waiting
For a bus next to a greasy pylon.
You're consumed in travel, in just
Getting through. You take care of
Yourself. Time takes care of itself.
The ship with lowered sail
Arrives to bear you back. Moon's out.
But there comes a moment, be it in Wales
Or deep in the hold of that ship plowing
Deadhead through the night
That it's back again to the essential.
The cup of tea is here, not so elusive
As snow on Snowdon or Fuji.
So what's the use of Tokyo?
The work room's shared with a cricket
Or a flea, and the cup of tea, the napkin,
Light, and time that is taking care of itself.

David Ignatow

Reflections Upon The Past
With Robert Bly

I first met Robert Bly by telephone, either at my apartment or at the bindery where I was employed; but I am inclined to believe that I received the call at home because I was in the relaxed state which I never could have been in the shop. Robert's was a voice that I had never before heard, strong, as if exulting in its strength, a voice in joy of itself that seemed to carry a message of some extraordinary dispensation towards others, particularly the one being addressed at that moment. I was all attention. He had demanded to know whether I was David Ignatow. Surprisingly, after my reply, his voice dropped a full octave to begin speaking confidentially, identifying itself as the voice of Robert Bly. Had I heard of him, it asked. I had to confess I had not. The voice went on, and here I can only paraphrase his remarks which, in brief, spoke of his admiration for my poems. Out of nowhere, it seemed, had come a voice to give me heart again, to set me up in my own eyes as poet.

It is difficult to remember what followed between us, but as I sit here typing it comes back to me that I probably next visited him at his apartment in Greenwich Village. I had taken time off from my demanding routine at the bindery, just enough time in which to pay a courtesy call in return for his phone call. The pressure on me to return to work that afternoon was strong, as usual, much as I was filled with guilt for having told my father, the boss, that I had urgent shop business on the outside. I remember sitting with Robert in his apartment, but I do not remember in detail what we talked about. I would think it had to be about poetry and, if my fading memory can be relied on, he did ask me about the circumstances under which I made my living. About that I was always self-conscious—a poet working in a bindery shop. It didn't accord with the conventional version of a poet seated in a cafe over a glass of wine with his fellow poets or seated in a locked room bare of furniture, except for a desk, a bed and a table. Robert himself didn't seem to fit that conventional mode either so the self-consciousness I felt about describing my way of making a living was eased by his warm, sympathetic and even admiring manner in speaking with me. When finally I left, having to excuse myself on account of business—I was angry at myself for having to say it and angry at the job which forced me to leave—I resolved to learn more about Robert's poetry.

Instantly on meeting him, I recognized an out-of-towner, a Midwesterner by his demeanor and accent. In fact, first speaking to him by phone the week before, I had vaguely sensed from his diction and speech tones that he was from out of town and so, seeing him for the first time as he was and as he spoke I became doubly admiring of him for having the insight and empathy to feel and know city poetry, the kind I was writing then. I was amazed at his pleasure in city themes—this from a Midwesterner who I sensed was of the wide open spaces, miles from urban life, a man who had probably grown up amid fields of corn, wheat, barley and rye, amid horses and wild flowing grasses that stretched toward the horizon for endless miles.

Apparently, as I came to realize, Robert had called me on the phone after the publication of an anthology, edited by Louis Simpson, Donald Hall and Robert Pack, in which Robert was represented by his poems. It was an anthology dedicated to a new mode of poetry. At the moment, the title escapes me. Robert's poems, when I read them after our first meeting, seemed traditional both in rhyme and stanzaic forms. Well done, yes, but disappointing by comparison with Robert's strong, uplifting sense of himself as poet and as missionary to the poets. The last came across to me during our first visit together. That he should have spent the brief visit with me in his apartment praising my work and speaking with such interest—curiosity would be more appropriate—in my life and conditions, and in my vision of the city—all this had prepared me for a different kind of poetry from him. And so I suspected he was in the midst of an inner struggle or conflict. I had to remember that I had consciously chosen to take the road opposite his and that I had persisted in it and was persisting in it defiantly in the face of opprobrium of the then established poets. Already I had published two volumes, both influenced by the poetry of William Carlos Williams. I suspected that Robert was undergoing a conversion of spirit, while learning to understand and appreciate the virtues of the principles of freely organized form, and I suspected that he was having a difficult time of it as a conventionally trained Midwestern poet living in the uproar and violence of New York City. Perhaps, the thought occurred to me, I was his cicerone in his journey towards the then forbidden and denigrated, if not totally despised, principles of free form. Had he, living in New York, come to see that these principles were precisely what fit poetry that tried to communicate city life? These were my thoughts after meeting with him that afternoon.

Thereafter, we met infrequently. I really can't recall our next city meeting, but I do remember Carol Bly's coming to visit me in the shop shortly after my meeting with Robert. Why Robert was not with her I never found out or thought of asking, but to see her coming to visit me in my place of business was, to me, at first an awkward surprise, since I too was yet in conflict with myself about the course I had taken in poetry, isolated as I was from the "kingly" realm of rhyme and meter. Carol had come to watch me at work, to admire the proficiency with which I managed the workers at their machines, the speed and effectiveness with which I answered the phones and wrote out orders for scheduled jobs. Listening to her admiring words, I began to feel proud of my occupational skills. After all, I was doing the antipoetic thing poetry needed for vitality, and I was being admired for it. As Carol finally left, after walking slowly through the shop turning her head this way and that to catch the rhythms, tensions and sounds of the machines and their workers, I knew I had made a new and solid friendship on, of all things, the basis of my work here in the bindery, which, to confess, until that moment I had hated and despaired of ever leaving. It was a strange paradox to me but an exciting one suddenly, and I had Carol and Robert to thank for this new view I could have of myself. And so I was not alone in my commitment to the daily life of most men and women, at work in factories and offices and behind sales counters. I was not alone in dedicating my poetry to writing about this ordinariness. Robert's and Carol's introduction to and admiration for my life made it a triumph of vindication for me who had had secret doubts about my efforts to portray in poetry the people I knew, the conditions I lived in, the life I had to live.

Now I remember one more meeting with Robert in his apartment, and it had to do with one of James Wright's most famous and beautiful poems, "Lying in a Hammock at William Duffy's Farm in Pine Island." Robert let me see it in manuscript, which he had gotten from Jim by mail, I believe—Jim was then teaching at the University of Minneapolis. I was astonished, flabbergasted by the last line, "I have wasted my life."—this after the superb description of such beauty that I could not equate that last line with what came before it. I thought of the last line as a complete anomaly, an aberration, a total misunderstanding and misrepresentation of himself, the poet who could write with surpassing beauty, but Robert smiled at my excited disagreement. He understood something more. He argued with me gently. I argued passionately that the marvelous lines that came before that last one gave the lie to Jim's statement of a wasted life. How could a poet think of having wasted his life when those lines showed exactly the opposite, an achievement of such great strength and love of life and its details. Robert argued gently that the point was not the beauty of those lines but the insight into the order and calm lives of others, a calm and order that was their achievement, of which Jim had nothing to compare in his life that this last line revealed. I'm afraid it took me several years to absorb that insight; eventually I did, but not before undergoing, in my way, experiences such as Jim had gone through. This was no ordinary run of the mill Midwesterner, Robert Bly, who had argued gently with me for his understanding of the poem. Robert had been there ahead of me. He had hold of something I then did not know or was not then fully conscious of in myself, despite my dark poems of city life. I had not yet faced the fact that life in the city was in itself a waste, as lived in shops, factories, offices. Though I knew of it in others, I who was writing the poems, the successful poems, had not been prepared to know it in my own life. Jim had been confronting himself on this issue in his particular circumstances and Robert had known it.

At that time and perhaps at that very same meeting I got to read Robert's city poems, his attempt at recording the city from his standpoint as a Midwesterner. I was not so much impressed with as admiring of his effort. Except for one or two poems, I thought something of the city rhythms and tone was missing. There was too much of the prophetic voice, precisely what could not apostrophize nor perhaps hope to reform a city that by its very nature ran on strict concern with money, with pleasures derived from money, with rewards derived from money, a life style in itself that lived by money and was the city's existence; in sum, a kind of managed disorder and violence which flowed from precisely this drive in each individual: anarchic for its emphasis upon the person to the exclusion of the city as a living whole. Who, then, of the city would assume that the city could be laid low with a prophetic blast, such a city of stone and heedless traffic? In brief, Robert's poems lacked the insider's view of it: the sarcasm, the weariness with money, with pleasures made paltry with excess of them, the scorn of oneself and of others caught up in and enthusiastically pursuing spiritual desuetude. I could praise several of his poems, those that caught the outsider's wonder about the disorder in adults who could raise their violent, unhappy voices at night when one as a Midwesterner, could remember only the silence and peace of the open fields and sky at night.

Then Robert left for home, and I was to hear from him again through the receipt of his first volume of poems, *Silence in the Snowy Fields*. I knew I held in my hand a masterpiece of western sensibility. Nothing in it moved me so much as that sense of awe of his environment, the order and beauty he found in it. I knew I was in the presence of a spirit unique to the American experience in the Midwest, something I had never before encountered, and I became aware of a different America from what I had come to think was the one and only kind, the city.

Robert eventually accepted a poem of mine, in fact two, on two separate occasions for two separate issues of the magazine, *The Sixties*. The first poem, if I'm not mistaken, was "The Dream." A man is pounding his head upon the sidewalk in front of a department store in a huge city, a nightmare poem of city life. Robert saw it for what it meant; he could see clear through to the actual event as a true city poem. But the next poem he accepted had been written under the spell of his *Silence in the Snowy Fields*. I had admired the book so much, I was envious of the beauty and rest, calm and faith he had found in his surroundings, and I was made to realize I was ignoring my own experience. It had been something I had yearned for and loved in my adolescence when I had lived in the spacious suburbs that were then Brooklyn, its open fields, its trees, its silent night sky, the summer evening of fireflies and the long leisurely walks across the fields with friends. All this I had bitterly left behind me to merge with the city to earn my living from it. I sent Robert a poem that was partly a salute to him, in remembrance of my own lost paradise that yet in memory was real to me, as real as was Robert actually living in the Midwest. The poem, "Earth Hard," was very brief. Robert accepted it and let me know that, master of natural description and response that he was, he had found my poem authentic. It set me off to write in that vein again and again; I was thrilled to have recovered that part of me out of the muck and fury of city life, not that I was through with writing about the city, but I had this past to balance it with and with which to help me keep my balance at last.

The Vietnam War that followed this euphoric period was the climactic experience for us both in the 60s, but Robert did something about its frightening face and form, its horrific insanity. Almost singlehandedly, he launched a campaign of speeches, demonstrations, readings and read-ins and writing of poems across the college campuses of the nation. He withheld paying his taxes as yet another form of personal resistance to the war and published *The Light Around the Body,* a complete turn around from *Silence in the Snowy Fields. The Light Around the Body* was a statement of national anguish, of the sense of national betrayal by those in power, drunk and arrogant with power. The book won the coveted and then highly respected National Book Award. I for one was already electrified by his heroic fight in the latter half of the 60s. I joined him and Galway Kinnell in a car trip to Harvard University where we read each from our anti-war poems to a packed audience of students and faculty members. A year or so earlier, with Robert as an inspiration, I had gathered my courage to participate in a protest march down the main street of Lawrence, Kansas, where I was then teaching at the university. It was at least four years since I had given up the bindery at my father's death. At the protest march, we were being photographed every step of the way by FBI agents and local detectives. On our return to campus where we sat down in front of the administration building, we were threatened by the savage expressions of hatred by youths who could always be seen in their expensive Oldsmobiles and Cadillacs. There were cops there too on campus who carried their sidearms openly and came to look down on us impassively, as if we were objects for inspection and disposal in some form at their discretion. We knew the Vietnam savagery was there upon us, but we sat the scheduled time.

The Light Around the Body brought Robert the National Book Award when I was back from Kansas and teaching at Vassar. I and all his friends knew that accepting the prize in front of a huge audience, as was the custom, would give Robert a superb opportunity to speak out against the war. To Robert, at first, the idea of accepting a prize in the middle of a war of devastation upon innocent people was obscene and a travesty of the high purpose of poetry itself. He was for rejecting the prize outright with a written, scathing denunciation, but talking this out with Paul Zweig, James Wright and me, as I remember, he decided finally to accept the award on condition that he be allowed to speak as he wished. It was an unusual request to make to the committee, since it was the custom then simply to accept the prize with a short but graceful thank you and depart from the stage. However, the climate of the times being what it was, and Robert's passionate efforts against the war being already known, permission was reluctantly granted, and Paul, Jim, Saul Galin, and I sat down to rewrite a speech that Robert had begun. After reading through what he had written so far, we realized, as Robert came to realize in discussions with him, that the speech had to be written in a measured and calm rhetoric to be the more convincing to the august atmosphere of the occasion. The speech finally was written among us just hours before the ceremony was to start, and it was an amazing moment in the hall when Robert, after quietly receiving the check, turned to the audience with his speech in hand and began to read it in his measured but angry voice. He denounced the war, those who had begun it and were pursuing it; he denounced the writers in the audience who had been sitting by idly, letting the war take its frightful course without a word of protest or expression of conscience; and, finally, he denounced the publishers themselves who had contributed towards the prize money and his own publisher in particular for its silence during the war in the face of its overwhelming significance as an onslaught upon the liberty and civil rights of an entire nation, a fact that could by extension be applied to the developing condition in this country in which publishing itself could be threatened by governmental censorship and intimidation. It was a fact that was already being felt in the publishing world without a word of protest from anyone in the field. He ended by accepting the check only with the intention of then and there handing it to a representative of the War Resister's League who would then receive it for use in helping to resist the war in whatever manner it saw fit. A hush fell upon the audience as he called out the name of the representative to come to the platform and to receive the check from Robert's hand. As the check passed between them, Robert offered the recipient a final admonishment—to refuse to register for the draft upon his, Robert's, urging. Such a refusal and the open encouragement of such a refusal was tantamount to a violation of a law that had recently been passed in Congress. There was silence in the hall for a moment, the silence of extreme tension, until, finally, a small scattering of handclapping began. We had been fore-warned that there would be FBI agents in the audience, and, as we looked around we became aware that about ten men dressed in dark suits rose up from their seats in different parts of the hall and walked out in a body. The rest of the audience now had be-gun an uproar of talk mixed with boos and cheers. The die had been cast for Robert and for us. We had thrown down the chal-lenge to the government. I was apprehensive that the worst was yet to come, but who at that moment would let that fear over-ride the exhilaration, that victory of spirit that swept through us who had helped Robert with his speech? We knew that whatever government reprisal might follow, we could deal with it as it happened. For now we had won the day and put on notice the government and this distinguished audience, composed of most of the major literary figures of the day and their publishers, that this war could not be suppressed in our thoughts, nor in our lives, but had to be met honestly and with conscience. Donald Hall and Ted Weiss, two of the three judges who had given Rob-ert his prize, were also seated in the audience.* Although they were keeping their own counsel, we knew very well what had motivated their decision. And so, for me the moment meant a complete and overwhelming affirmation and vindication of all that Robert stood for as a crusading, visionary figure in the lit-erary world and in the politics of the nation. He had endured in-sults, threats and condemnation to make his stand before the ar-tistic and intellectual elite at the full height of his career and po-etic talents. He was a man for all seasons. He had done it with all the style, gusto and political passion on the highest level. It was Robert's finest hour and we who were attached to him through admiration, faith and common goals were affirmed through him and made to feel our significance before the world.

For the present, I would prefer that others, with their ver-sions, continue this account of Robert's fortunes as poet, man and crusader, but this much I can state in conclusion. Robert is

---

* Editor's note: Harvey Shapiro, the third judge, was in Europe at the time of the awards ceremony.

a man in change, growing deeper into himself and into the consciousness of his readers and audience, precisely because of his deepening life and new ways of writing it. Much already is emerging in his poems and in his choice of poets to translate that is significant for an understanding of where he is headed as poet. I am willing to state here that he has only now begun to see the outlines of his future as poet and that, as I see it, that future is extraordinary and of central importance to American writing yet to come.

Robert Bly and the Ants

"And what, O my master, would become of me, if I should ever attain with my mind to that, where no creature is? Must I not cry out, 'I am undone!'"

—The Disciple, in Jacob Boehme's
"Of the Supersensual Life"

"I bend over an old hollow cottonwood stump, still standing, waist high, and look inside. Early spring. Its Siamese temple walls are all brown and ancient. The walls have been worked on by the intricate ones."

—From "A Hollow Tree"

The generation of American poets to which Robert Bly belongs has among its considerable strengths that it has included animals memorably in its poetry. One thinks of Galway Kinnell's porcupine and crow and sow (and of course his bear, though that poem is actually about the bear's hunter, moving deep in a dream); of James Wright's ponies, his mother bear with her cubs, his birds that appear like epiphanies in various poems—a floating chicken hawk, a blue jay on a bending branch, an owl rising suddenly in the dark from the cutter bar of a hayrake; of James Dickey's animals in heaven and in "cage country" and his deer among cattle. A list of examples could go on and on.

Animals are plentiful and of great importance in Bly's poetry. He has said in an interview that "what is precious in poetry is the inwardness and the love of animals," and the conjunction of those two elements is not just coincidental. Some of his "tiny poems" on animals are superb—

The Loon

From far out in the center of the naked lake
the loon's cry rose...
it was the cry of someone who owned very little.

—and *The Morning Glory* particularly among his books, with
its many careful yet wildly imaginative descriptions, gets much
of its energy from the presence of animals. He has written beautiful elegies to them: "Looking at a Dead Wren in My Hand,"
"A Hollow Tree," "The Dead Seal Near McClure's Beach,"
"The Hunter." It is one of Bly's gifts in his poetry that he is
moved and excited by animals, fellow travelers on this planet
and in this stream of time, with us but not with us.

In *Silence in the Snowy Fields* Bly walked out alone late on
a summer night, and "a dark thing hopped near [him] in the
grass." That was probably a toad. The animals that figure most
importantly in Bly's poetry are not bears or lions or eagles; even
horses do not touch his imagination as persistently as less con-
spicuous, less glamorous creatures do. Like Theodore Roethke,
he is drawn to write about animals that inhabit crannies and low
places. Salamanders, caterpillars, turtles, moles, a starfish, an
octopus, the "tiny white shell-people on the bottom [of a tide
pool], asking nothing, not even directions!"—such as these appear often in his work, and insects also interest him a great deal.
I have noticed in particular a recurrence of ants, and I would like
briefly to look at three poems with an eye to the possible significance of the ants that crawl through them.

"In the Courtyard of the Isleta Mission," from *The Morning
Glory,* tells a story. Something strange happens in this New Mexico mission, now seemingly abandoned by the Church. Every
spring the coffins of the priests buried inside rise, an event the
people of the mission observe with reverence. Once a new priest,
a German, arrived to take charge of the mission. Apparently he
didn't like things to be too mysterious, for he said that the coffins rise only because of the water table beneath them and
ordered the ones that would not stay down reburied outside.

Before this could be done, however, the Indians carried him bodily away from the mission one night, dumped him along the road somewhere, and padlocked the church.

The ants appear in the paragraphs that precede and follow this story. They are described first "on the old flagstones... [trailing] after each other between a fireweed and a rock chip, as they did when the European friars awoke and walked here in the morning." That suggests nicely the steadiness of the animal universe carrying on below or beyond the level of human conflicts and changes, and also sets up a link between the human and the insect worlds: the ants and the friars both walking across the sun-lit stones of the courtyard seem oddly to resemble each other. Then after the German priest has been thrown out and we return to the present, Bly says, "Now the courtyard is left to the ants and the wind, and the priests rise and fall as they wish..."; then he makes a leap from the shadows on the adobe walls to "the airiest impulses we have," which he says will live "if we agree to put ourselves in the hands of the ants."

A strange statement. I am not sure which of our impulses are "airiest," though perhaps Bly is suggesting something beyond the reach of proofs, an area of faith, an openness to possibilities and mysteries that people such as autocratic priests oppose and repress. But it is the second part of the statement that jumps out. It's one thing to play with the pathetic fallacy, as Bly has long done, but isn't it going too far, isn't it sentimental or irresponsible to what it means to be human, to suggest that we should "put ourselves in the hands of the ants"? And what would it mean to do so anyway?

Obviously ants have been anthropomorphized and used in moral lessons for a long time. But is there any connection between us and the ants that has a deeper authenticity than that which a fable sets up?

In *This Tree Will Be Here for a Thousand Years* there is a six-line poem called "Ant Heaps by the Path." It begins with three lines, patented Bly, expressing pleasure at close perceptions of the ordinary, and then switches in the second stanza to a different sort of statement.

Ant Heaps by the Path

I love to stare at old wooden doors after working,
the cough the ant family makes in the ground,
the blackish stain around screwheads.

How much labor is needed to live our four lives!
Something turns its shoulders. When we do work
holes appear in the mountainside, no labor at all.

As with many of Bly's poems, a question that needs to be
dealt with here is the relationship among the parts. Typically,
the coherences within the poem are intuitive or associative rather
than rational. The first stanza is held together by the pleasure
felt, looking at those things, but more importantly by a criss-
crossing of associations, two half-submerged motifs: work and
doorways. The poet has just finished working, maybe physical
work, maybe writing; those old doors and their dark screwheads
represent work performed by someone many years ago; an ant
heap is both a kind of doorway and the product of enormous
amounts of minuscule, anonymous labor. (The word "cough" is
interesting. I think it is the compact roughness of the word that
makes it appropriate for describing an ant hill. Also there is perhaps an association with miners slipping in.)

Doorways are openings into other places, whether barns, underground tunnels, or parts of our lives and psyches. The poem
picks up something like this idea when it jumps to the "labor
. . . needed to live our four lives." The reference here is likely
to Jung's four functions. Then, suddenly, "something turns its
shoulders." The picture I get from this is of something out there
ahead of us, glancing back to see if we are coming. "When we
do work / holes appear in the mountainside, no labor at all."
Needless to say, we are not dealing with the Protestant Ethic
here, but something more subtle and joyous. Those holes could
possibly be made by that one out ahead of us, further up the
mountainside, perhaps by its walking stick; or possibly they are
the doorways of ant heaps, doorways to hidden corridors, which

while they are the result of intense work, from our perspective appear rather miraculously. The last lines suggest the way work not only accomplishes some immediate task, but is also involved with some much larger, longer labor, which we may someday find done without ever having consciously worked on it. They also describe the way work sometimes opens us up: the way effort, fatigue, and satisfaction can clear the mind, opening circuits that had become clogged with unused energy.

I've been following hunches with this poem, but I feel pretty sure that underlying it are the ideas that we are surrounded by work, some of it our own, some of it carried on without us yet still somehow connected with us; that outward work is connected with inward work; and that all of it is involved with a progress up a mountainside.

In his biographical essay "Being a Lutheran Boy-God in Minnesota"—a wonderful piece of writing—Bly makes an interesting comment in describing his father:

> He had a gift for deep feeling. Other men
> bobbed like corks around his silence, and around
> his swift decisions; that did not bring him more
> company, but did help carry the burdens higher
> up the mountain.

Bly uses the image of the mountain here naturally, assuming that it needs no explanation or justification. It's an old enough metaphor, but I don't think many modern writers would employ it instinctively as Bly does. In the Twentieth Century many people spend much of their lives wondering whether there is a mountain at all. This is called, among other things, alienation, despair, drifting, malaise, and cynicism. For Bly, the mountain exists, and I think his strong sense of the mountain in human life is connected with his attraction to the tiny mountains of ant heaps by the path.

In *This Body Is Made of Camphor and Gopherwood,* Bly's weirdest and most extravagant book, there is an enigmatic poem called "How the Ant Takes Part," which shares certain image patterns with the poem just discussed. Again there is a mountain, here with a climber "far up the mountainside," and again the mountain is juxtaposed with an ant hill. Also there is another turning of the face and shoulders. In both poems ants appear briefly, an image among several, yet in both cases the titles direct our attention toward them. The title "How the Ant Takes Part" goes further, and asks us to see the ant as part of some larger scheme. Since the subject of *Camphor and Gopherwood* is essentially the flow of energy itself within the body and the universe, the scheme would appear to be a very fundamental and far-reaching one.

The poem is a dream-like, sometimes ominous collage of images: a girl walking by water "near where we sleep," the mountain climber, the ant, a man and a woman between whom some division or tension has arisen, and finally "the bacteria [that] go in swarms through the ocean-salted blood." If the poem is a kind of collage, the main point is to sense the total effect created by the various pieces. The association between the climber and the ant is distinct, but other links are obscure and unsteady. In fact the last two images—the girl suddenly stirring the images or reflections in the water, and the bacteria swarming —both seem deliberately to set the poem swirling. The effect is cloudiness, jostling, but at the center of the poem is the ant, hurrying up his mound, carrying on his simple, mysterious business. The mountain climber is perilously high up on the mountain, "pick[ing] his way up the rocky scrap," but the other climber, the ant, moves quickly and sure-footedly. He is a small anchor, rushing about but reliable, within a complicated arrangement of levels, conflicts, and processes.

Human beings may ascend high up their mountainsides, may, for example, write *The Divine Comedy* or become martyrs for a belief. We also have relationships with one another (and within ourselves) which our complicated emotional natures often unravel or rip apart. We are spoken to in dreams. All of this, however, is supported by a vast world of relationships and agreements in nature. A single ant is a sign. Bly calls our attention to this world again and again in his poetry, and even in the difficult arc of images of "How the Ant Takes Part" he seems to be saying, "look down, look down."

In response to the question of ants and their possible connections to humanity, so far the leads we have come up with are that they do work, climb mountains, pass through dark doorways, and go about their lives with steadiness and perseverance—a part, no doubt, of "the life of faithfulness [that] goes by like a river, / with no one noticing it." In his essay on Wallace Stevens, Bly mentions that concentration on ants sometimes delivers a reminder that we will someday die. That intuition could be studied further, and I think it is related to the other ideas that have been emerging, as the awareness of death shadows all our thoughts about what our lives are and mean. But instead I want to try to get at a significance of ants in Bly's poetry by crossing a bridge from *Camphor and Gopherwood* to a different, related book.

The bridge is the dedication of another poem, with no less a title than "The Origin of the Praise of God": "for Lewis Thomas, and his *The Lives of a Cell*." Thomas's book deals with ants and other social insects a number of times, and two of its essays, "On Societies as Organisms" and "Social Talk," contain ideas that seem especially revealing with regard to an ant-human correspondence I sense running underneath Bly's poems.

Thomas is acutely aware of the resistance his fellow scientists, and people in general, have to comparing human beings to insects, "perfectly tooled but crazy little machines" that they are. But he continually pokes, delicately but firmly, at that resistance. He compares termites to artists, and scientists to termites. There is one link in particular that Thomas emphasizes which is also, I think, intimated in the poems. That is the idea of the Hill. Thomas says:

> What makes us most uncomfortable is that [the ants], and the bees and termites and social wasps, seem to live two kinds of lives: they are individuals, going about the day's business without much evidence of thought for tomorrow, and they are at

the same time component parts, cellular elements, in the huge, writhing, ruminating organism of the Hill, the nest, the hive.

I've mentioned Bly's natural use of the mountain to express his sense of human life and purpose. A serious, deeply felt action or decision helps to "carry the burdens higher up the mountain." But seeing an ant hill as an entity, an organism—what is the human equivalent of that, disregarding well-worn and mildly depressing comparisons to cities and our social organization? One possibility is evolution, and the evolution of consciousness in particular. If we take a long enough view, we can say that every time a human being makes a moral choice, or thinks carefully or brilliantly, or feels deeply, or makes a discovery through a microscope or a poem, the life of the hill of consciousness is maintained, possibly even extended. I suspect that one reason why Bly is as adventurous and energetic a writer as he is is that he has a strong sense of this hill. He knows he is working within something old and sprawling, so he follows his genius and hopes to contribute. This way of looking at things in general, and comparisons to ants in particular, may seem to crush individualism a bit, yet each ant, though not indispensable, is an amazingly strong, persistent, purposeful, and intense being.

In "Societies as Organisms" Thomas similarly compares the ants' hill to human awareness, conceived in terms of scientific knowledge, "the storage, processing, and retrieval of information." But in "Social Talk" he hits on another idea of what the Hill might be:

It begins to look, more and more disturbingly, as if the gift of language is the single human trait that marks us all genetically, setting us apart from all the rest of life. Language is, like nest-building or hive-making, the universal and biologically specific activity of human beings. We engage in it communally, compulsively, and automatically. We cannot be human without it; if we were to be separated from it our minds would die, as surely as bees lost from the hive.

. . . .

If language is at the core of our social existence, holding us together, housing us in meaning, it may also be safe to say that art and music are functions of the same universal, genetically determined mechanism. These are not bad things to do together. If we are social creatures because of this, and therefore like ants, I for one (or should I say we for one?) do not mind.

That may be a good point on which to end an essay on a poet. Conceived of as either consciousness or the language and art which express, extend, enrich, and sharpen it, the Hill is what our species has and labors on. It is a markedly different emphasis from that which thinks of art as a kind of existential stand or bid for immortality. Such a conception may in part account for an admiring fascination with ants. The poet, off in solitude, writing strange, haunting poems that probe and celebrate, that include war, religion, walks across fields at dusk, dreams, silence, hollow stumps, and animals, is engaged in the Hill's long work.

Howard McCord

Hunting Canaries With Robert Bly

I want the one, sd Robert
with the yellow eyes, the
eyes that wd be green if
his feathers were.

I nodded, and raised the net.

I wish I had irridescent
skin, he sd, so fingers
to fist wd be a rainbow,
or a trout in shallows.

Light alone is not
enough: refraction
is the elm root of light
breaking out toward summer

(This is the golem in the shadow
of the tree who speaks)

And in the spaces of the net,
Tezcatlipoca, the bird who
is a smoking mirror, defines
interstices.

He strokes its beak
and tells its eyes
be calm.

With Steve Mooney (center), editor of *Tennessee Poetry Journal* in Martin, Tennessee, 1969. Mooney is wearing an Indian amulet that Bly had just given him.

WILLIAM STAFFORD

Leif Sjöberg

The Poet as Translator:
Robert Bly and Scandinavian Poetry

What are we as readers entitled to expect from poets? Is it not enough that they manage to stay alive, despite unfavorable circumstances, cynicism, neglect, and ignorance on the part of critics, publishers, and the book-buying public? No, this is not enough! We expect lyrical outbursts, new insights, succinct presentations of new problems and glimpses of possible alternatives, fantasies, ecstasies, new ways of seeing things, and more. We demand that they charm, enlighten, liberate us, occasionally summon us to political action or remind us of lofty ideals. And more. We think it appropriate that they exhibit a rare awareness of the world within and the world without, worlds close by and worlds far away. But there is even more that we expect.

We want genuine poets not only to be masters of their mother tongue but also knowledgeable in other languages, at least in the major ones such as Spanish, German, French, or Russian. We like them to order foreign books, pay for them, take the time to read whatever good poetry there is, identify the best of it, then work through several drafts to finished translations. And we expect the poet-translator to maintain all the tonal values and interconnections of the original, to find equivalents when a word will not work in English, and also to sustain musical effects—the pitch, rhythm, dynamics, and register—while retaining the parallels and special effects, recognizing the hidden allusions, quotations, reminiscences, etc., etc. We ask that they treat the original, if not with awe and reverence, at least with respect and care and a measure of humbleness, before finally choosing any of the possible alternatives among the words and expressions at their disposal, trying to balance gains and losses, fidelity and infidelity, freshness and immediacy, the conventional and the unconventional. And more: some readers even insist that the poets who translate should also be scholars who make their versions poetical *and* scholarly editions, simultaneously.

And always we expect more.

*

But are poets also expected to know the "critical" languages, such as one or more of the five Scandinavian languages?

In Europe, where professors are of the "ordinarius" type (that is, *one* and *only one* per department), scholars are certainly not expected to translate modern foreign poetry. Perhaps no one would even want them to. Such unremunerative, supposedly insignificant chores are usually delegated to poets, those outside the university. In other words, to be properly introduced in, say, Sweden, an American poet will have to wait for the *initiative of another poet*—which often may involve a very long wait.

Even if Scandinavian publishers, especially the Norwegians, have a reputation for recognizing poetry as a slightly worthwhile activity, poetry in translation does not travel very fast. Before Roethke's death in 1963, there were only a few individual poems of his translated into Swedish. His friend and admirer, W. H. Auden, was more fortunate. He had one book of essays, one opera libretto (*The Rake's Progress* translated by Östen Sjöstrand), one play (*The Ascent of F6* translated by Erik Lindegren), and one selection of poetry (*Och i vår tid* translated by Petter Bergman) as well as numerous individual poems translated into Swedish before he died. In recent years tremendous efforts have been made by Swedish poets to introduce American poets in Sweden. Offhand I can think of these books: Bly's *Sleepers Joining Hands* (*Alla sovande i världen* translated by Eva Bruno), Gary Snyder's *Turtle Island* (*Sköldpaddsön* translated by Reidar Ekner), Lawrence Ferlinghetti's *A Coney Island of the Mind* (*Själens cirkus* translated by Thomas Kjellgren), as well as books by Jerome Rothenberg, Richard Brautigan, Kenneth Rexroth, Anne Sexton, Denise Levertov, Muriel Rukeyser, Sylvia Plath, Louis Simpson, Robert Hass, John Matthias, and many others.

In the United States, with several professors within the same department, there is fortunately sometimes room for a poet who might wish to translate a foreign poet writing in a "critical" language. This should be a positive situation, and it would be if only there were *more* competence and willingness to work for unknown, yet outstanding poets abroad. Of course, it would be much better if there were not what might be called a Gold Curtain preventing much worthwhile foreign poetry from appearing in English.

Among American poets who have taken on the often thankless responsibility of translating Swedes are W. H. Auden, Muriel Rukeyser, Judith Moffett, Rika Lesser, John Matthias, Yvonne Sandström, Siv Cedering, Thomas and Vera Vance, W. S. Merwin, Samuel Charters, Lennart Bruce, and others. But no one has been as efficient or determined at sponsoring Scandinavian poets in recent decades as Robert Bly.

*

Robert Bly makes his living not from university teaching, like most poets, but as a freelance. This means that in order to translate and promote Scandinavian poets he has had to donate his time and talents for a good purpose without any guarantee of adequate remuneration and attention. Yet he has helped win some international recognition for Swedish poets, among them Gunnar Ekelöf, Harry Martinson, and Tomas Tranströmer, with that invaluable book, *Friends, You Drank Some Darkness.* He has also championed Tranströmer's poetry in several books, the latest one being *Truth Barriers,* and Ekelöf's work in two books, *Late Arrival on Earth* and *I do best alone at night.*

Thinking of Bly's Swedish translations, a wonderful poem by Werner Aspenström comes to mind:

Fall

The shuffling mists, morning and evening.
The old oak stands there and coughs.
How easy it was to breathe during the days
The gold wagtails collected horsehair in the wild
    rose bushes.

Bly included his translation of this poem in his book of tiny poems, *The Sea and the Honeycomb*. Another successful translation is "Henhouse" by Harry Martinson, from *Friends, You Drank Some Darkness:*

Henhouse

The hens drift in early from the day's pecking.
They take a few turns about the henhouse floor
and arrange themselves according to who's the
    favorite.
Then, when all that is clear,
the leaping up to the roost begins.
Soon they're all sitting in rows and the rooster is
    present.
He tests out sleep
but there is to be no sleep right away.
The hens shove to the side and cause trouble.
He has to straighten them out, with his beak and
    a cawkle.
Now it's shifting and settling down.
One of the hens tries to remember the last worm
she caught today.
But the memory is already gone down,
on its way through the crop.
Another hen, just before she falls asleep, recalls,
the way the rooster looked, the white of her eye-
    balls fluttering,
her shutterlike lids closing out the world.

A fine example of Ekelöf's short poems in Bly's translation is "I do best alone at night":

> I do best alone at night
> alone with the secrets my lamp has
> set free from the day that asks too much
> bent over a labor never finished
> the combinations of solitaire. What then
> if the solitaire always defeats me
> I have the whole night. Somewhere
> a truth has been said once already
> then why worry? Can it ever
> be said again? In my absentmindedness
> I will listen to the wind in the night
> to the flutes of the Corybanths
> and to the speech of the men who wander forever.

Bly does not only translate the famous Swedes. In a recent article the Norwegian poet Jan-Erik Vold selected four Norwegian poetry collections from 1979 which he felt "communicated something permanently new"—the books by Einer Økland, Pål-Helge Haugen, Oskar Stein Björlykke, and Rolf Jacobsen. These are all outstanding Norwegian poets. But who has ever heard of them in America—even though they have made significant contributions—apart from a few Norwegian scholars in Madison, Wisconsin, and Minneapolis, Minnesota? The answer is: Robert Bly. Bly already has translated two of these poets, Pål-Helge Haugen and Rolf Jacobsen.

Perhaps two more samples of Bly's translations, from *Rolf Jacobsen: Twenty Poems,* will suffice to illustrate his prowess as a translator. In his lucid introduction to the book Bly compares Jacobsen to Antonio Machado, Theodore Roethke, and Thomas Hardy—no mean comparison. Not since I read Tarjej Vesaas' *Lóynde eldars land* (an American translation, *Land of Hidden Fires,* by F. Köning and J. Crisp is available) have I been so impressed and uplifted by a book of Norwegian poetry. There is a wealth of beauty and a rare kind of wisdom in Jacobsen's poems, especially in "Stave Churches," "The Age of the Great Symphonies," and "Towers in Bologna." Here is a poem called "Old Age":

> I put a lot of stock in the old
> They sit looking at us and don't see us,
> and have plenty with their own,
> like fishermen along big rivers,
> motionless as a stone
> in summer night.
>
> I put a lot of stock in fishermen along rivers
> and old people and those who appear after a long
>   illness.
> They have something in their eyes
> that you don't see much anymore
> the old, like convalescents
> whose feet are still not very sturdy under them
> and pale foreheads as if after a fever.
>
> The old
> who so gradually become themselves once more
> and so gradually break up
> like smoke, no one notices it, they are gone
> into sleep
> and light.

What a seemingly complete picture of a miniature world Jacobsen/Bly conjure up in "Country Roads," a poem about an ant starting to work at 4 a.m. on a June morning:

> A pale morning in June 4 A M
> the country roads still greyish and moist
> tunnelling endlessly through pines
> a car had passed on the dusty road
> where an ant was out with his pine needle working
> he was wandering around in the huge F of Fire-
>   stone

that had been pressed into the sandy earth
for a hundred and twenty kilometers.
Fir needles are heavy.
Time after time he slipped back with his badly
    balanced load
and worked it up again
and skidded back again
travelling over the great and luminous Sahara lit
    by clouds.

A wonderful poem and a fine translation.

*

With the reasonable and unreasonable expectations we may have of the poet as translator, can there be anything but failure, in the final analysis? Do we have to concede, with Benedetto Croce, that translation of poems is virtually impossible? At best it is a re-creation, a reflection of the original. These are questions that cannot, perhaps, be answered. There is no hiding that some of Bly's translations contain shortcomings; he makes surprising and unnecessary small errors. But it is senseless to nit-pick when you are given such a marvelous treat in general. And besides, in most of his books of translations, especially the Scandinavian ones, the originals and the English texts are on facing pages.

If we could only get Robert Bly to translate a Norwegian, a Danish, and a Finnish companion to the Martinson, Ekelöf, and Tranströmer book, in bilingual editions, it would be possible to teach courses in Scandinavian poetry! The best Norwegians, Danes, and, particularly, the Finns, are great. But is this merely wishful thinking? Are we again expecting too much? Especially from somebody who has found time to translate *Twenty Poems of Georg Trakl* (with James Wright), *Neruda and Vallejo* (with James Wright and John Knoepfle), *Lorca and Jiménez: Selected Poems, Rilke: Ten Sonnets to Orpheus, The Kabir Book: Forty-Four of the Ecstatic Poems of Kabir,* and so many other books of poetry and prose?

Although not perfect in his translation efforts, Bly has accomplished such publishing feats that he is a hero to many, not least in Scandinavia. It seems to be no exaggeration to claim, in Kenneth Rexroth's words, that Bly, as poet, editor of magazines, and translator, has become "one of the leaders of a poetic revival which has returned American literature to the world community."

With daughters Biddy and Mary in Norway, spring 1968. Bleie-land, Bly's
ancestral home, is across the cove in the background.

Translation Worksheets

Following are the working drafts of "Street Crossing," by the Swedish poet Tomas Tranströmer, which appeared in *Poetry East* #1. Bly worked through four versions of the poem, then sent the fourth to Tranströmer who responded with a letter commenting on "Street Crossing" and other poems that were later included in Bly's translation of Tranströmer's *Truth Barriers*. The final version and the Swedish original are reprinted here.

[1]

Cold wind in the eyes, several suns dance
in the cold's kaleidoscope of tears
as I cross the street so long with me
where the summer of Greenland shines from
    ponds.

The whole energy of the street seethes around me;
it remembers nothing and it wants nothing.
The unborn forest motionless for a thousand years
is waiting in the earth deep under the traffic.

I get the idea the street can see me.
Its eyes are so dim the sun
is only a gray ball of yarn in black space.
For this moment I shine! The street sees me.

[2]

Cold winds hit my eyes, and suns dance
in the kaleidoscope of tears, as I cross
this street so familiar,
where the Greenland summer shines from
    snowpools.

The street's energetic life swirls around me;
it remembers nothing and desires nothing.
Far under the traffic, deep in earth,
the unborn forest waits, still, for a thousand years.

I have the sense the street knows I am here.
It sees so poorly that to it the sun
is a gray ball of yarn in black space.
But for this instant I am lit! The street knows I
    am here.

[3]

The eyes receive a cold blast, and suns dance
in the kaleidoscope through tears, as I cross
this street I have known so long, a street
where the Greenland summer shines from
    snowpools.

The street's powerful life swarms around me;
it has no memories and no desires.
Far under the traffic, deep in earth,
the unborn forest waits, still, for a thousand years.

I have the sense the street knows I am here.
Its seeing is so shadowy the sun itself
is a gray ball of yarn in black space.
But for this instant I am lit! The street is aware
    of me.

Cold winds get my eyes, and suns dance
in the kaleidoscope of tears, as I cross
this street so familiar to me,
where the Greenland summer shines from
    snowpools.

The street's massive life swirls around me;
it remembers nothing and desires nothing.
Far under the traffic, deep in earth,
the unborn forest waits, still, for a thousand years.

I get the notion that the street can see me.
Its eyesight is poor, so that the sun
is a gray ball of yarn in black space.
But for a second I am in the light! It sees me.

(Sent to Tomas in a letter)

Västerås Dec 2nd —79
Dear Robert,
              again a little time for my own benefit (the martyr
is speaking), a small amount of time to sit down and talk about
Truth Barrier. Weather is gray, I don't feel healthy and Emma
has a crisis with her boy friend, which shakes the whole family.
How good to know that somebody over there takes trouble to
translate even

"Street Crossing"

                                which is untranslat-
able, so I give it to you—make whatever you can. I hesitate to
discuss it, I want to trust you. After all, you are a great poet in
English. BUT. I object to the last line. I want to have "But for
a second I am luminous (or lit, or shining). The street sees me."
In your version here "It" could as well mean "the sun." Or
even "the light." I don't know exactly what it means to "be in

the light,'' it sounds symbolic to me. If you insist on ''I am in the light,'' I can take it, but you must add ''The street sees me''. The line will be a little too long, but never mind.

''The Clearing''

Your secretary made a mistyping in line 2—instead of ''be found be those'' it should be ''be found by those''. The whole tone of your translation sounds like good Bly prose poem tone to me, I am happy for that. I have a few reservations though. ''The name sleeps somewhere'' should be plural: ''The names sleep'' etc... I think a whole family has been living in the house. I want to have ''the gypsy tribe'' instead of ''gypsy race''. ''Race'' is a difficult word to use, and in this connection I am not thinking of the gypsies as a race, but as a group with a tradition (non-literate tradition). ''This house, where the hired man lived''. OK I can understand that for some reason ''the croft'' is not the right word, but isn't it too much to explain it by saying ''where the hired man lived''? What is wrong with croft? Maybe you should say simply ''the simple house'' or ''little house''. Or ''The cottage''? Think it over. *There is a sentence missing.* After ''hums with voices'' comes a sentence: ''Det är världens centrum.'' (It is the centre of the world.) Did your secretary forget it? (Send my best to her, I hope to see her again soon.)

''First Chapter of a Late Autumn Novel''

I don't know the quality of the word ''reek''. Does it mean very bad smell? In that case I would like to have a more neutral word, like ''smell''. I don't like oil but I don't think it stinks. Don't forget to italicize the word ''is'' in the sentence ''if night really *is* something''. A point to discuss is the expression ''That world is also this one''. Maybe it's right. The last sentence: ''wonders'' is for me a little too positive, I want to have a word more in the monster direction. How is ''prodigies''? Good translation probably.

I just got the report from my tax authorities. I got an after taxation of 13.000 Swedish crowns ($3100), which should all be paid before May 1980. So I propose you look for a very generous publisher for *Truth Barrier!* The moment of truth has arrived. I write soon again. Let me hear something from you!

Love

Tomas

Övergångsstället

Isblåst mot ögonen och solarna dansar
i tårarnas kaleidoskop när jag korsar
gatan som följt mig så länge, gatan
där grönlandssommaren lyser ur pölarna.

Omkring mig svärmar gatans hola kraft
som ingenting minns och ingenting vill.
I marken djupt under trafiken väntar
den ofödda skogen stilla i tusen år.

Jag får den idén att gatan ser mig.
Dess blick är så skum att solen själv
blir ett grått nystan i en svart rymd.
Men just nu lyser jag! Gatan ser mig.

Street Crossing

Cold winds hit my eyes, and two or three suns
dance in the kaleidoscope of tears, as I cross
this street I know so well,
where the Greenland summer shines from
    snowpools.

The street's massive life swirls around me;
it remembers nothing and desires nothing.
Far under the traffic, deep in earth,
the unborn forest waits, still, for a thousand years.

It seems to me that the street can see me.
Its eyesight is so poor the sun itself
is a gray ball of yarn in black space.
But for a moment I am lit. The street sees me.

Translated from the Swedish
by Robert Bly

David Seal

Waking to "Sleepers Joining Hands"

Critics can be obsessed with tidying things up. When they interpret a particularly difficult poem, the urge to clean can result in a poem that looks like it has never been lived in. Like a bank at night, the poem becomes an empty and severe attempt to be friendly.

For some poems, however, this excessive orderliness is wrong. One such poem is Robert Bly's "Sleepers Joining Hands," a long poem of four parts in the volume of the same name, published in 1973. Charles Molesworth complained after *Sleepers* came out that it was largely ignored; regrettably, he was correct.[1] A few critics came to the aid of the reader, which is good because the poem is difficult, but the result was still to make the poem too clean.

What is deceptive about "Sleepers" is that it is clearly indebted to Jung. All four parts bear Jungian allusions in their titles alone. This of course brings the systematizers out in force. The briefest acquaintance with Jung reminds us that the process of individuation has four parts—persona, shadow, animus/anima, and Self—and it is clearly tempting to read the poem as a Jungian drama. This may even be the best way to begin reading the poem. As Martin Luther says, sin boldly. But it is not the proper destination. "Sleepers Joining Hands" is only apparently a Jungian drama. If we lift up the rug of individuation we'll find a lot of "matter out of place" (Mary Douglas's definition of dirt). I think the poem will ultimately be read more for what Bly swept under the rug than for the pattern he wove into it.

Briefly, there is a substantial part of "Sleepers" that cannot be made sense of by Jung's individuation scheme. Furthermore, this "matter out of place" is a quarrel precisely with the Jungian ideas that apparently dominate. And it seems to me that the poem is not "really" about this quarrel, but also about it. Bly consciously uses Jung, and unconsciously resists Jung. The poem, then, contains an unconscious conflict within itself. The critic's function is not to gain unity at the expense of a real, if subliminal conflict; nor is it to point to the conflict, label it some kind of pathology, and then dismiss it in favor of more normal poems. A good critic has to be part healer. The critic helps the reader (and in some cases even the poet) talk about the poem so that the interpretive process heals the wounds of the poem. The critic is both cleaner and healer because the poet's house, the poem, is both material and psychic. To imagine that poems can't be wounded is to indulge in a New Critical fantasy.

My strategy will be to read the four (actually five) parts of the poem with the Jungian frame in mind. I'll then concentrate on what I perceive to be the anomalies in the Jungian model of interpretation. The anomalies won't force us into a whole new paradigm, but they will make us complicate the old. The poem will come out of this a little messier, but I hope this also makes it more liveable.

II

Part One is titled, "The Shadow Goes Away." The poet begins by uttering fears of drowning, of being overwhelmed and eaten by sea monsters and predators. But these vague fears quickly reduce to a sense of loss, a loss both of a brother and of part of the self. Even in this brief tenure of the poem, we can feel the movement from all-encompassing terror through ambivalence to a dim perception of local guilt, immediate loss, the movement from anxieties known only by symptoms to the pathology of their cause. Repression is lifting. Consciousness realizes the extent of its loss, and takes its first steps in repair: it begins a search for its "shadow," and finds its signs everywhere. At first the search is directed toward the "Dark Peoples." But then the lines turn inward, to the enemies inside. The section ends with the consequences of internal troubles: hints of divorce, rape, incest, Napoleon's mulatto mistress framed against "the white dusk" all suggest sexual problems connected with projection, predation, religious rigidity. The huts of the "Shadowy People" that are destroyed suggest the military's predilection to project and prey upon the North America "owned" by Indians and upon Vietnam. It ends with the psychic consequence of shadow antagonism grinding on:

> My mother's bed looms up in the dark.
> The noose tightens,
> servants of the armor brain, terrified hired men
> whom the sharks feed,
> scales everywhere, "glittering on their bodies as
> they fall."
>
> The Sea of Tranquility scattered with dead rocks,
> and black dust resembling diesel oil.
> The suppressed race returns: snakes and transistors
> filling the beaches,
> pilots in armored cockpits finding their way home
> through moonlit clouds.

Clearly the shadow that goes away is related to Jung's concept of shadow. Jung argues that unless our social egos, our "personas," are connected to our unconscious energies, they dry up in routine, harden into set defensive postures. The first stage of the individuation process is the recognition that our personas cannot be purely consciously determined; that when they are, we "encounter" our unconscious as projections upon other people, which we erroneously interpret as their flaws. We have collective as well as individual shadows, and this first section of the poem explores the shadow problem in both areas: the loss of the poet's shadow, the loss of the national shadow, the consequences of both. It moves from mythological to historical time, ending in the contemporary allusions to Vietnam, with the mythological allusions abiding in the background, instead of the foreground, as in the beginning. The hardening of our national attitudes is caught by the reptilian imagery at the end, recalling Bly's essays in *Leaping Poetry*, where the equation is made between the primitive "reptile" part of the brain and paranoia and military reaction. But there is internal guilt as well, as is clear from the following lines:

> Walking through the camp, I notice an old chest
> of drawers.
> I open a drawer and see small white horses gallop
> away toward the back.
> I see the birds inside me,
> with massive shoulders, like humpbacked Puritan
> ministers,
> a headstrong beak ahead,
> and wings supple as a stingray's,
> ending in claws, lifting over the shadowy peaks.

The suggestion in these lines is the relation of predation and Puritan rectitude, but making that explicit barely captures the forces of the lines, which also, by suggestion, bury the heart under wads of muscle and deformity, connect the head to an instrument of carnivorous tearing, and yet give to that psychic murderousness the awful beauty of the stingray beating rhythmically over a Satanic landscape.

"The Shadow Goes Away" is, among other things, a poetic rendition of a Jungian concept. No problem here. If we stand back a little, we can see that it is part of a vein that Bly is mining in several places in the *Sleepers* volume, mainly in his other long poem, "The Teeth Mother Naked At Last," but also in the shorter pieces, "Condition of the Working Classes: 1970" and "Hair." Relative to the rest of its own poem, this part has more of a collective feel than anything except the chorus. While it has historical and mythical dimensions, it is basically Bly's attempt to place his political vein of poetry into a psychological context. The part of the psyche that this part of the poem concerns itself with is the persona, the more public, social part of each of us. Jung's ideas amplify the central poetic figure of the shadow; they give the psychic equivalents for the narrative events of the poem.

The next section, "'Meeting the Man Who Warns Me,'" is substantially different in mood, action, psychic landscape, from the first. It begins in a fairy tale setting: "I wake and find myself in the woods, far from the castle." The suggestion here is both that the first part's desultory search has become the more structured journey or quest, and that the wandering occurs in the unconscious, in the woods, far from the community. The context becomes more narrowly psychic, rather than domestic or political: "fragments of the mother lie open in all low places."

The poet falls asleep, and meets a man from a milder planet, Christ's. His circumcising touch is soporific. The encounter is a religious one, and the results are mixed: the fierce light of consciousness is won at the price of sexual energy. Christ energy denies cock energy, and puts the speaker in a sleep within a sleep, where he dreams of the dying of the fathers. The dying religious fathers serve to put transcendental religious energy back into its chthonic "grave" where it functions as "great conductors / carrying electricity under the ground." In the jump in imagery characteristic of Bly, the poem moves from subterranean electrical energy to subterranean water moving with great force. The poet senses his shadow underneath him, and then we find a locational shift: under transforms to inside.

> I taste the heaviness of the dream,
> the northern lights curve up toward the roof of
>   my mouth.
> The energy is inside us....
> I start toward it, and I meet an old man.
>
> [Bly's ellipses]

Jung speaks of the "Wise Old Man" as an archetype which occurs when a positive father complex produces a kind of credulity with regard to authority that has, ultimately, a spiritual cast.

From this father figure decisive beliefs, prohibitions, and wise counsel emanate.[2] Furthermore, he appears when the hero "is in a hopeless and desperate situation from which only profound reflection or a lucky idea—in other words, a spiritual function or an endopsychic automatism of some kind—can extricate him."[3] This old man in the poem is obviously "the man who warns me," and the warning first produces a hesitation in the poet. The old man then challenges him to speak or to go back. The speaker then confesses.

This confession is crucial, both to the section and the whole poem. It begins with the line, "I am the dark spirit that lives in the dark," showing that the shadow work has been done. His confession then recounts a quest, complete with a three-day immersion in the belly of a whale. Michael Atkinson comments brilliantly on the abruptness of the confession:

> When the protagonist pauses for breath and begins to account for his experience, the rendering is more startling; for it comes from a greater completeness, and a greater mythic awareness than either reader or dreamer knew he had. He begins by announcing his own shadow-including nature and proceeds to recount a mythical journey which neither we nor he knew he had taken.[4]

Some kind of unconscious transformation has occurred within. Its seeming gratuitousness is one way of showing how extended unconscious development quite suddenly rises up. The tongue finds itself saying what had only been dimly felt or dreamt.

It is clear that this confession closes off the second part of the Jungian scheme, as it demonstrates that the ego can do shadow work when it follows the increasingly bright guiding light of the Self. But the confession raises some issues that it doesn't resolve. If the poet already, even if unconsciously, possesses a kind of wisdom, what is the role of the Old Man? He merely prompts the telling of the quest. What seems to be a crucial encounter is actually anti-climactic. Second, the confession itself is dense, dream-like, highly "poetic." The point is not only that the speaker is startled by what comes out of his mouth. In Freud's terms, the lines the speaker speaks are already "secondary revision." Something is being hidden even as something else is revealed. We'll flag this part and return to it later. The poem shows symptoms here of bulging from something not said, although it has accomplished its shadow mission satisfactorily.

"The Night Journey in the Cooking Pot," the third section, is a rebirth, told in symbols that Jung had analyzed in *Symbols of Transformation*. As Atkinson says, it is an expanded version of the trenchant story the speaker tells to the old man. The opening lines move from mythical time to real, poetic time:

> I love the snow, I need privacy as I move,
> I am all alone, floating in the cooking pot
> on the sea, through the night I am alone.

Just as snow is transformed water, with a "solidtude" of its own, the speaker is a local version of the myth, finding in winter privacy an interior time and growth that makes the myth real in his life. The poet will move from mythic time to historical time, which is not so much national, as in the first section, as autobiographical, to real poetic time, where most of this section abides. The second group of lines, set off typographically by asterisks and indentations, is a kind of immersion in poetic time, so intense that it "forgets" the form that the poem is in and takes its own.

The "us" in this section is the union of the poet and his interior side, which Bly, following Jung, calls feminine. As he says in the essay in the *Sleepers* volume,

> All of my poems come from the Ecstatic Mother;
> everyone's poems do. Men in patriarchies try to
> deny the truth that all creativity lies in feminine
> consciousness; it is part of the fight with the
> Mother. But if the Mothers are immense force
> fields, then men are receiving magnets, who fly

about in inner space. The masculine soul in a woman is pulled in a similar way.

Jung said that the unconscious in general appears as feminine to a man, and is personified in dream or artistic images as a particular woman. Jung calls this function the anima; its complement for women is the animus, the masculine image that often pictures the woman's exterior bearing. For Bly, whose interior side is linked to mother consciousness, matriarchal thinking is intuitive and moves by leaps, and tends to favor the left side of the body, the feeling side. It writes poems; father consciousness revises them. Father consciousness thinks logically, controls "mammal nature" through rules, commandments, morality.

Given this polarity, it is not surprising to see "Night Journey" as a love poem, feeling-centered, bursting into moments of ecstasy, as a dancer sustains relevé for a sweeping instant before releasing. The poet has grown into joy:

For the first time in months I love the dark.
A joy pierces into me, it arrives like a runner.

The images are maternal, joy piercing, the baby whirling in the womb, "Nuns with faces smoothed by prayer." And the section itself moves into Mother Earth, as the poet follows the mouse down the hole, sees "owls with blue flames coming from the tops of their heads," and meditates on the dead who sleep in anguish in the earth. Once again the direction is downward, into the earth, which stands for a movement into the psyche that is part archaeological (to put it patriarchially) and part intuitive. Down there are

Men with large shoulders covered with furs,
eyes closed, inexplicable.
Holy ones with eyes closed,

The suggestion is that of meditation intensity. Just as meditation brings the poet onto the crest of present time, it also brings him into the timeless realms of the interior. Bly does not know which to prefer: the blackbird whistling, or the owls with blue flames coming from the tops of their heads.

The poet in his epiphanies has pierced the earth. But he must also return to the mundane, to himself, which can even be more dangerous than the journey outside the self. At first the ecstatic energy begins to swell in the body, and the poet sings and leaps about his room, "the happy genius of my own household," as Williams would say. The culmination is a love poem:

> I am not going farther from you,
> I am coming nearer,
> green rain carries me nearer you,
> I weave drunkenly about the page,
> I love you,
> I never knew that I loved you
> until I was swallowed by the invisible,
> my black shoes evaporating, rising about my
>   head....
>
> For we are like the branch bent in the water...
> Taken out, it is whole, it was always whole....
>
> [Bly's ellipses]

This is the emotional climax of the poem, not just of this section. In a moment we will see the ecstasy disintegrate, as it must for any of us fortunate enough to live it. Yet, as Kabir says in Bly's translation, "Kabir saw that for fifteen seconds, and it made him a servant for life." Ultimately the branch is whole; it will not break.

The reversal follows hard. The body is not up to the leaping the mind makes, and its clumsiness takes revenge. Since "body" is Bly's term of terms, we are located in his legacy, not the Platonic-Christian-Cartesian tradition which disparages the body. The poet ends up in a ditch, "wasting energy talking to idiots," while in mythical/historical time, King Herod "sends his wise men out along the arteries" to find the child and kill him. "Night Journey" ends in painful self-excoriations:

I sit down again, I hit my own body,
I shout at myself, I see what I have betrayed.
What I have written is not good enough.
Who does it help?
I am ashamed sitting on the edge of my bed.

We will need the calm of the first few lines of the next section to put this collapse in perspective. Then it will be clear that men laugh in their sleep even when one man, no matter that he figures centrally in the poem, sits on the edge of his bed in grief. The ecstatic moment of "Night Journey" is the climax of the poem, and as if to insure that it will stand as a thing in itself, Bly in a sense dissociates his own career from it.

But here again we note how much of the drama of this section goes beyond the Jungian scheme. All a treatment of the anima would require is the ecstatic moment, the union with the feminine. And if a dissolution of ecstasy were to continue along the anima lines, we would expect the Teeth Mother again, or some Stone Mother or Death Mother, to show us that the archetype is not merely salubrious but also dangerous. But the dissolution here does not proceed along those lines. In fact the major image, Herod and Christ, is masculine, not feminine. There is an autobiographical cast to this particular return from the psychic interior. In its particularity it constitutes no threat to the general scheme of moving into the interior. But it may alter our reading of this poem, for this poem is not merely a poetic validation of Jung. It is, to some extent—and we must determine how much—Bly's reworking of Jung. This is the second significant departure from the Jungian scheme. We will return to it later.

The fourth section, "Water Drawn Up Into the Head," resolves in one stroke the disparagements of the previous section, and draws us back in a phrase to the new community implied in the title of the whole poem: "Now do you understand the men who laugh all night in their sleep?" This establishes more firmly the ecstatic mood, which in each of us seems so transitory and fragile, but which is an undeniable reality in the community. The prose that follows, "Once there was a man who went to a far country to get his inheritance and then returned," is a root of many fairy tales and parables, and it is now more clear that the "far country" is inside. And the lines, "I am passive, listening to the lapping waves, / I am divine, drinking the air," show us the poet beginning to enlarge his utterance, speaking not merely privately but cosmically with the voice that will soon dominate in the "Extra Joyful Chorus."

The next group of lines begin the primary voice of "Water Drawn Up," and that voice is argument:

> We know the world with all its visible stars,
> earth, water, air, and fire,
> but when alone we see that great tomb is not God.

The lines seem to echo those at the end of Wallace Stevens's "Sunday Morning," but the sentiments are not quite the same:

> She bears, upon that water without sound,
> A voice that cries, "The tomb in Palestine
> Is not the porch of spirits lingering.
> It is the grave of Jesus, where he lay."

As J. Hillis Miller says, the lady in Stevens is left in a world of "exquisite particulars" larger than any interpretation of them,[5] while the man in Bly, who might agree that doctrine screens us from the exquisite particulars, will claim,

> So rather than saying that Christ is God or he is not,
> it is better to forget all that
> and lose yourself in the curved energy.

Like Stevens, Bly will reject the external world as the signature of God. Like Stevens, Bly will find doctrine a deadening influence. There is a hint of William Carlos Williams in the lines,

> We have no name for you, so we say:
> he makes grass grow upon the mountains,

which sound like they were written by a Psalmist who has read Williams. We can almost hear "no ideas but in things." But the following line takes us beyond Williams, and beyond pantheism:

> and gives food to the dark cattle of the sea.

Stevens could have written "Dark cattle of the sea," but he would not have made them the recipients of divine care. The argument of "Water Drawn Up" and its allusions are clearly meant to address what we will broadly call a "religious" issue all but abandoned in modern and post-modern poetry. There is a much stronger claim here than Stevens's "fictions which do not pretend to be more than fictions."

This may be seen most clearly in the final lines of the section:

> That is why I am so glad in fall.
> I walk out, throw my arms up, and am glad.
> The thick leaves fall,
> falling past their own trunk,
> and the tree goes naked,
> leaving only the other one.

In these lines we once again go beyond the naked trees of Williams, and while we move into a poetic fiction in the manner of Stevens, this is a fiction which asks to be taken as a metaphor, not as supreme fiction. They are lines which would claim to be not merely ultimately linguistic, but experiential. We are called by the final two lines to the great poem of Jiménez, "I am not I."

> I am not I.
>   I am this one
> walking beside me whom I do not see,
> whom at times I manage to visit,
> and whom at other times I forget;
> who remains calm and silent when I talk,
> and forgives, gently, when I hate,
> who walks where I am not,
> who will remain standing when I die.

"Water Drawn Up Into the Head" is unlike the previous parts of the poem. It is a congeries of argument, image-scenes, allusions, and metaphorical descriptions. There is virtually no action: no drama of discovery, no embodiment of psychic energy, no reversal of mood. That the water goes to the head and not the heart predicts argument. Some kind of mental wound has been healed by the unconscious. But while argument tends to dominate "Water Drawn Up," it is only a peroration. The pure poetry that ends the section has become an instance of the argument; it attains what the poem as a whole is aiming at. By "forgetting all that" and losing itself in the "curved energy" the poem repeats the larger drama noted by Jung in *Symbols of Transformation:* conscious attainments are sacrificed in order to let the unconscious well up and heal. By drawing upon poetic forebears, Jiménez and Kabir, Stevens and Williams, Bly is able to heal not strictly by argumentative claims but by affective metaphor.

Jung's fourth and final stage in the individuation process is Selfhood, and this fourth section of the poem clearly is indebted to this concept. Recalling Jung's treatment of Christ as an individual instance, perhaps the very paradigm, of Selfhood, we are better able to understand the following Bly lines:

> We know of Christ, who raised the dead, and
> started time.
> He is not God, and is not called God.

Clearly Bly is plowing conventional theology back under, hoping that debates over orthodoxy can be forgotten and attention turned toward interior energies. By the end of this section the interior energy has become a being:

> There is another being living inside me.
> He is looking out of my eyes.
> I hear him
> in the wind through the bare trees.

The gladness of the final lines shows the poet in touch with his

Self. The Christ emblem of the archetype of Self has been bent into a particularity that meets the needs of the poem. If the crucifixion is the outstanding example of sacrificing conscious attainments in order to make way for the healing work of the unconscious, then its poetic analogue is surrender of the Self, the very thing we have fought so hard to attain. And so the end of the section on Self is appropriately death—but death as transformation. As the ego surrenders to Self, so Self surrenders to "the other one." "Otherness" is working as a signifier here: relative to ego, otherness is Self; relative to Self, it is the release in death of "the other one." Selfhood includes its own end, even if that end is only relative to our particular human estate.

Appended to the poem, and obviously a break from the stable quaternity of sections, is "An Extra Joyful Chorus for Those Who Have Read This Far." Atkinson reminds us that the long lines of this chorus recall Whitman, even as the title of the whole poem, "Sleepers Joining Hands," reminds us of Whitman's "The Sleepers," and that both poets work within the tradition of the psychic quest.[6] The reader is also implicated in the quest. All the Whitmanic "I am"'s that Bly borrows are not autobiographical, but typical, the kind a reader can try on, as the title encourages him to do. Bly's "I am"'s play out over not only a physical landscape, where empathy and identity become the poet's tools as in Whitman, but also over a psychic landscape, where empathy must be extended to forms of the Self. Indeed, Bly's "I am"'s have a mythological cast to them recalling the powers of Proteus and Jove to become serially the forms of Creation.

The final tercets drop the first person singular for the plural of community, but do so in lines that are clearly and beautifully Bly's:

> Our faces shine with the darkness reflected from
>   the Tigris,
> cells made by the honeybees that go on growing
>   after death,
> a room darkened with curtains made of human
>   hair.

The panther rejoices in the gathering dark.
Hands rush toward each other through miles of
    space.
All the sleepers in the world join hands.

The Miltonic oxymoron of the first line is both part of the conceit of the whole poem and part of a poetic tradition. The poem means to explore, not the light around the body, but the light inside, a special kind of light that tumbles paradoxically into its opposite. This first line remembers the fireball floating in the corner of the Eskimo's house, the owl with blue flames, dark bodies on the horizon trailing lights, the moonlit villages of the brain, the light that makes the flax blossom at midnight. Its oxymoronic nature owes much to Milton, while the enormity of the reversal implied by the conceit, it being the product not of clever wit but of consciousness plowed under, borrows not a little from Blake. And the buried nature of the image, the fact that it is meant to work not on our wit but on our unconscious, owes much to Coleridge, who, in *Biographica Literaria,* reminds us that

> But again; of all intellectual power, that of superiority to the fear of the invisible world is the most dazzling. Its influence is abundantly proved by the one circumstance, that it can bribe us into a voluntary submission of our better knowledge, into suspension of all our judgment derived from constant experience, and enable us to peruse with the liveliest interest the wildest tales of ghosts, wizards, genii, and secret talismans. On this propensity, so deeply rooted in our nature, a specific *dramatic* possibility may be raised by a true poet, if the whole of his work be in harmony: a *dramatic* probability, sufficient for dramatic pleasure, even when the component characters and incidents border on impossibility.[7]

Coleridge's claim works two ways: he reminds us of the extent to which this effect is consciously shaped as a work of art; but he also reminds us of our "propensity" to suspend knowledge and common sense, that the very power of poetry is to work subliminally. Today, with our heritage of Freud, Jung, and beyond we might state the case even more strongly: it is precisely the physical impossibility of dogma, religious or poetic, that helps the imagination grow, not randomly but in defined ways. This is the core of a conceit which reverses not merely poetic convention but even the psychological conventions of Freud and Jung. It is not darkness that has now been made visible—the id dredged up and tamed by the ego, or even the shadow brought into union with the self—by the light of consciousness. Instead it is a deepened consciousness that learns to see the way in which darkness shines. When our faces shine with that darkness we are at last on our way to an Edenic recovery.

If the first line in the first tercet recalls the conceit upon which the whole poem is built, the succeeding two lines reinforce by means of parallels the mood of the first line, and extend the psychic location beyond death. It might be confusing to treat the lines eschatologically, for they primarily refer to psychic phenomena: the King is dead, long live the King; the hero dies and is reborn; the ego dies to itself and is transformed. But the words "darkness," "darkened," and "dark" remind us that death at least means the absence of light, whether psychic or physical death is meant.

If the first tercet draws the curtains, the second moves behind them with joy. Some fierce but beautiful animal part of our psyche feels joy at the same time that the human part wants to share the joy. "All the sleepers in the world join hands." We may ultimately find this line to be more than a metaphor. But for now it is enough to see what Bly has done poetically. If Stevens awakened us to the morning of a new day, Bly puts us into a special kind of sleep in the evening of a new night.

III

Reading "Sleepers Joining Hands," whatever its excellences, is an arduous task. Any reading of it ought to take caution from Bly's own difficulties in writing it. In one interview he recalled that "Sleepers" has 480 lines in it although he wrote about 5000 lines for it, "of which 4500 were written by some other part of me, or by my memory—they didn't have the tone!"[8] In another interview he said that "I didn't know what the poem was about so I worked in confusion for four years."[9] But with a provisional reading under our belt, we can draw closer to the peculiar powers and limitations of the poem, to its dark as well as its light side. In particular, we should return immediately to those two instances that seem to flow over the edges of their Jungian containers. It is apparent that the poem as a whole is deeply indebted to Jung's fourfold individuation scheme. But significant departures from it may force us out of the easy chair of systematics and onto the hard floor of the poem itself.

The title of the second section, "Meeting the Man Who Warns Me," signals a dramatic encounter. "Warning" arouses the reader's expectations: clearly danger is present, and the art of warning is nothing if not an attempt to be brief and yet salient at one and the same time. The warning clearly is brief:

"Who is this who is ascending the red river?
Who is this who is leaving the dark plants?"

A few lines later the old man "cries out":

"I am here.
Either talk to me about your life, or turn back."

What begins as interrogation ends abruptly as imperative. The mood grows more severe, and despite the initial density of "red river" and "dark plants," which suggests a movement upward toward greater consciousness, what the two passages have in common is the issue of identity, or more exactly, autobiography.

The demand for autobiography produces the following:

> "I am the dark spirit that lives in the dark.
> Each of my children is under a leaf he chose from
>   all the leaves in the universe.
> When I was alone, for three years, alone,
> I passed under the earth through the night-water,
> I was for three days inside a warm-blooded fish.
> 'Purity of heart is to will one thing.'
> I saw the road...." "Go on! Go on!"
> "A whale bore me back home, we flew through
>   the air....
> Then I was a boy who had never seen the sea!
> It was like a king coming to his own shores.
> I feel the naked touch of a knife,
> I feel the wound,
> this joy I love is like wounds at sea...."
>
>   [Bly's ellipses]

This confession is a game of hide-and-speak. It acts like a dream: there are some nuggets of factual residue, but most of the images are symbolic, presenting a picture of a poetic career elliptically. Bly did live alone for three years; he was a young Minnesota farm boy when he graduated from high school and joined the navy. There are allusions to his teachers: Whitman, Machado, Kierkegaard. There is a mythological allusion to Jonah, and the fairy tale plot of the return of the king. But most important are the opening and closing lines. The opening line shows us that shadow work has been done, this being the major theme of the second section. But it also suggests that the confession is of the dark. This is an important claim. But to understand its significance, we must turn to the last lines.

The knife wound is the cut of consciousness, wounds which identify the hero with the sacrificial wounds sustained by gods, wounds which, in particular, as Jung shows, deliver the body up out of the maternal thrall and into a spiritual dimension. As Jung argues in the closing chapter of *Symbols of Transformation*, mother-libido must be sacrificed in order to create the world. The fear of incest, and deeper fear of being devoured, can cut itself loose from the maternal embrace and return to the surface of consciousness with new possibilities.[10] This is the spiritual rebirth that we know of in many religions, and in many forms. Jung goes on to argue something which has a substantial bearing for this part of the poem. He argues that the essential motive of the sacrificial drama is the unconscious transformation of energy. Now we know why, in Atkinson's terms, the speaker did not know what sort of a journey he had taken until he opened his mouth. And Jung concludes by saying that this process of transformation goes on in the unconscious whose contents are unknown but become visible indirectly to the conscious mind by stimulating the imaginative material, "like dancers clothed in the skins of animals."[11]

In the terms of the poem, some kind of unconscious transformation had occurred in the poet. Meeting the old man provided an occasion for that transformation to manifest itself. The point is not simply, as Atkinson would have it, that the speaker is startled by what comes out of his mouth, as if, once spoken, it is thereby understood by the speaker himself. In Freud's terms, the lines the speaker speaks are already "secondary revision." Something is being hidden even as something else is revealed. As in a dream proper, we must read back through the images to the "dreamwork" which assembled them. The speaker is speaking deliberately in dreamlike or mythical statements. To put it in another way, the poet is speaking particularly densely at a moment when, dramatically, the poem is promising something not merely conscious but saliently conscious. What we are given is an unconscious *fait accompli*. To sum up, perhaps the speaker is not simply representing an unconscious experience he has had; perhaps his lines also still are in themselves a piece of the unconscious of the poem.

Before probing into the dream-work of this particular passage, let us be sure of where we stand. At a place in the poem where the reader expects something both dramatic and clear, we find neither. The episode is not dramatic because there is no collision or even significant confrontation between the old man and the speaker. True, the old man prompts a confession of sorts, but one which implies that all the essential psychic work has already been done. The old man is in some way superfluous. He does not give wise counsel. He merely produces an opportunity to speak. The speaker upstages him. Second, the episode is not clear. The confession is dream-like and obscure. After all, this is our speaker's first major utterance. Quite obviously, he is speaking from the dark. What does that imply?

One thing it does imply is a burden on the reader. That in itself is neither unfair nor new these days. It's part of the fine print in the poet's contract with readers. If we are to make sense of the dense lines and truncated action of the second section, we'll have to read the lines as possible symptoms of some other conflict, something trying to be said at the expense of what is apparently being said. We'll have to range beyond "Sleepers Joining Hands" as well, but we won't have to go far.

The place to start looking for signs of the poem's dream-work is in the passage a little before the encounter with the old man. There is great movement in the lines that follow the passage about the fathers dying and precede the group which speaks of the integration of the shadow. It is worth quoting them in their entirety:

> Who is this that visits us from beneath the earth?
> I see the dead like great conductors
> carrying electricity under the ground,
> the Eskimos suddenly looking into the womb of
>   the seal. . . .
> Water shoots into the air from manhole covers,
> the walker sees it astonished and falls;
> before his body hits the street
> he is already far down the damp steps of the
>   Tigris,
> seeing the light given off under the door by
>   shining hair.
>
> [Bly's ellipses]

The subject of these lines is "water under the earth,'" and appropriately enough there is a poem in the *Sleepers* volume with that title. It is about how much is moving deep in the unconscious, and how much must still come out:

> Oh yes, I love you, book of my confessions,
> when the swallowed begins to rise from the earth
> again,
> and the deep hungers from the wells.
> So much is still inside me, like cows eating in a
> collapsed strawpile
> all winter to get out.
> Everything we need now is buried,
> it's far back into the mountain,
> it's under the water guarded by women.
> These lines themselves are sunk to the waist in the
> dusk under the odorous cedars,
> each rain will only drive them deeper,

A few lines further the poet says, "I see how carefully I have covered my tracks as I wrote." And later still: "So much is not spoken!" The poem "Water Under The Earth" makes explicitly clear the link in Bly between the image of water moving under the earth and repression, the not-said. It is possible that "Water Under the Earth" is an out-take from the "Sleepers" poem, and possible that it fits right here. At least it is a close cousin. It also seems to have a blood-connection to the earlier lines in "Meeting the Man Who Warns Me" on the deaths of fathers, for we find the following lines:

> I see faces looking at me in the shallow waters
> where I have thrown them down.
> Mother and father pushed into the dark.

And the final group of lines of the "Water" poem read,

> There is a consciousness hovering under the
> mind's feet,

advanced civilizations under the footsole,
climbing at times up on a shoelace!
It is a willow that knows of water under the earth,
I am a father who dips as he passes over underground rivers,
who can feel his children through all distance and
time!

This restates the chthonic theme, and tells us that the energy under the earth is civilizing. But more important is the father theme. In the above first instance, the father is repressed. In the second, he has been assimilated. Yet in "Meeting," the fathers die out, and when the water moves swiftly under the earth, what results is not the father, but the old man, a spiritual father figure. The relative paucity of the old man's contribution tells us that the father archetype behind the poem has not entirely surfaced. Yet there is great energy present, shadow-retrieving energy: water shoots into the air, the walker is swept away. And the occasion for this burst of energy is the immediately preceding reflection that "the fathers are dying."

Granted, the speaker in "Meeting," like the speaker in "Water," has somehow become a father to himself. But the salient point in "Meeting" is that the process is repressed, "not spoken," and its very absence becomes an important part of the drama of "Meeting." The poet who "passed under the earth through the night-water" has chosen not to speak of the cause of the transformation. There is something invested in keeping the father conflict from fathering openly the poet's first utterance.

As is often the case with an unresolved conflict, it will surface again. The third section, "The Night Journey in the Cooking Pot," is largely about the poet's union with his feminine side. This anima encounter is part of the psychic quest toward Selfhood. In particular it is identified with art, with the Muses, with writing poetry. The anima encounter, in this poem as well as in experience, is a typical experience. It may be rare, but in principle it is available to all.[12] "Night Journey," however, does not content itself with the typical; it goes beyond that into autobiographical particularity. Here the poet is not generic but individual, Robert Bly, and the action that is represented is the falling out of the ecstatic state, the self-perception of his limitations and failures, the grief of not being good enough. We have already claimed that this autobiographical part, even if seen as failure, does not damage the integrity of the ecstatic state, the union with the feminine.[13] But at this point it is appropriate to investigate the causes of the parting from the Ecstatic Mother. It at least has autobiographical pertinence, and may help us read the poem more accurately.

Just when the poet cries out that he sees the road ahead, the wholeness of things, the body takes revenge and brings the poet back to earth, literally into the ditch. In an excellent essay on Bly's attempts to domesticate religious ecstasy, Charles Molesworth notes that, for Bly, the body becomes the 'field of consciousness' within which ecstasy can become divine. "What Bly's religion does is to substitute the body for the soul as the privileged term in the traditional body-soul dichotomy. (The negative term then is not soul, but conscious rationality.)"[14]

> I think I am the body,
> the body rushes in and ties me up,
> and then goes through the house....
> [Bly's ellipses]

Here the "negative term" is clearly getting its comeuppance. The group of lines that follows this sense of shame and clumsiness jumps into historical / mythical time: King Herod orders his wise men to find and kill the child, saying that "There cannot be two rulers in one body." Jung has suggested that Christ is, among other things, an image of the Self, while the king is a symbol of the ego or persona. So we have here a regression, an attack on the emerging sense of self by the old self, old habits, weaknesses, postures. The scene of battle is "in the old moonlit villages of the brain":

> The mind waters run out on the rug.
> Pull the mind in,
> pull the arm in,
> it will be taken off by a telephone post.

The first line foreshadows the resolution of the next section, where water will be drawn up into the head. But here the mind has overflowed (Jung would say inflated), as if to say that for the poet, the old ego was a kind of mental king who armed himself intellectually against the body, against the unconscious. "I think I am the body." The fault is the former's, not the latter's. Oddly enough, a childish fragment, like Eliot's nursery rhymes in "The Hollow Men," warns of the danger.

What we have here is a sub-plot that nearly becomes dominant. The action for most of "Night Journey" is internal, and we do not ever find personified projections such as the shadow or The Wise Old Man. The anima, for instance, is not personified as a woman, merely as the grammatical "you." Only when the body severs itself from the speaker does the action become external, and that suggests immediately a masculinization of the problem, for if in Jung's terms the interior is feminine, then the movement to the exterior is typically masculine. Furthermore the quarrel of poet and body is not a lover's quarrel. It is a quarrel among men, principally among rulers. Finally, the cause lies in the thinking function: "I think I am the body" is a mental error; "There cannot be two rulers in one body" is a mental rule, "Pull the mind in" is the child's prescription for a cure. Why the shift in images from feminine to masculine, from the feeling function to the thinking function? To resolve this, we must return to "the old moonlit villages of the brain."

The context of King and Divine Child suggests the nature of the dispute. Historically this is Herod and Christ, but mythologically it is a Saturn dispute, the King-Father determined to kill his Successor-Son. Saturn, we recall, killed his father Uranus, and then devoured his children in turn, all but Jupiter, who grew up in secret, protected by a strategem of his mother Rhea. Jupiter then dethroned Saturn, but instead of killing him, he allowed Saturn to become the God of Harvests: the devourer ironically becomes a patron of food.

Saturn may be more than the presiding god of the Herod-Christ conflict; he may preside over the fall out of the ecstatic state as well, at least in this particular case. If the King is rising up against the new interior Self, his analogue in the struggle is the mind, which has become inflated, presumptuous, hardened, jealous of the ecstasy not of the body but of the psychic body. And the fact that the struggle is occurring here, at this point of the poem, suggests something more disturbing: a quarrel with the Jungian scheme that provides the structure of the poem. The quarrel is not open, external, but "along the winding tunnels, into the mountains." Characteristic of projection, the action becomes external exactly when the wounds are dimly perceived to be internal. The poem seems to recognize that Jung's very scheme is too mental for its own life. And so the ecstasy dissolves in a quarrel with the scheme itself. But perhaps most importantly, the quarrel is hidden, repressed, kept in the dark. It is camouflaged by the autobiographical excoriations.

IV

To argue for two anomalies in the Jungian model of interpretation of "Sleepers Joining Hands" is just a way of letting the poem speak for itself against attempts to leash it to some doctrine. Poems are made things, not philosophical or psychological press-agents. And yet to argue that such anomalies are bits of unconsciousness is clearly to personalize the poem, to make it more the creature than the creation.

The interpreter accedes to such charges, but only because of faith in the interpretive process. Some problems in poems are clearly flaws, mistakes, inanimate cleavages, chips, scratches, what have you. Other mistakes, however, speak from the unconscious of the poet, and have not succeeded in congealing and separating themselves from the poet's psyche: unintended entendres, pathological twists in the plot, indeed, all the literary versions of the psychopathology of everyday life. In these instances, and only these, does the interpreter function as therapist: he provides the occasion whereby what can't be said, what can't be said directly, what can be said but not felt, and so on, can be said effectively and affectively. The interpretive process explains and understands, but must also on occasion heal.

In "Sleepers Joining Hands," there are two such instances where the poem is trying to say something that its general form does not permit. The encounter with the Old Man is either dramatically deficient, if the Old Man's scaring into consciousness is truly necessary, or it is dramatically superfluous, if the poet already has done his psychic shadow work and knows himself. If the Old Man is instrumental to the telling, not the doing, then a second, largely subliminal theme is emerging: the development of the poet apart from the speaker's development of Selfhood. The speaker's Selfhood is bound up with becoming a poet, even though the poem is also about anyone becoming his or her Self, regardless of whether that Self includes being a poet.

A second anomaly occurs in the third section, "The Night Journey in the Cooking Pot." Recall that the journey into the unconscious is what is being referred to, and following Jung, who personified the unconscious as feminine—hence the womb-like cooking pot as vehicle—the movement of this section will require a journey into the anima and a return from it. That is exactly what happens. As is often the case, the journey into the unconscious leads to moments of ecstasy, while the return can lead to decompression sickness, psychic bends, which in this case was the poet's self-blame and even self-pity—the line "Who does it help?" is the one moment when self-pity overcomes what otherwise is genuine remorse. So far, so good. But the particular nature of the poet's grievances against himself—the psychic inflation, whose perverse charms are largely intellectual, the masculine imagery of infanticide—suggest either that the quarrel is on the masculine side or has been shifted there from the feminine, more feeling side by intellectualizing. Furthermore, there is no content to the quarrel. That is precisely the reason for the hypothesis that the "mind waters" running out on the rug contain the repressed father or spiritual father.

It is my claim that the poem itself has a kind of unconscious conflict occurring within it, the perception of which must alter not only our notions about this poem but also a little about reading poems in general. To say that poems have an unconscious is a risky claim. On the one hand, those of the New Critical persuasion or habit of mind see the poem as all consciousness, and not only of its tenor but of its vehicle as well. A perfect poem is so rounded and glassy that no unconscious cracks or holds can be found. On the other hand, the Deconstructionists see a poem all too often as a field for their own projections, a kind of unconscious Eliza Doolittle waiting to be made over into an appropriate Fair Lady—all too often the critic's anima, and not an independent woman. If we can tread somewhere in between, admitting that a poem may not totally know itself, but recognizing too that it doesn't want to become us or our dream of it, we might be able to enhance our sense of what is going on—and perhaps our appreciation of its aims, achievements, or both.

"Sleepers Joining Hands" is a poem about a journey into the interior of the psyche. The journey has definable stages and predictable ends, and knowing Jung makes this clear. But the poem is also in conflict with itself, on precisely this issue: it is in conflict with the source of its scheme. To put it mildly, the poem has some ambivalence about Jung. The poem's ambivalence may reflect the poet's. Bly does say that this poem is autobiographical.[15]

To borrow the poem's terms, the Old Man in "Meeting the Man Who Warns Me" is Jung. He is more than Jung, but still Jung in part. Bly says in the essay in *Sleepers,* "I don't expect these ideas to help writers write better poems, nor should anyone examine my own poems for evidence of them, for most of my poems were written without benefit of them." In these terms, then, Bly had already, although unconsciously, arrived at the knowledge that Jung gives. The Old Man does act as a "Transformer," for he forces the unconsciously won knowledge up into the mouth of the speaker, where it emerges as poetry, not merely as testament to an archetype. This raises an immediate question: to what extent should Bly use Jung, if the psychic journey has been made unconsciously without him? Should he use the Jungian scheme or make up his own, one faithful to his own development? If so, will he stand to lose the small plurality of readers Jung has already won? Or, on the other hand, is this transforming moment more crucial than we think? If the latter, perhaps we ought to change our reading of Jung, and see him less as intellectual—whether you use the terms "psychologist," "scientist," "prophet," or "critic of mass man"—and more of a shaman figure, a sort of Socrates in touch with his feminine side. And again even if this is the case, then the encounter in the poem between the Old Man and the speaker ought to be more explicit, as well as more dramatic. The shaman's arts and wiles must be more than mechanical, although no doubt less than totally exposed.

Bly decides to use Jung, but this does not resolve the dilemma. By making Jung the spiritual father in "Meeting," but depriving him of any power other than that of prompter, the old Cronus/Saturn castration temptation is at work. By allowing the individuation scheme to govern the poem overtly, Saturn is put out to pasture with apparent honor. Bly, then, feels both halves of the father dilemma: castration/murder on the one hand, honor and tenure on the other. The poem manages to wound the spiritual father and do him some homage anyway. That both could be done without buckling the whole frame of the poem is a tribute to the control Bly had on it. But that it still bulges the poem in two places suggests that another poem is trying to be written. Perhaps it is yet to be.

Because of the more public and inclusive nature of the fourth and fifth parts, "Water Drawn Up Into the Head" and the "Extra Joyful Chorus," the conflict between Bly and Jung within the terms of the poem has little room to grow. "Water Drawn Up" is by turns lyric and didactic, but in either case the issues are no longer intra-Self, but rather the Self's role relative to God and death. The Chorus, which must perhaps be called "extra joyful" because it senses something wrong underneath and so must compensate, turns to Whitman's typicality as a way of invoking a poetic communion that the more intellectual communion of Jung may not achieve: Besides, the speaker all along has aspired to poetry, and here he is turned loose. He has earned it. Furthermore, the journey into Self must bring a sense of community if it is to be of any value at all—otherwise its knowledge is solipsistic. And the whole force of the title militates against solipsism.

It is the second and third sections, then, that disrupt the wholeness of the poem. There is a tension with Jung that mars in particular the autobiographical third section. But rather than calling these flaws in the poem, and perhaps dismissing it, it may serve us better to call them wounds and dress them. As James Hillman reminds us, "Healing comes then not because one is whole, integrated, and all together but from a consciousness breaking through dismemberment."[16]

It is enough to suggest here that "Sleepers Joining Hands" has a kind of Manichean tension to it: its light parts honor Jung and require background in his ideas; its dark parts struggle against those ideas in ways we have called "unconscious." "Sleepers" is both a poem about the psychic journey into our interior, and about one poet's implicit resistance against his guide. In the long run the latter, inchoate part may be of more interest to the reader of Bly's poetry.

Notes

[1] Charles Molesworth, "Thrashing in the Depths: The Poetry of Robert Bly," *Rocky Mountain Review of Language & Literature,* Vol. 29 (1974), p. 104.

[2] C. G. Jung, "The Phenomenology of the Spirit in Fairy Tales," in *Psyche and Symbol* (Anchor, 1958), p. 69.

[3] Jung, pp. 72-3.

[4] Michael Atkinson, "Robert Bly's *Sleepers Joining Hands:* Shadow and Self," *Iowa Review,* Vol. 7:4 (Fall 1976), p. 143.

⁵ J. Hillis Miller, *Poets of Realtity* (Atheneum, 1974), p. 222.

⁶ Atkinson, p. 150.

⁷ S. T. Coleridge, *Biographia Literaria,* in *Selected Poetry and Prose of Coleridge,* ed. Donald A. Stauffer (Random House, 1951), p. 405.

⁸ Robert Bly, *Talking All Morning* (University of Michigan Press, 1980), p. 136.

⁹ Bly, p. 280.

¹⁰ C. G. Jung, *Symbols of Transformation* (Princeton University Press, 1967), p. 420.

¹¹ Jung, *Symbols,* p. 430.

¹² Jung thought that the unconscious of a woman had a largely masculine imprint. He called this the animus, and it corresponded to the feminine anima for men. He admitted that both were "intuitive concepts" and refused to define them too specifically. See "Aion," p. 13, in Jung, *Psyche and Symbol.* For our purposes here, poetry is identified with the feminine whether it appears in men or women.

¹³ See Bly's essay, "I Came Out of the Mother Naked," in *Sleepers Joining Hands* (Harper and Row, 1973) for Bly's version of Neumann's fourfold approach to Mother Consciousness. Bly links poetry with the Ecstatic Mother, the archetype of, among other things, the Muses.

¹⁴ Charles Molesworth, "Domesticating the Sublime: Bly's Latest Poems," *Ohio Review,* Vol. XIX: 3 (Fall 1978), p. 64.

¹⁵ Bly, *Talking,* p. 257.

¹⁶ James Hillman, "Puer Wounds and Ulysses' Scar," *Puer Papers* (Spring, 1979), p. 117.

DAVID ROBENS

At the Mother Conference, Tanglewood Island, Oregon, June 1979.

William V. Davis

"At the Edges of the Light":
A Reading of Robert Bly's
Sleepers Joining Hands

Robert Bly's early poetry moved from the simple, lovely lyrics of *Silence in the Snowy Fields* (1962) to the outspoken, hate-filled diatribes of *The Light Around the Body* (1967). His most recent major collection, *Sleepers Joining Hands* (1973), synthesizes the themes and styles of these earlier collections and moves out in a new and fascinating direction completely unique in contemporary American poetry.

Bly's initial interest in the "deep image" was quickly buttressed by his reading in other, earlier, poets as well as thinkers such as Boehme and Jung. Jung's notions of the personal and collective unconscious and of the role of the shadow-side of the psyche Bly immediately found intriguing. As Bly developed his own thinking along these lines, his poetry developed simultaneously along similar lines. His obsession with "inwardness" led him toward the archetypal base upon which Jung built, and he found in one of Jung's disciples, Erich Neumann, the very source of what he had been seeking all along. Neumann's elaboration of the myth of "Great Mother culture" provides a ready theoretical arena within which Bly's *Sleepers Joining Hands* can be examined.

Neumann suggests that the key to understanding the "primordial image" of man is to be found in the archetype of the Great Mother, which he describes as "an inward image" working within the psyche which effects both conscious and unconscious processes. As such, this Great Mother archetype is the *"dynamis"* which corresponds to an unconscious 'conception.' "[1] Within "the uroboric state of perfection where body and psyche are identical...the metabolic symbolism of mutual exchange between body and world is paramount" since the "original tie with the body as with something 'peculiarly one's own' is the basis of all individual development."[2]

Now, since poetry "is animated by the same primordial images as myth,"[3] poetry rises "spontaneously from the unconscious."[4] Therefore, Neumann argues, "the key to a fundamental understanding, not only of man, but of the world as well, is to be sought in the relation between creativity and symbolic reality."[5]

Bly takes up Neumann's work on the Mothers in the long prose statement, "I Came Out of the Mother Naked," which makes up the central section of *Sleepers*. For Bly, the psyche, crushed under centuries of "Father consciousness," must make the slow, painful return to the Mother.

This process of the psyche's return to the Mother is similar to the struggle of the poet with his poem, as Bly has suggested in a recent interview: "One can describe all struggles in poetry, as in religion, as struggles between Mother consciousness, on the one hand, and Father consciousness, on the other."[6] *Sleepers* then is a poetic, religious, psychological struggle in which Bly, following Neumann and Jung, attempts to understand himself and the world around him by exploring the substrata of the psyche. Bly describes the process as a kind of "psychic archaeology": "When a culture begins to return to the Mother, each person in the culture begins to descend, layer after layer, into his own psyche."[7]

As the result of such "psychic archaeology" Bly believes that modern culture can begin to regain a proper psychic balance. Bly believes this balancing is imminent:

> The increasing strength of poetry, defense of
> earth, and mother consciousness, implies that
> after hundreds of years of being motionless,
> the Great Mother is moving again in the psyche.

Every day her face becomes clearer. We are becoming more sensitive, more open to her influence. She is returning, or we are returning to her; everyone who looks down into his own psyche sees her, just as in leaves floating on a pond you can sometimes make out faces. The pendulum rushes down, the Mothers rush toward us, we can all feel the motion downward, the speed increasing.

"The Teeth Mother Naked At Last," the long poem which precedes the prose section, is Bly's vision of the apocalypse demanded by man's inhumanity to man as a result of his allegiance to the Teeth Mother. The Teeth Mother, in opposition to the Ecstatic Mother, an "abundant Mother on the spiritual plane," works to destroy psychic life by "dismembering" the psyche. The most specific evidence of man's inhumanity is the travesty of war, and the most specific evidence of the travesty of war is the Vietnam War—which here becomes a paradigm for all wars, or at least all modern wars. In modern warfare man's natural tendency toward conflict has been made unnatural through the perversion of his natural resources for unnatural ends. This perversion, which begins with man, which allows him to lie, extends to the use of man's sophisticated industrial developments, initially invented to improve his life, which he turns into engines of destruction manned by the mindless, inhuman and inhumane man he has become. Such men force even nature herself to be made accomplice to the perversion they have initiated. Such a world, one in which the Teeth Mother reigns supreme, can only suggest the last stage of man's existence, a world bent on its own destruction, mindlessly rationalizing its travesties as progressive necessities.

"Teeth Mother" is Bly's most bitter anti-war poem. The biting satire of poems like "The Executive's Death," "Johnson's Cabinet Watched by Ants," "Those Being Eaten by America," "Listening to President Kennedy Lie About the Cuban Invasion," "The Current Administration," "Asian Peace Offers Rejected without Publication," "War and Silence," "Counting

Small-Boned Bodies," "As the Asian War Begins," "At a March Against the Vietnam War," "Hatred of Men with Black Hair," and "Driving through Minnesota During the Hanoi Bombings" in *Light* is here extended, drawn out and made all-inclusive. Along with the politicians, still the most heinous sinners in Bly's vision of the hell on earth created by the world at war, now even "The ministers lie, the professors lie, the television lies, the priests lie.... These lies mean that the country wants to die."

> And a long desire for death flows out, guiding the
>   enormous caravans from beneath,
> stringing together the vague and foolish words.
> It is a desire to eat death,
> to gobble it down,
> to rush on it like a cobra with mouth open
>
> It's a desire to take death inside,
> to feel it burning inside, pushing out velvety
>   hairs,
> like a clothes brush in the intestines—
>
> This is the thrill that leads the President on to lie

*   *   *

> Now the Chief Executive enters; the press con-
>   ference begins:
> First the President lies about the date the Appa-
>   lachian Mountains rose.
> Then he lies about the population of Chicago,
>   then he lies about the weight of the adult ea-
>   gle, then about the acreage of the Everglades
>
> He lies about the number of fish taken every year
>   in the Arctic, he has private information about
>   which city *is* the capital of Wyoming, he lies
>   about the birthplace of Attila the Hun.

He lies about the composition of the amniotic
   fluid, and he insists that Luther was never a
   German, and that only the Protestants sold in-
   dulgences,

That Pope Leo X *wanted* to reform the church,
   but the "liberal elements" prevented him,
that the Peasants' War was fomented by Italians
   from the North.

And the Attorney General lies about the time the
   sun sets.

                *   *   *

These lies are only the longing we all feel to die.
It is the longing for someone to come and take
   you by the hand to where they are all sleeping:
where Egyptian pharaohs are asleep, and your
   own mother,
and all those disappeared children, who used to
   go around with you in the rings at grade
   school. . . .

Do not be angry at the President—he is longing
   to take in his hand
the locks of death hair—
to meet his own children dead, or unborn. . . .
He is drifting sideways toward the dusty places[8]

Bly asks, "Why are they dying? I have written this so many
times." There is no answer. Here at the end of "Teeth Mother,"
there is only the imminent sense of impending destruction, the
description of the world on the verge of an apocalyptic upheaval
which promises to destroy it.

   Now the whole nation starts to whirl,
   the end of the Republic breaks off,

> pigs rush toward the cliff,
> the waters underneath part: in one ocean lumi-
>   nous globes float up (in them hairy and ec-
>   static men—)
> in the other, the teeth mother, naked at last.

Before we turn to the long title poem which concludes the volume, where Bly points to a path of renewal, we should consider the series of shorter poems which precede "Teeth Mother," which hint not only at the apocalyptic travesty which "Teeth Mother" attempts to define but also suggest the solution which will be provided by the title poem.

Of the ten poems in the first section of the volume, two, "Six Winter Privacy Poems," and "The Turtle" are particularly important. Both "Six Winter Privacy Poems" and "The Turtle" turn on familiar Bly themes, the dichotomy of light and darkness, of light shining in and through darkness, the metaphor of the reborn body.

"Six Winter Privacy Poems" (which may owe a nod to Stevens' "Six Significant Landscapes") suggest the movement toward a great Mother culture, away from the domination of "the Fathers."

> More of the fathers are dying each day.
> It is time for the sons.
> Bits of darkness are gathering around them.
> The darkness appears as flakes of light.
> . . . .
> When I woke, new snow had fallen.
> I am alone, yet someone else is with me,
> drinking coffee, looking out at the snow.

The poet, "Sitting in this darkness singing" says, "I can't tell if this joy / is from the body, or the soul, or a third place."[9]

The turtle, a creature who inhabits the chiaroscuro of the water, both the dark and the light, suggests the necessary intrusion of the one upon the other.

How shiny the turtle is, coming out
of the water, climbing the rock, as if
the body inside shone through!
As if swift turtle wings swept out of darkness,
and found new eyes.

The turtle has come out of the water to lay her eggs. She lays
her eggs in darkness on the dried up ocean, an old symbol of
birth. Those that would find the eggs must search for them just
as the young turtles, when born, must search to find the source
of their lives in the waters beyond "the floor of the old sea"
where they were born.

Of the eight other poems in this section, several deserve mention. In "Water Under the Earth," a poem which seems inevit-
ably to follow "The Turtle," Bly suggests the possibility of rebirth and renewal which he is beginning to sense. Here, however, as in all these poems, the renewal is not yet clearly visible.
The speaker realizes that he is still much in the dark, even
though he is standing "at the edges of the light." He realizes
that he must somehow mine his own inwardness because even
"these lines...are sunk to the waist in the dusk." Still, he
senses the true, necessary direction ahead of him, available:

There is a consciousness hovering under the
    mind's feet,
advanced civilizations under the footsole,
climbing at times up on a shoelace!
It is a willow that knows of water under the earth,
I am a father who dips as he passes over under-
    ground rivers,
who can feel his children through all distance and
    time!

In this world where the dead and dying huddle together in
despair, unable to "leap like rough marble into the next world"
and, at the same time, unable to endure the present world where
"The building across the street suddenly explodes," where "The

weeping child [is] like a fish thrown from the herring block,"
where "Women...hear the cry of small animals in their furs /
and drive their cars at a hundred miles an hour into trees," and:

> All those things borne down by the world,
> corpses pulled down by years of death,
> veins clogged with flakes of sludge,
> mouths from which bats escape at death,
> businessmen reborn as black whales sailing under
>   the Arctic ice...;

here these "newly dead kneel" to await their end, an end, one
can only say, that they have earned—or been too foolish to
avoid.

It is into this world, tipped precariously toward destruction,
that the "Teeth Mother" intrudes. This intrusion, which at first
augers only ill, has the opposite effect because it catapults the
poet so deep into darkness that he is finally able to see the light
of his own "inwardness" and thus initiate an upward "leap" into the reborn being whose spirit reigns when the sleepers join
hands, as they do in the final section of the volume.

Before looking at the long title poem, we should examine the
theoretical underpinning, upon which Bly builds "Sleepers Joining Hands."

Bly's latest theoretical notion, that of the "three brains," is
an outgrowth, however tenuous, of his earlier notions of "leaping poetry" and, as well, his reading of myth and the archetypes
in Jung, Neumann and others. Since Bly has never been a systematic critic, his reader is required to make "leaps" from one
point to another, as he himself does.

Bly developed his theory of the "three brains" through his
exposure to the work of Paul MacLean, Arthur Koestler and
Charles Fair.[10] MacLean, a neurologist, argues:

> Man finds himself in the predicament
> that Nature has endowed him essentially with
> three brains which, despite great differences in

structure, must function together and communicate with one another. The oldest of these brains is basically reptilian. The second has been inherited from lower mammals, and the third is a late mammalian development, which in its culmination in primates, has made man peculiarly man.[11]

Arthur Koestler applies MacLean's theory to creative endeavors. Arguing that "...maturation seems to mean a transition from the domination of the old brain towards the domination of the new,"[12] Koestler shows how:

> Poetry could thus be said to achieve a synthesis between the sophisticated reasoning of the neocortex and the more primitive emotional ways of the old brain. This *reculer pour mieux sauter,* draw-back-to leap process, which seems to underlie all creative achievement, may reflect a temporary regression from over-concrete, neocortical thinking to more fluid and "instinctive" modes of limbic thinking—a "regression to the id in the service of the ego...." The consequences of the innate "schizophysiology" of man thus range from the creative to the pathological. If the former is a *reculer pour mieux sauter,* the latter is a *reculer sans sauter....* In extreme cases, the distinction between the outer and inner world can become blurred—not only by hallucinations, but also in other ways; the patient seems to regress to the magic universe of the primitive.... "In other words, internal feelings are blended with what is seen, heard or otherwise sensed in such a way that the outside world is experienced as though it were inside. In this respect there is a resemblance to children and primitive peoples."[13]

Thus, "...the creative act always involves a regression to earlier, more primative levels in the mental hierarchy...."[14] Furthermore, "the poetic image attains its highest vibrational intensity as it were, when it strikes archetypal chords—when eternity looks through the window of time."[15] Thus, among various archetypes, the one with "special significance for the act of creation ...is variously known as the Night Journey, or the Death-and-Rebirth motif...." This "Night Journey" involves "a regression of the participatory tendencies, a crisis in which consciousness becomes unborn—to become reborn in a higher form of synthesis."[16]

It is not surprising that Bly would be attracted to such suggestions. Of course, he adapts these suggestions to his own ends. The "third brain" (which Bly prefers to refer to as the "new brain") is symbolized by light:

> As the reptile brain power is symbolized by cold,
> the mammal brain by warmth, the mark of the
> new brain is light.... The reptile and the new
> brains are now trying to make themselves visible.[17]

As for poets:

> ...it is clear that poets, like anyone else, can be
> dominated by one of the three brains. Chaucer is
> a great poet of the mammal brain; clearly St. John
> of the Cross and Kabir are great poets of the new
> brain.[18]

Among modern poets Rilke is "surely...the greatest spiritual poet of the twentieth century, and the greatest poet of the new brain."[19] Rilke's poetry, for Bly, "leaps;" it is what he calls poetry of "steady light."[20]

Surely, Bly would classify himself among the poets of the "new brain." In order to investigate this claim we must look at "Sleepers Joining Hands." Before we look specifically at the individual long title poem, it is helpful to see that "Sleepers Joining Hands" is, in embryo, what *Sleepers Joining Hands* itself is, writ large.

Whitman's poem "The Sleepers" may well stand behind Bly's *Sleepers* in several ways. Beyond the obvious parallel suggested by the titles, the works share a number of other similarities. Whitman begins his poem alone, in the grip of a private vision, just as Bly begins his volume with the "Six Winter Privacy Poems;" Whitman's poem traces a kind of psychic journey which delves into the subconscious reaches of the human psyche, just as Bly's prose section attempts to grasp deep psychological verities of man in an attempt "to right our own spiritual balance;" Whitman's poem climaxes with the vision of an integrated self, at peace with its own being, and reconciled with the world, just as Bly, in the "Sleepers Joining Hands" section which concludes his volume, rises to a similar vision in which "All the sleepers in the world join hands."[21]

In "The Shadow Goes Away," the first section of "Sleepers Joining Hands," private myth is interpreted in terms of public myth as dream reality supersedes waking reality. The poem begins with several visions of death as the poet plumbs the layers of his collective dream reality to uncover the source of the archetypal mythos in the ancient world. To the anonymous possibilities of death, first by water for "the woman chained to the shore" while "the cold ocean rise[s]," and next by the natural death which nature participates in as, "The owl senses someone in the hole in his tree, / and lands with wings closing, claws out...." he adds an allusion to the Joseph story from Genesis 37 ("Now I show the father the coat stained with goat's blood.... I sent my brother away / ...I gave him to the dark people passing") and links this myth to the American Indian mythos ("I heard he was near the Missouri, taken in by traveling Sioux"). This mixing of myth and fracturing of time is accomplished by the dream reality which links the various mythical traditions in the collective unconscious and traces them back to the seat of Great Mother culture in ancient Egypt. Such juxtapositions are appropriate and acceptable in dreams; indeed, they can be, and often are the inevitable stays against the waking reality of death. As the poet here says, "I don't want to wake up in the weeds, and find the light / gone out in the body." Thus, as "The

suppressed race returns," and is held up for view within the unconscious consciousness of dream reality, the poet rises to that
"body not yet born" which exists "like a light around the
body."[22]

"Meeting the Man Who Warns Me," the second poem in
the sequence, begins with the brief awakening of the poet. He
finds that "fragments of the mother lie open in all low places,"
that "The body surrounds me on all sides." He "walk[s] out
and return[s]" to sleep, to participate again in the dream reality.
He knows that "the dead [are] great conductors / carrying electricity under the ground." In this dream he dreams "that the
fathers are dying," that the mother consciousness is being reborn
again. Since what is most important to him is buried "underneath," the poet must try to get back to "The energy [which] is
inside us." He starts toward it. The drive toward inwardness is
described in terms of the myth of Jonah. "I was for three days
inside a warm-blooded fish." When the body, caught in the
body of the whale, is vomited out a symbolic, bodily rebirth has
been accomplished and the poet rejoices in the joy of his new-
born body.

> "A whale bore me back home, we flew through
>   the air . . . .
> Then I was a boy who had never seen the sea!
> It was like a King coming to his own shores.
> I feel the naked touch of the knife,
> I feel the wound,
> this joy I love is like wounds at sea . . . ."

This rebirth is the beginning of the "Night Journey" which
Koestler has described: "Among the many variations of the
Night Journey in myth and folklore, one of the most forceful is
the story of Jonah and the whale . . . ."[23] Like Jonah, the poet
sees that both he and the world have been asleep in the midst of
catastrophe, clinging to what Koestler calls "the Trivial Plane:"[24]
they have failed to follow their true callings.

Here then Bly points to the true calling, the true direction, in which "consciousness becomes unborn—to become re-born."[25] This rebirth is specifically dealt with in the next section of the poem, "The Night Journey in the Cooking Pot," which is the climactic section not only of this poem but of the whole of *Sleepers*.

"The Night Journey in the Cooking Pot" opens with the poet's acknowledgment of his rebirth through his participation in the Jonah-like burial and rebirth of the body already described: "I was born during the night sea-journey. "Floating in the cooking pot / on the sea" he has gone through the death of the body and been reborn in the new body. Having discovered the hidden "inwardness, inwardness, inwardness, / the inward path I still walk on," the poet rejoices with nature to which he is now attuned like a "face shining far inside the mountain." He "feel[s] the blood galloping in the body, / the baby whirling in the womb." As "The tree becomes naked and joyful," as "Leaves fall in the tomby wood," the poet rejoices:

> Suddenly I love the dancers, leaping
> in the dark, jumping
> into the air, and the singers and dancers and
> leapers!
> . . . .
> I am not going farther from you,
> I am coming nearer,
> green rain carries me nearer you,
> I weave drunkenly about the page,
> I love you,
> I never knew that I loved you
> until I was swallowed by the invisible,
> my black shoes evaporating, rising about my
> head. . . .
>
> For we are like the branch bent in the water. . . .
> Taken out, it is whole, it was always whole. . . .

*   *   *

> I see the road ahead,
> and my body cries out, and leaps into the air,
> and throws itself on the floor, knocking over the
>   chairs.
> I think I am the body,
> the body rushes in and ties me up,
> and then goes through the house....

Having gone through this conversion, the poet "decide[s] that death is friendly" even though he acknowledges that "What I have written is not good enough" to explain the full significance of the mystery he has experienced.

The final section of the poem, "Water Drawn Up Into the Head," begins with the inevitable question one puts to an oneiric mystery: "Now do you understand the men who laugh all night in their sleep?" And as the question is clouded with mystery so too is the response. Obviously, the question cannot be logically answered. The body, born through death, can only be defined by poetry and even poetry betrays the true answer since such ecstasy is ultimately inexpressible. The poet knows that:

> There is another being living inside me.
> He is looking out of my eyes.
> I hear him
> in the wind through the bare trees.

But the poet knows, also, that "I am the one whom I have never met," that he has yet a long way to go into the deeper mysteries of the night journey. He says: "Sometimes when I read my own poems late at night, / I sense myself on a long road." Still, in spite of everything, there is "An Extra Joyful Chorus for Those Who Have Read This Far"—it is a chorus of all that has gone before and for all that is yet to come, the wish, which is almost a prayer, that "Hands rush toward each other through miles of space;" that "All the sleepers in the world join hands."

Donald Hall has said, quite rightly, " 'Sleepers Joining

Hands' is the earliest and latest of Bly's work. It has taken this long for him to use material which leaves him so vulnerable."[26]

Notes

[1] Erich Neumann, *The Great Mother: An Analysis of the Archetype,* translated by Ralph Manheim (New York: Bollingen Foundation, Inc., 1963), pp. 3, 15.

[2] Erich Neumann, *The Origins and History of Consciousness,* translated by R. F. C. Hull (Princeton: Princeton University Press, 1970), pp. 290-291.

[3] Erich Neumann, *Amor and Psyche: The Psychic Development of the Feminine,* translated by Ralph Manheim (New York: Bollingen Foundation, Inc., 1956), p. 65.

[4] Neumann, *Great Mother,* p. 297.

[5] Erich Neumann, *Art and Creative Unconscious,* translated by Ralph Manheim (Princeton: Princeton University Press, 1971), p. 170.

[6] Kevin Power, "Conversation with Robert Bly," *The Texas Quarterly,* XIX:3 (Autumn, 1976), 86.

[7] Robert Bly, *Sleepers Joining Hands* (New York: Harper & Row, 1973), pp. 34-37. Hereafter, all quotations and references are to *Sleepers* except where noted.

[8] An earlier version of this part of "Teeth Mother" appeared as an individual poem, entitled "Lies," in *The Nation,* March 25, 1968. A portion of this section of "Teeth Mother" also appeared, in somewhat different form, in Bly's *The Satisfaction of Vietnam: A Play in Eight Scenes, Chelsea,* 24-25 (October, 1968), 32-46.

[9] Bly here suggests in embryo the idea of the "new mind" which he elaborates in considerable detail later (see below).

[10] See Robert Bly, *Leaping Poetry: An Idea with Poems and Translations* (Boston: Beacon Press, 1975), pp. 59-67, passim.

[11] Paul MacLean, "New Findings Relevant to the Evolution of Psychosexual Functions of the Brain," *Journal of Nervous and Mental Disease,* 135:4

(October, 1962), 289. MacLean has elaborated considerably on his theory of the "three brains." See his "Psychosomatic Disease and the 'Visceral Brain,'" *Psychosomatic Medicine*, II (1949), 338-353; "Contrasting Functions of Limbic and Neocortical Systems of the Brain and their Relevance to Psychophysiological Aspects of Medicine," *American Journal of Medicine*, XXV:4 (October, 1958), 611-626; "Psychosomatics," *Handbook of Physiology-Neurophysiology*, III (1961), and "Man and his Animal Brains," *Modern Medicine*, (March 2, 1964), 95-106. See also, Charles M. Fair, *The Dying Self* (Middletown, Connecticut: Wesleyan University Press, 1969), pp. 15-53. It might be interesting to compare Bly's theory of the "three brains" as he develops it with Jean Paul Sartre's three "ontological dimensions of the body." [See *Being and Nothingness: An Essay on Phenomenological Ontology*, translated by Hazel E. Barnes (New York: Philosophical Library, 1956), pp. 303-359.]

[12] Arthur Koestler, *The Ghost in the Machine* (New York: The Macmillan Co., 1968), p. 286.

[13] Koestler, *Ghost*, pp. 288-289. The last portion of this quotation is from MacLean's "Psychosomatics" referred to above. Compare in this regard Koestler's earlier remarks on "draw-back-to-leap:" "The essence of the process which I have described is an evolutionary *retreat* from specialized adult forms of bodily structure and behaviour, to an earlier or more primitive, but also more plastic and less committed stage—followed by a sudden advance in a new direction.... I shall try to show that this *reculer pour mieux sauter*—is a favorite gambit in the grand strategy of the evolutionary process; and that it also plays an important part in the progress of science and art." (*Ghost*, p. 167)

[14] Arthur Koestler, *The Act of Creation* (New York: The Macmillan Co., 1964), p. 316.

[15] Koestler, *Act of Creation*, p. 353.

[16] Koestler, *Act of Creation*, pp. 358, 360.

[17] Bly, *Leaping Poetry*, pp. 62-63.

[18] Bly, *Leaping Poetry*, p. 66.

[19] Bly, *Leaping Poetry*, p. 73.

[20] Bly surely knows and certainly would agree with Erich Heller's analysis of Rilke in his famous essay "The Artist's Journey into the Interior: A Hegelian

Prophecy and Its Fulfillment," in *The Artist's Journey into the Interior and Other Essays* (New York: Vintage Books, 1968). Indeed, it is possible that Heller's essay helped influence Bly's thinking in some significant ways. Here, for instance, are Heller's comments on Rilke's great Elegies:

> *The Duino Elegies,* concerned as they are with the seemingly contradictory task of rescuing the *visible* world in the *invisibility* of inwardness, touch upon the mystery within which the perishable bread, remaining bread, is invisibly transubstantiated, and the perished body, restored to its bodiliness, is invisibly resurrected. If Hegel has tried to convert this mystery into dialectic philosophy, Rilke has turned it into the apocalyptic poetry of a human inwardness that takes over the divine agency of salvation: "Nowhere will be world but within." (p. 170) For another analysis of Rilke which Bly would surely agree with see Geoffrey H. Hartman, *The Unmediated Vision: An Interpretation of Wordsworth, Hopkins, Rilke, and Valery* (New York: Harcourt, Brace & World, Inc., 1966), pp. 70-96.

[21] Indeed, the similarities between these two works are so manifold that a comment like the following one, made specifically with respect to Whitman's poem, might apply, as well, to Bly's book:

> "The Sleepers" is indeed Whitman's masterpiece in the genre we have called "the inward journey...." Whitman begins...with a true sense of guilt and of psychic disorder: ...the journey metaphor in "The Sleepers" may well imply (as Richard Chase has suggested) a descent into the unconscious where, in a dream of terror and bewilderment, the ego or conscious self confronts the lawless energies of the id and feels its very existence threatened. Nonetheless, the dominant impulse in this poem, as everywhere else in the 1855 *Leaves of Grass,* is toward psychic recovery and self-assurance, toward a wholeness of *self* that produces a sense of harmony and reconciliation throughout the surrounding *world.*

[Cleanth Brooks, R. W. B. Lewis, Robert Penn Warren, *American Literature: The Makers and the Making,* Vol. I (New York: St. Martin's Press, 1973), pp. 938-939.] George S. Lensing and Ronald Moran have recently suggested that Bly's "Teeth Mother" is "Whitmanesque in the use of sprawling and oracular lines which constitute catalogues of denunciation, such as the presidential lines in Part II. The poet himself assumes the role of the Civil War nurse of

Whitman's *Drum Taps....*" [See *Four Poets and the Emotive Imagination: Robert Bly, James Wright, Louis Simpson, and William Stafford* (Baton Rouge, Louisiana: Louisiana State University Press, 1976), p. 83.] Bly would, of course, be sympathetic to Whitman's call, in the Preface to the 1855 edition of *Leaves of Grass,* for "the perfect equality of the female with the male."

22 See the title poem of *The Light Around the Body,* "Looking into a Face" (New York: Harper and Row, 1967), p. 53

23 Koestler, *Act of Creation,* p. 360.

24 Koestler, *Act of Creation,* p. 361.

25 Koestler, *Act of Creation,* p. 360.

26 Donald Hall, "Notes on Robert Bly and *Sleepers Joining Hands,*" *The Ohio Review,* XV:1 (Fall, 1973), 92.

Selected Bibliography

n.d. = date of publication unknown
n.p. = place of publication unknown

Poetry by Robert Bly

Silence in the Snowy Fields (Middletown, Conn.: Wesleyan University Press, 1962; London: Cape, 1967).

The Light Around the Body (New York: Harper & Row, 1967; London: Rapp & Whiting, 1968).

Chrysanthemums (Menomenie, Wisc.: Ox Head Press, 1967).

Ducks (Menomenie, Wis.: Ox Head Press, 1967).

The Morning Glory: Another Thing That Will Never Be My Friend: Twelve Prose Poems (San Francisco: Kayak Books, 1969; revised 1970).

The Teeth Mother Naked At Last (San Francisco: City Lights Books, 1970; Millwood, NY: Kraus Reprint Company, 1973).

Christmas Eve Service at Midnight at St. Michael's (Rushden, Northamptonshire, U.K.: Sceptre Press, 1972).

Water Under the Earth (Rushden, Northamptonshire, U.K.: Sceptre Press, 1972).

The Dead Seal Near McClure's Beach (Denver: Straight Creek Journal, 1972; Rushden, Northamptonshire, U.K.: Sceptre Press, 1973).

Jumping Out of Bed (Barre, Mass.: Barre, 1973).

Sleepers Joining Hands (New York: Harper & Row, 1973).

The Hockey Poem (Duluth, Minn.: Knife River Press, 1974).

Old Man Rubbing His Eyes (Greensboro, N.C.: Unicorn Press, 1974).

Point Reyes Poems (Half Moon Bay, Cal.: Mudra, 1974).

Grass From Two Years (Denver: Ally Press, 1975).

The Morning Glory (New York: Harper & Row, 1975).

Climbing Up Mount Vision with My Little Boy (Pittsburgh: Slow Loris Press, 1976). (broadside)

4 Poems (Birmingham, Ala.: Thunder City Press, 1976). (broadside)

The Loon (Marshall, Minn.: Ox Head Press, 1977).

Walking at Night (New York: Poetry in Public Places, 1978). (poster)

This Body is Made of Camphor and Gopherwood (New York: Harper & Row, 1979).

Visiting Emily Dickinson's Grave (Madison, Wisc.: Red Ozier Press, 1979).

This Tree Will Be Here For a Thousand Years (New York: Harper & Row, 1979).

What the Fox Agreed to Do (Athens, Ohio: Croissant & Company, 1979). (pamphlet)

The Man in the Black Coat Turns (New York: Dial, 1981).

Translations by Robert Bly

Hans Hvass, *Reptiles and Amphibians of the World* (New York: Grosset & Dunlap, 1960).

Georg Trakl, *Twenty Poems of Georg Trakl*, trans. Bly and James Wright (Madison, Minn.: Sixties Press, 1961).

Selma Lagerlöf, *The Story of Gösta Berling* (New York: New American Library, 1962).

Cesar Vallejo, *Twenty Poems of Cesar Vallejo*, trans. Bly, James Wright and John Knoepfle (Madison, Minn.: Sixties Press, 1962).

Tomas Tranströmer, *Three Poems*, trans. Bly, Eric Sellin and Thomas Buckman (Lawrence, Kans.: T. Williams, 1966).

Knut Hamsum, *Hunger* (New York: Farrar, Straus, 1967; London: Duckworth, 1974).

Gunnar Ekelöf, *I Do Best Alone At Night*, trans. Bly and Christina Paulston (Washington, D.C.: Charioteer Press, 1968).

Ekelöf, *Late Arrival on Earth: Selected Poems of Gunnar Ekelöf*, trans. Bly and Christina Paulston (London: Rapp & Carroll, 1967).

Yvan Goll, *Selected Poems*, trans. Bly and others (San Francisco: Kayak Books, 1968).

Pablo Neruda, *Twenty Poems of Pablo Neruda,* trans. Bly and James Wright (Madison, Minn.: Sixties Press, 1968; London: Rapp & Whiting, 1968).

Issa Kobayashi, *Ten Poems* (n.p. Privately printed, 1969).

Juan Ramón Jiménez, *Forty Poems of Juan Ramón Jiménez* (Madison, Minn.: Seventies Press, 1970).

Tranströmer, *Twenty Poems by Tomas Tranströmer* (Madison, Minn.: Seventies Press, 1970).

Neruda and Vallejo, *Neruda and Vallejo: Selected Poems,* trans. Bly, James Wright and John Knoepfle (Boston: Beacon Press, 1971).

Kabir, *The Fish in the Sea is not Thirsty: Versions of Kabir* (Northwood Narrows, N.H.: Lillabulero Press, 1971; Calcutta: A Writers Workshop Publication, 1972).

Tranströmer, *Night Vision* (Northwood Narrows, N.H.: Lillabulero Press, 1971; London: London Magazine Editions, 1972).

Rainer Maria Rilke, *Ten Sonnets to Orpheus* (San Francisco: Zephyrus Image, 1972).

Miguel Hernandez and Blas De Otero, *Selected Poems,* trans. Timothy Baland, Bly, Hardie St. Martin and James Wright (Boston: Beacon Press, 1972).

Basho, *Basho* (San Francisco: Mudra, 1972).

Garcia Lorca and Jimenez, *Lorca and Jimenez: Selected Poems* (Boston: Beacon Press, 1973).

Tranströmer, *Elegy, Some October Notes* (Rushden, Northamptonshire, U.K.: Sceptre Press, 1973).

Kabir, *Grass From Two Years* (Denver: Ally Press, 1975).

Kabir, *Kabir: Twenty-eight Poems* (New York: Siddha Yoga Dham, 1975).

Harry Martinson, Ekelöf, Tranströmer, *Friends, You Drank Some Darkness* (Boston: Beacon Press, 1975).

Kabir, *The Darkness of Night* (Ruffsdale, Pa.: Rook Press, Inc., 1976). (broadside)

Kabir, *The Love Swing* (Pittsburgh: Slow Loris Press, 1976). (broadside)

Kabir, *Try to Live to See This: Versions of Kabir* (Denver: Ally Press, 1976; Rushden, Northamptonshire, U.K.: Sceptre Press, 1976).

Vicente Aleixandre, *Twenty Poems of Vicente Aleixandre* (Madison, Minn.: Seventies Press, 1977).

Rolf Jacobsen, *Twenty Poems of Rolf Jacobsen* (Madison, Minn.: Seventies Press, 1977).

Kabir, *The Kabir Book: Forty-Four of the Ecstatic Poems of Kabir* (Boston: Beacon Press, 1977).

Rilke, *The Voices* (Denver: Ally Press, 1977; London: Sceptre Press, 1977).

Antonio Machado, *I Never Wanted Fame: Ten Poems and Proverbs* (St. Paul, Minn.: Ally Press, 1979).

Tranströmer, *Truth Barriers* (San Francisco: Sierra Club Books, 1980).

Rilke, *October Day and Other Poems* (Cal.: Calloipea Press, 1981).

Rilke, *Selected Poems of Rainer Maria Rilke* (New York: Harper & Row, 1981).

Other Books by Robert Bly

A Broadsheet Against the New York Times Book Review (Madison, Minn.: Sixties Press, 1961).

The Lion's Tail and Eyes: Poems Written Out of Laziness and Silence, includes poetry by Bly, James Wright and William Duffy (Madison, Minn.: Sixties Press, 1962).

A Poetry Reading Against the Vietnam War, edited by Bly and David Ray (Madison, Minn.: American Writers Against the Vietnam War, 1966).

The Sea and The Honeycomb: A Book of Tiny Poems, edited by Bly (Madison, Minn.: Sixties Press, 1966; Boston: Beacon Press, 1971).

Forty Poems Touching on Recent American History, edited by Bly (Madison, Minn.: Sixties Press, 1966; Boston: Beacon Press, 1970).

Poems for Tennessee, Bly, William Stafford and William Matthews (Martin, Tenn.: Tennessee Poetry Press, 1971).

McGrath, Bly and others (Stone Marrow Press, 1972).

Leaping Poetry: An Idea with Poems and Translations, edited by Bly (Boston: Beacon Press, 1975).

David Ignatow: Selected Poems, edited by Bly (Middletown, Conn.: Wesleyan University Press, 1975).

News of the Universe: Poems of Two-fold Consciousness, edited by Bly (San Francisco: Sierra Club Books, 1980).

Articles by Robert Bly

"Five Decades Of Modern American Poetry." *Fifties* 1 (1958), p. 36-39.

"Interview with the Head of the *New York Times Book Review.*" *Fifties* 1 (1958), p. 47-51.

"On English and American Poetry." *Fifties* 2 (1959), p. 45-47.

"Some Thoughts on Lorca and Rene Char." *Fifties* 3 (1959), p. 7-9.

"On Current Poetry In America." *Sixties* 4 (1960), p. 28-29.

"Poetry in an Age of Expansion." *Nation* 192 (April 22, 1961), p. 350-54.

"Some Notes on French Poetry." *Sixties* 5 (1961), p. 66-70.

"On the Necessary Aestheticism of Modern Poetry." *Sixties* 6 (1962), p. 22-24.

"Prose Versus Poetry." *Choice* 2 (1962), p. 65-80.

"Rewriting as Translation." *Hudson Review* 15, #3 (Autumn 1962), p. 469-75. (omnibus translation review)

"Translations from Gunnar Ekelöf." *Hudson Review* 15, #4 (Winter 1962-63), p. 546-47. (translation and note)

"A Wrong Turning in American Poetry." *Choice* 3 (1963), p. 33-47.

"Henrik Ibsen: On the Murder of Abraham Lincoln." *Nation* 196 (February 16, 1963), p. 142. (translation and note)

"The Surprise of Neruda." *Sixties* 7 (Winter 1964), p. 18-19.

"Voznesensky and his Translators." *Kayak* 9 (1966), p. 46-48.

"Concerning the Little Magazines: Something Like A Symposium." *Carleton Miscellany* 2 (Spring 1966), p. 20-22.

"The Dead World and the Live World." *Sixties* 8 (Spring 1966), p. 2-7.

"Recent German Anthologies." *Sixties* 8 (Spring 1966), p. 84-88.

"Robert Lowell's *For The Union Dead.*" *Sixties* 8 (Spring 1966), p. 93-96.

"The First Ten Issues of *Kayak.*" *Kayak* 12 (1967), p. 45-49.

"Answers to Correspondents." *Kayak* 13 (1967), p. 28-31.

"Looking for Dragon Smoke." *Stand* 9, #1 (1967), p. 102.

"The Collapse of James Dickey: *Buckdancer's Choice.*" *Sixties* 9 (Spring 1967), p. 70-79.

"Leaping Up into Political Poetry." *London Magazine* 7 (Spring 1967), p. 82-87.

"On Political Poetry." *Nation* 204 (April 24, 1967), p. 522-24.

"A Poet on Vietnam: Murder as Prudent Policy." *Commonweal* (March 22, 1968), p. 17.

"On Pablo Neruda." *Nation* 206 (March 25, 1968), p. 414-18.

"Not Very Near the Ocean." *Michigan Quarterly Review* 7 (Summer 1968), p. 211-12. (review of Robert Lowell's *Near the Ocean*)

"Poetry—What is it Saying and to Whom?" *American Dialogue* 5 (1968-69), p. 28.

"Private Gardens, Cloisters, Silent Women." *Nation* 209 (July 7, 1969), p. 17-18.

"Tomas Tranströmer." *Field* 1 (Fall 1969), p. 60-61.

"James Wright." *Cafe Solo* 2 (1970), p. 69.

"A Conversation About Hernandez: Interview with Pablo Neruda." *Sixties* 9 (Spring 1970), p. 4-6.

"Some Notes on Donald Hall." *Field* 2 (Spring 1970), p. 57-61.

"What About Poetry?" *Prairie Schooner* 44, #2 (Summer 1970), p. 146-50.

"Symposium: What's New in American and Canadian Poetry." *New* 15 (April/May 1971), p. 17-20.

"A Letter." *Poet and Critic* 11 (Summer 1971), p. 30.

"American Poetry: On the Way to the Hermetic." *Books Abroad* 46 (Winter 1972), p. 17-24.

"Developing the Underneath." *American Poetry Review* 2, #2 (1973), p. 44-45.

"The Network and the Community." *American Poetry Review* 3, #1 (1974), p. 19-21.

"Reflexions on the Origins of Poetic Form." *Field* 10 (Spring 1974), p. 31-35.

"Growing Up in Minnesota." *American Poetry Review* (January/February 1975), p. 4-6.

"The Writer's Sense of Place." *South Dakota Review* 13, #3 (Autumn 1975), p. 73-75.

"Being a Lutheran Boy-god in Minnesota." *Growing Up in Minnesota: Ten Writers Remember Their Childhood,* Chester G. Anderson, editor. (Minneapolis: University of Minnesota Press, 1976), p. 206.

"A Note on James Wright." *Ironwood* 10 (1978), p. 64.

"Reviewing Poetry: Where Have All the Critics Gone?" *Nation* 226 (April 22, 1978), p. 456.

"Holding On To One Rope." *Modern Swedish Poetry in Translation,* Gunnar Harding and Anselm Hollo, editors. (Minneapolis: University of Minnesota Press, 1979), p. v-viii.

"Tranströmer and The Memory." *Ironwood* 13 (Spring 1979), p. 84-87.

"The Stages of an Artist's Life." *Georgia Review* 34, #1 (Spring 1980), p. 105-09.

"Recognizing the Image as a Form of Intelligence." *Field* 24 (Spring 1981), p. 17-27.

"Form that is Neither In nor Out." *Poetry East* 4/5 (Spring/Summer 1981), p. 29-34.

Articles and Books on Robert Bly

"Alienation and Acclaim." *Times Literary Supplement* #3481 (November 14, 1968), p. 1285. (review of *Twenty Poems of Pablo Neruda*)

Altieri, C.F. "Varieties of Immanentist Experience: Robert Bly, Charles Olson and Frank O'Hara." *Enlarging The Temple* (Lewisburg, Pa.: Bucknell University Press, 1979).

Atkinson, Michael. "*Sleepers Joining Hands*: Shadow and Self." *Iowa Review* 7, #4 (Fall 1976), p. 135-53.

Baker, Deborah. "Making a Farm: A Literary Biography of Robert Bly." *Poetry East* 4/5 (Spring/Summer 1981), p. 145-89.

"Bibliography and Biographical Note on Robert Bly." *Great Lakes Review* (Summer 1976), p. 66-69.

Blackman, Jennings. "The Kabir Book." *Midwest Quarterly Review* 19 (Winter 1978), p. 219-20.

"Books in Brief." *Beliot Poetry Journal* 28 (Spring 1978), p. 40. (review of *Old Man Rubbing His Eyes*)

Brooks, Cleanth. "Poetry Since the Waste Land." *Southern Review* 1 (1965), p. 498-99.

Brownjohn, Alan. "Pre-Beat." *New Statesman* 76 (August 2, 1968), p. 146. (review of *The Light Around the Body*)

Calhoun, Richard. "On Robert Bly's Protest Poetry." *Tennessee Poetry Journal* 2 (Winter 1969), p. 21-22.

Carroll, Paul. "Bly's Kabir." *American Poetry Review* 8, #1 (1979), p. 30-31. (review of *The Kabir Book*)

Carruth, Hayden. "Critic of the Month." *Poetry* 112 (September 1968), p. 418-27. (review of *The Light Around the Body*)

———— "Poets on the Fringe: *This Tree Will Be Here for a Thousand Years.*" *Harper's* 260, #1556 (January 1980), p. 79.

Case, L.L. "Robert Bly and David Ray, eds.: *A Poetry Reading Against the Vietnam War.*" *El Corno Emplumado* 23 (July 1967), p. 148-50.

Cavich, David. "The Poet as Victim and Victimizer." *New York Times Book Review* (February 18, 1973, p. 2-3. (review of *Sleepers Joining Hands*)

"Chained to the Parish Pump." *Times Literary Supplement* #3394 (March 16, 1967), p. 220. (review of *Silence in the Snowy Fields*)

Clayre, Alasdair. "Recent Verse." *Encounter* 29 (November 1967), p. 78-79. (review of *Silence in the Snowy Fields*)

Colombo, John Robert, "Poetry Chronicle." *The Tamarack Review* 26 (Winter 1963), p. 86-94. (review of *Silence in the Snowy Fields*)

Cotter, James Finn. "Poetry Reading." *Hudson Review* 31, #1 (Spring 1978), p. 214-15. (review of *This Body is Made of Camphor and Gopherwood*)

Cox, C.B. "Ox, Mule and Buzzard." *Spectator* 217 (March 24, 1967), p. 342-43. (review of *Silence in the Snowy Fields*)

Dacey, Philip. "This Book is Made of Turkey Soup and Star Music." *Parnassus: Poetry in Review* 7 (Fall/Winter 1978), p. 34-45. (review of *This Body is Made of Camphor and Gopherwood*)

Daniels, Kate and Richard Jones, editors. *Of Solitude and Silence: Writings on Robert Bly* (Boston: Beacon Press, 1982).

Davis, William Virgil. "Defining the Age." *Moons and Lion Tailes* 2, #3 (1977), p. 85-89. (review of *The Morning Glory*)

———— "Hair in a Baboon's Ear: The Politics of Robert Bly's Early Poetry." *The Carleton Miscellany* 18, #1 (1979-80), p. 74-84.

———— "At the Edges of the Light: A Reading of Robert Bly's *Sleepers Joining Hands.*" *Poetry East* 4/5 (Spring/Summer 1981), p. 265-82.

Davison, Peter. "New Poetry: The Generation of the Twenties." *Atlantic Monthly* 221 (February 1968), p. 141-42. (review of *The Light Around the Body*)

Delonas, John, Untitled. *Library Journal* 92 (October 15, 1967), p. 3647. (review of *The Light Around the Body*)

Dodsworth, Martin. "Towards the Baseball Poem." *The Listener* (June 27, 1968), p. 842. (review of *The Light Around the Body*)

Donadio, Stephen. "Some Younger Poets In America." *Modern Occasions,* Philip Rahv, editor. (New York: Farrar, Straus, and Giroux, 1966), p. 226-46.

Faas, Eckbert. "Robert Bly." *Boundary* 4, #2 (Spring 1976), p. 707-25.
See also *Towards A New American Poetics: Essays & Interviews* (Santa Barbara: Black Sparrow Press, 1978), p. 203-43.

Feinsod, Ethan. "Kayak." *Chicago Review* 22, #2-3 (January/February 1971), p. 156-59. (review of Goll's *Selected Poems*)

Fowlie, Wallace. "Not Bards So Much as Catalyzers," *New York Times Book Review* (March 12, 1963, p. 36. (review of *Silence in the Snowy Fields*)

Friberg, Ingegard. *Moving Inward: A Study of Robert Bly's Poetry* (Göteborg: Acta University Göthoburgenis, 1977).

Friedman, Norman. "The Wesleyan Poets—III:The Experimental Poets." *Chicago Review* 19 (1967), p. 52-73. (review of *Silence in the Snowy Fields*)

Garret, George. "Against the Grain: Poets Writing Today." *American Poetry,* Irvin Ehrenpreis, editor. (New York: St. Martin's Press, 1965), p. 221-39.

Gifford, Henry. "The Master of Pain." *Poetry* 105, #3 (December 1964), p. 196-97. (review of *Twenty Poems of Cesar Vallejo*)

Gitlin, Todd. "The Return of Political Poetry." *Commonweal* 94 (July 23, 1971), p. 375-80. (review of *40 Poems Touching on Recent American History*)

Gitzen, Julian. "Floating On Solitude: The Poetry of Robert Bly." *Modern Poetry Studies* 7, #3 (Winter 1976), p. 231-40.

Goedicke, Patricia. "The Leaper Leaping." *Poetry East* 4/5 (Spring/Summer 1981), p. 64-84.

Goldman, Michael. "Joyful in the Dark." *New York Times Book Review* (February 18, 1968), p. 10, 12. (review of *The Light Around the Body*)

Graubart, Rose. "Drawing of Robert Bly." *Chelsea* 24/25 (October 1968), p. 107; Slow Loris Broadsides (Buffalo: Slow Loris Press, 1973); *Poetry East* 4/5 (Spring/Summer 1981), cover.

Guest, Barbara. "Shared Landscapes." *Chelsea* 16 (March 1965), p. 150-52. (review of *Silence in the Snowy Fields*)

Gunn, Thom. "Poems and Books of Poems." *Yale Review* 53 (October 1963), p. 142. (review of *Silence in the Snowy Fields*)

Haines, John. "Robert Bly: A Tiny Retrospect." *Poetry East* 4/5 (Spring/Summer 1981), p. 190-93.

Hall, Donald. "American Expressionist Poetry." *Serif* 1 (December 1964), p. 18-19.
"Notes on Robert Bly and *Sleepers Joining Hands.*" *Ohio Review* 15, #1 (Fall 1973), p. 89-93.
"Poetry Food." *Poetry East* 4/5 (Spring/Summer 1981), p. 35-36.

Halley, Anne. "Recent American Poetry: Outside Relevancies." *Massachusetts Review* 9 (Fall 1968), p. 696-713.

Hammer, Louis Z. "Moths in the Light." *Kayak* 14 (April 1968), p. 63-67. (review of *The Light Around The Body*)

Harnack, Curtis. "Week of the Angry Artist." *Nation* 204 (February 20, 1967), p. 246-47.

Harris, Victoria. "'Walking Where the Plows Have Been Turning': Robert Bly and Female Consciousness." *Poetry East* 4/5 (Spring/Summer 1981), p. 123-38.

Helms, Alan. "Two Poets." *Partisan Review* 44, #2 (1977), p. 284-88. (review of *Sleepers Joining Hands*)

Hertzel, L.J. "What About Writers in the North?" *South Dakota Review* 5 (Spring 1967), p. 3-19.

Heyen, William. "Inward to the World: The Poetry of Robert Bly." *The Far Point* 3 (Fall/Winter 1969), p. 42-50.

Hill, Douglas. "Scattered Literature." *Ambit* 49 (1971), p. 16-17. (review of *The Teeth Mother Naked at Last*)

Hoffman, Frederick J. "Contemporary American Poetry," *Patterns of Commitment in American Literature,* Marston La France, editor. (Ottawa: University of Toronto Press, 1967), p. 193-207.

Holmes, Theodore. "Wit, Nature and the Human Concern." *Poetry* 100 (August 1962), p. 319-24. (review of *Twenty Poems of Georg Trakl*)

Howard, Richard. "Poetry Chronicle." *Poetry* 102 (June 1963), p. 182-92. (review of *Silence in the Snowy Fields*)

"Robert Bly." *Alone With America* (New York: Atheneum, 1969; 1980 revised), p. 57-67.

Hughes, D.J. "The Demands of Poetry." *Nation* 196 (January 5, 1963), p. 17-18. (review of *Silence in the Snowy Fields*)

Ignatow, David. "Reflections Upon the Past with Robert Bly." *Poetry East* 4/5 (Spring/Summer 1981), p. 197-206.

Janssens, G.A.M. "The Present State of American Poetry: Robert Bly and James Wright." *English Studies* 51 (April 1970), p. 112-37.

Jones, Richard and Kate Daniels, editors. *Of Solitude and Silence: Writings on Robert Bly* (Boston: Beacon Press, 1982).

Kenner, Hugh. "Review." *New York Times Book Review* (January 1, 1978), p. 10 (review of *This Body is Made of Camphor and Gopherwood*)

Kirby, Martin. Untitled. *The Georgia Review* 32 (Fall 1978), p. 686-88. (review of *This Body is Made of Camphor and Gopherwood*)

Komie, Lowell. "Ecstasy and Poetry in Chicago: A Middle-Age Lawyer Goes to his First Poetry Reading." *Harper's* 256 (March 1978), p. 129-31.

Lacey, Paul A. "The Live World." *The Inner War: Forms and Themes in Recent American Poetry* (Philadelphia: Fortress Press, 1972), p. 32-56.

Leibowitz, Herbert. "Questions of Reality." *The Hudson Review* 21 (August 1968), p. 553-57. (review of *The Light Around the Body*)

Lensing, George S. and Ronald Moran. *Four Poets and the Emotive Imagination: Robert Bly, James Wright, Louis Simpson and William Stafford* (Baton Rouge: Louisiana State University Press, 1976), p. 71-85.

Levis, Larry. "Some Notes on Grief and the Image." *Poetry East* 4/5 (Spring/Summer 1981). p. 140-44.

Libby, Anthony. "Fire and Light: Four Poets to the End and Beyond." *Iowa Review* 4, #2 (Spring 1973), p. 111-26.

"Robert Bly: Alive in Darkness." *Iowa Review* 3 (Summer 1972), p. 78-91.

Logan, John. "Poetry Shelf." *Critic* 21 (January 1963), p. 84-85. (review of *Silence in the Snowy Fields*)

Lyne, Sandford. Untitled. *Poetry East* 3 (Fall 1980), p. 80-83. (review of *News of the Universe* and *Talking All Morning*)

McPherson, Sandra. "You Can Say That Again. (Or Can You?)" *Iowa Review* 3 (Summer 1972, p. 70-75.

Malkoff, Karl. *Escape from the Self: A Study in Contemporary American Poetry and Poetics* (New York: Columbia University Press, 1977), p. 143-44.

Mazzocco, Robert. "Jeremiads at Half-Mast." *New York Review of Books* 10 (June 20, 1968), p. 22-25. (review of *The Light Around the Body*)

Mersmann, James F. "Robert Bly: Watering the Rocks." *Out of the Vietnam Vortex: A Study of Poets and Poetry Against the War* (Lawrence: University Press of Kansas, 1974), p. 113-57.

Mills, Ralph J. "Four Voices in Recent American Poetry." *The Christian Scholar* 46 (Winter 1963), p. 324-45. (review of *Silence in the Snowy Fields*)

Contemporary American Poetry (New York: Random House, 1965), p. 210-17.

"Five Anthologies." *Poetry* 109 (February 1967), p. 345-50. (review of *A Poetry Reading Against the Vietnam War*)

"Robert Bly's Recent Prose Poems." *New Mexico Humanities Review* 4, #2 (1981).

Molesworth, Charles. "Thrashing in the Depths: the Poetry of Robert Bly." *Rocky Mountain Review of Language and Literature* 29 (August 1975), p. 95-117.

"Contemporary Poetry and the Metaphors for the Poem." *The Georgia Review* 32 (Summer 1978), p. 319-31.

"Domestication of the Sublime: Bly's Latest Poems." *Ohio Review* 19, #3 (Fall 1978), p. 56-66.

" 'Rejoice in the Gathering Dark': The Poetry of Robert Bly." *The Fierce Embrace: A Study of Contemporary American Poetry* (Columbia: University of Missouri Press, 1979), p. 112-38.

Moran, Ronald and George Lensing. "The Emotive Imagination: A New Departure in American Poetry." *The Southern Review* 3 (January 1967), p. 51-67. (review of *Silence in the Snowy Fields*)

Mueller, Lisel. "Five Poets." *Shenandoah* 19 (Spring 1968), p. 65-72. (review of *The Light Around the Body*)

Murray, Philip. "Perilous Arcady." *Poetry* 120 (August 1972), p. 304-12.

"National Book Awards." *Nation* 206 (March 25, 1968), p. 413-14.

Nelson, Howard. "Welcoming Shadows: Robert Bly's Recent Poetry." *Hollins Critic* 12 (April 1975), p. 1-15.

——— "Robert Bly and the Ants." *Poetry East* 4/5 (Spring/Summer 1981), p. 207-15.

"19th National Book Awards Stir Controversy in New York: Poetry Prizewinner Robert Bly Scores Vietnam War Policy." *Library Journal* 93 (April 1, 1968), p. 1395-96.

Nordell, Frederick. "From the Bookshelf: A Poet in Minnesota." *The Christian Science Monitor* 55 (January 23, 1963), p. 9.

"Notes on Current Books." *Virginia Quarterly Review* 39 (Winter 1963), p. xxii. (review of *Silence in the Snowy Fields*)

"Notes on Current Books." *Virginia Quarterly Review* 44 (Winter 1968), p. xviii. (review of *The Light Around the Body*)

Novak, Robert. "What I have Written is not Good Enough: The Poetry of Robert Bly." *Windless Orchard* 18 (1974), p. 30-34.

Oates, Joyce Carol. "When They All Are Sleeping." *Modern Poetry Studies* 4 (1973), p. 341-44.

Orr, Gregory. "The Need for Poetics: Some Thoughts on Robert Bly." *Poetry East* 4/5 (Spring/Summer 1981), p. 116-22.

Palmer, Penelope. "Review of *Twenty Poems of Pablo Neruda*." *Agenda* 6, #3-4 (Autumn/Winter 1968), p. 124-28.

"Photographs of Robert Bly." *Poetry East* 4/5 (Spring/Summer 1981), p.

"Poetry International." *Times Literary Supplement* #3445 (March 7, 1968), p. 231. (review of *Late Arrival on Earth*)

Punter, David. "Robert Bly: Gone Fishing for the Sign." *Modern Poetry Studies* 10, #2/3 (1981), p. 241-45. (review of *Talking All Morning*)

Ramsey, Paul. "American Poetry in 1973." *Sewanee Review* 82, #2 (Spring 1974), p. 401-02.

Ray, David. "Robert Bly." *Epoch* 12 (Winter 1963), p. 186-88. (review of *Silence in the Snowy Fields*)

——— "Robert Bly." *Contemporary Poets of the English Language,* Rosalie Murphy, editor. (Chicago and London: St. James Press, 1970), p. 110-13.

——— "On Robert Bly" and "Two Poems for Robert Bly." *Poetry East* 4/5 (Spring/Summer 1981), p. 194-96.

Reid, A.S. "A Look at the Living Poem: Rock Protest and Wit." *Furman Magazine* (Spring 1970), p. 6-11.

Rexroth, Kenneth. "The New American Poets." *Harper's* 230 (June 1965), p. 65-71.

——— "The Poet as Responsible." *Northwest Review* 9 (Fall/Winter 1967-68), p. 116-18. (review of *The Light Around the Body*).

"Robert Bly and David Ray: A Poetry Reading Against the Vietnam War." *South Dakota Review* 4 (Winter 1966), p. 89.

Root, William P.H. "Comment." *Poetry* 123 (October 1973), p. 34-56. (review of *The Sea and the Honeycomb* and *Twenty Poems of Tomas Tranströmer*)

Rosenthal, M.L. *The New Poets: American and British Poetry Since World War II.* (New York: Oxford University Press, 1967), p. 25, 320-21.

Rudman, Mark. "New Mud to Walk Upon." *Poetry East* 4/5 (Spring/Summer 1981). p. 99-104.

Ruffin, Carolyn F. "From the Book Reviewer's Shelf: Three Poets of the Present." *The Christian Science Monitor* 59 (October 9, 1967), p. 9. (review of *The Light Around the Body*)

"The Sea and the Honeycomb." *El Corno Emplumado* 21 (January 1967), p. 111 (review of *The Light Around the Body*)

Seal, David. "Waking to 'Sleepers Joining Hands.'" *Poetry East* 4/5 (Spring/Summer 1981), p. 234-63.

"Seventy Poets on Robert Bly." *Poetry East* 4/5 (Spring/Summer 1981), p. 105-15.

Simmons, Charles. "Poets in Search of a Public." *Saturday Review of Literature* 46 (March 30, 1963), p. 48. (review of *Silence in the Snowy Fields*)

Simon, John. "More Brass than Enduring." *Hudson Review* 15, #3 (Autumn 1962), p. 455-68. (review of *Twenty Poems of Georg Trakl*)

Simpson, Louis. "New Books of Poems." *Harper's* 237 (August 1968), p. 73-77. (review of *The Light Around the Body*)

——— "Poetry Chronicle." *The Hudson Review* 16 (Spring 1963), p. 130-40.

Sjöberg, Leif. "The Poet as Translator: Robert Bly and Scandinavian Poetry." *Poetry East* 4/5 (Spring/Summer 1981), p. 218-25.

Smith, Ray. Untitled. *Library Journal* 87 (November 1, 1962), p. 4025. (review of *Silence in the Snowy Fields*)

"Special Pleading." *Times Literary Supplement* #3468 (August 15, 1968), p. 867. (review of *The Light Around the Body*)

Stafford, William. "Notice: A Bly Prescription." *Poetry East* 4/5 (Spring/Summer 1981), p. 8.

Steele, Frank. "Three Questions Answered." *Tennessee Poetry Journal* 2 (Winter 1969), p. 23-28.

Stepanchev, Stephen. "Chorus of Versemakers: A Mid-1963 Medley." *New York Herald Tribune Books* 7 (August 11, 1963), p. 7. (review of *Silence in the Snowy Fields*)

"Eight Poets." *Shenandoah* 14 (Spring 1963), p. 58-65. (review of *Silence in the Snowy Fields*)

"The Subjective Image." *American Poetry Since 1945: A Critical Survey* (New York: Harper & Row, 1965), p. 185-87.

Stitt, Peter. "James Wright and Robert Bly." *Hawaii Review* 2 (Fall 1973), p. 89-94.

Taylor, W.E. "The Chief." *Poetry, Florida And...* 1 (Spring/Summer 1968), p. 12-16. (review of *The Light Around the Body*)

Thurley, G. "Devices Among Words: Kinnell, Bly, Simic." *The American Moment* (London: Edward Arnold, 1977), p. 210-28.

Tranströmer, Tomas. "Letters to Bly." *Ironwood* 13 (1979), p. 94-101.

"Letter to Bly." *Poetry East* 4/5 (Spring/Summer 1981), p. 229-31.

True, Michael D. "Robert Bly: Radical Poet." *Win* (January 15, 1973).

Tulip, James. "The Poetry of Robert Bly." *Poetry Australia* 29 (August 1969), p. 47-52.

Walsh, Chad. "Book World." *Washington Post* (April 1, 1973), p. 13 (review of *Sleepers Joining Hands*)

Wesling, Donald. "The Wisdom-Writer." *Nation* 233 (October 31, 1981), p. 447-48. (review of *The Man in the Black Coat Turns*)

Weinberger, Eliot. "Gloves on a Mouse." *Nation* 229 (November 17, 1979), p. 503-04.

Williamson, Alan. "Language Against Itself: the Middle Generation of Contemporary Poets." *American Poetry Since 1960: Some Critical Perspectives,* Robert B. Shaw, editor. (Chester Springs, Pa.: Dufour, 1974), p. 55-67.

"Music to Your Ears." *New York Times Book Review* (March 9, 1980), p. 8, 9, 14, 15. (review of *This Tree Will Be Here for a Thousand Years*)

Wright, Annie. "Joining Hands with Robert Bly." *Poetry East* 4/5 (Spring/Summer 1981), p. 37-42.

Zavatsky, Bill. "Talking Back: A Response to Robert Bly." *Poetry East* 4/5 (Spring/Summer 1981), p. 86-98.

"Talking All Morning: A Review." *Meridian* (Fall 1981).

Zinnes, Harriet. "Two Languages." *Prairie Schooner* 42 (Summer 1968), p. 176-78. (review of *The Light Around the Body*)

Zweig, Paul. "The American Outsider." *Nation* 203 (November 14, 1966), p. 517-19.

"A Sadness for America." *Nation* 206 (March 25, 1968), p. 418-20. (review of *The Light Around the Body*)

Dissertations on Robert Bly

Elliott, David Lindsey. *The Deep Image: Radical Subjectivity in the Poetry of Robert Bly, James Wright, Galway Kinnell, James Dickey, and W.S. Merwin* (Syracuse, N.Y.: Syracuse University, 1978), 280 pp. 39/06A, p. 3577 DDK78-23557

Harris, Victoria Frenkel. *The Incorporative Consciousness: A Study of the Poetry of Denise Levertov and Robert Bly* (Urbana, Il.: University of Illinois, 1977), 415 pp. 38/10A, p.6119 DDK78-04016

Justin, Jeffrey Arthur. *Unknown Land Poetry: Walt Whitman, Robert Bly and Gary Snyder* (Ann Arbor: University of Michigan, 1973), 189 pp. 35/01-A, p.457 74-15770

Piccione, Anthony. *Robert Bly and the Deep Image* (Athens, Oh.: Ohio University, 1969), 199 pp. 31/03A, p.1286 70-15288

Sage, Frances Kellog. *Robert Bly: His Poetry and Literary Criticism* (Austin: University of Texas, 1974), 228 pp.   35/08-A, p.5423   75-04450

Wosk, Julie Helen. *Prophecies for America: Social Criticism in the Recent Poetry of Bly, Levertov, Corso, and Ginsberg* (Madison: University of Wisconsin, 1974), 199 pp.   35/09-A, p.6169   74-28837

Interviews with Robert Bly

Talking All Morning (Ann Arbor, Michigan: University of Michigan Press, 1980). (collection of interviews)

*Chisolm, Scott. "On Unfinished Poets." n.p. (n.d.).

Clifton, Michael. "Interview with Robert Bly." *Poetry East* 4/5 (Spring/Summer 1981) p. 43-60.

*"A Conversation with Robert Bly." *Street* 2, #1 (1974?).

*Dodd, Wayne. "An Interview with Robert Bly." *The Ohio Review* 19 (Fall 1978), p. 32-48.

Faas, Ekbert. "An Interview with Robert Bly." *Boundary* 2, #4 (Spring 1976), p. 677-700.

*"Infantilism and Adult Swiftness." *Towards A New American Poetics: Essays & Interviews* (Santa Barbara: Black Sparrow Press, 1978), p. 223-43.

*Feroe, Paul, Neil Klotz and Don Lee. "Poetry is a Dream that is Shared with Others." *Sucking-Stones* (n.d.).

*Fortunato, Mary Jane and Cornelis P. Draves, and with Paul Zweig and Saul Galin. "Craft Interview." *New York Quarterly* (n.d.).

Froiland, Paul. "Of Shamans and Solitude: Robert Bly on the Meanings of Words." *TWA Ambassador* (December 1980), p. 33-36.

Holt, Patricia. "Robert Bly." *Publishers Weekly* 217 (May 9, 1980), p. 10-11.

"An Interview with Robert Bly." *The Lamp in the Spine* 3 (1972), p. 50-65.

*Martin, Peter. "On 'Losing the Road'." n.p. (n.d.)

Ossman, David. "Robert Bly." *The Sullen Art* (New York: Corinth Books, 1963), p. 39-42.

*Otto, Kathy and Cynthia Lofsness. "An Interview with Robert Bly." *Plaintiff* (Spring 1966). Reprinted in *Tennessee Poetry Journal* 2, #2 (Winter 1969), p. 29-48.

"Poet at Large: A Conversation with Robert Bly." Transcript of *Bill Moyer's Journal* #403, February 19, 1979 (New York: Educational Broadcasting Corporation, 1979).

*Power, Kevin. "Conversation with Robert Bly." *Texas Quarterly* 19, #3 (Autumn 1976), p. 80-94.

*Ratner, Rochelle. "On Writing Prose Poems." *Soho Weekly News* (n.d.).

*Siemering, Bill. "Interview with Robert Bly." *Dacotah Territory* 12 (Winter/Spring 1975-76).

*Yanella, Phil. "Two Halves of Life." *Tempest* 1, #1 (n.d.)

   *Reprinted in *Talking All Morning*

Special Features/Special Issues Devoted to Robert Bly and his Work

Ohio Review 19, #3 (Fall 1978), p. 29-66. Edited by Wayne Dodd. (feature)

Poetry East 4/5 (Spring/Summer 1981), p.1-293. Edited by Richard Jones and Kate Daniels. (whole issue)

San Francisco Book Review #19 (April 1971), p. 1-32. (whole issue)

Tennessee Poetry Journal 2, #2 (Winter 1969), p. 1-60. Edited by Stephen Mooney. (whole issue)

—*Compiled by James Doss and Kate Daniels*

Notes on Contributors

Deborah Baker is assistant editor of *Poetry East*. She lives in London.

Michael Clifton is finishing his dissertation in American literature for Indiana University where he won the Academy of American Poets award in 1979.

Michael Cuddihy edits the excellent literary magazine, *Ironwood*.

William Virgil Davis won the Yale Younger Poets prize in 1979. He is professor of English and Writer-in-Residence at Baylor University.

James Doss is currently working on new translations of Georg Trakl and has poems forthcoming in *Poetry East*.

Patricia Goedicke's books of poetry include *The Trail that Turns in on Itself* (Ithaca House) and *Crossing the Same River* (University of Massachusetts).

John Haines' book of essays was published this year by the University of Michigan Press. He is currently living in Alaska.

Donald Hall recently published a collection of his essays, *To Keep Moving* (Hobart & William Smith Colleges Press).

Victoria Harris has published criticism on a number of contemporary poets. She teaches at Illinois State University.

Richard Hugo edits the Yale Series of Younger Poets. His *Selected Poems* and *The Triggering Town* (prose) are available from Norton.

David Ignatow's *Tread the Dark* (Atlantic-Little) won the Bollingen Prize in 1978.

Larry Levis' second book, *The Dollmaker's Ghost* (Dutton), won the 1980 National Poetry Series.

Howard McCord's *Selected Poems* are available from Crossing Press.

Thomas McGrath's collected poems, *Movie at the End of the World,* are available from Swallow Press.

Howard Nelson is writing a critical study of Robert Bly for Columbia University Press.

Gregory Orr is currently writing a book on Stanley Kunitz for Columbia University Press. His chapbook, *Salt Wings,* is available from *Poetry East*.

David Ray edits *New Letters* and is currently traveling in India. He is the feature poet in the most recent issue of *Greenfield Review.*

Mark Rudman is writing a book on Robert Lowell. He lives in New York City and is poetry editor of *Pequod*.

David Seal teaches at Pacific Lutheran University in Tacoma, Washington.

Leif Sjöberg has translated extensively from Swedish; he is professor of comparative literature at State University of New York at Stonybrook.

William Stafford's recent book of prose, *Writing the Australian Crawl*, was published by the University of Michigan Press in 1978.

Annie Wright lives in New York City.

Bill Zavatsky edits *SUN* books and magazine and is the author of *Theories of Rain and Other Poems*.